S0-BRG-178

Cabrini College Library
Radnor, Pa. 19087

THE SPIRIT OF ENTERPRISE

THE SPIRIT OF ENTERPRISE

BY

EDGAR M. QUEENY

1943

CHARLES SCRIBNER'S SONS · NEW YORK

Printed in the United States of America

THIS BOOK IS
MANUFACTURED UNDER WARTIME
CONDITIONS IN CONFORMITY WITH
ALL GOVERNMENT REGULATIONS
CONTROLLING THE USE OF PAPER
AND OTHER MATERIALS

CONTENTS

I.	A.D.-1943	3
II.	The American Climate and Its Storm Clouds	17
III.	Black and White	36
IV.	Ten Years	48
V.	The Prophet and His Works	64
VI.	The Inquisition	74
VII.	Monopoly Bogey	88
VIII.	Bogey II	97
IX.	The Real McCoy	110
X.	Whose Feet Are Clay?	120
XI.	Sugar Daddy	149
XII.	Speck in the Milk	161
XIII.	The Speck Grows	168
XIV.	Disaster	177
XV.	The Skeleton Closet	195
XVI.	Hope	199
XVII.	An Alternative	205
XVIII.	Vision	229
Notes		243

PREFACE

WHEN I CONFIDED TO AN AUTHOR FRIEND THAT I INTENDED to buckle on my armor and break a lance in defense of business, he said, "Good! You will develop a whole economic philosophy for yourself. I don't believe anyone ever gets his ideas in order until he writes them down."

The idea of attempting this book held me because I believed that business and businessmen were misunderstood. Certainly, the majority of the friends I had made in the business world were taking what I thought an unjustified beating. Some were rich, but they were not wicked. Most were selfish, but so were many workers of my acquaintance. Occasionally a few might hit below the belt, but so would some labor leaders and some politicians. My businessmen friends were not saints, nor were they ogres feeding upon unfortunate fellow-beings, as some high priests of the social sciences were intimating; they were just boys grown into men, like the workers, and human virtues and human foibles were attributes common to both.

However, my friend was right. By the time my thoughts were on paper they consisted merely of a series of standard arguments against the New Deal "Hoyle" for business. But this did not constitute a philosophy nor explain satisfactorily, even to me, why I believed in business and the so-called American way of life of which it is a part. It was apparent I was too close to the picture—one side of it, anyway. Too much was missing, for instance, to make a convincing answer to the brilliant, lucid prophet of the New Deal—Stuart Chase.

He was writing that if you held your ear close to the ground you could hear a muffled roar echoing around the whole world. He said that it did not come from bombs, or thunder on the Russian front, but that it was the voice of the people demanding security and an end to the paradox of plenty. He called it a revolt of the masses asking for food which farmers let rot upon the ground.

Nor did my early notes answer the reverberations of this revolt that were coming from Britain, where The Malvern Doctrine, drawn by the Archbishop of Canterbury, primate of England, had been adopted by members of the Church of England who assembled to consider it. The Christian doctrine, these holy men resolved, has insisted that production exist only for consumption and that the industrial world of the past offended this principle. The method of industry, they continued, which treats human work as a means to monetary gain becomes a source of unemployment, so it is largely responsible for the problems of mass man, who, under the system, is conscious of no status—spiritual or social—who is a mere item in the machinery of production. The conference urged that the industrial system be so administered that the satisfaction of human needs be the only true end of production, and they propounded the question whether such a just order of society can be established so long as the resources necessary for the common life are privately owned.

And somewhat later the powerful British Labor party, assembled in convention, voted unanimously to socialize the basic industries and services of Britain and to plan production for community consumption as the only lasting foundation for a just and prosperous economic order.

To breast such an avalanche, much more was needed than offhand views of one indoctrinated with a laissez-faire philosophy, particularly in the case of one whose recent studies had consisted in too great part of balance sheets, production reports and legalistic briefs to be laid before our new administrative tribunals. These challenges called for a re-appraisal of one's past credo and a re-orientation as of today!

But to make such an appraisal, it was necessary to get off into space and get the perspective that time had of humanity. So I began to re-learn much of what I had forgotten and find out much more I had not known. I re-acquainted myself with the calm reasoning of Adam Smith and proceeded to the impassioned arguments of Karl Marx, and by the time I had finished "The Communist Manifesto" I was almost ready to cheer the red flag. Thus I recognized my two selves: a crusading idealist and a cold, granitic believer in the law of the jungle. For a time, the more I read the more confused I became. Business did not have clean hands; but its critics and detractors were not fair nor honest toward it, either!

One book recommended another; one field led to another. Although I had read some of Thorstein Veblen's essays years ago, I now labored through more of his writings, feeling certain I could never have liked the man in the flesh. Then back to my histories and through much of the testimony and monographs of the Temporary National Economic Committee, and so on.

During the progress of the inquiry my former beliefs slowly and finally evolved into reasoned conclusions, and it is this process which I am attempting to trace on the following pages.

Many friends have been kind enough to read the manuscript and even though their names are not mentioned individually I wish to express my gratitude to them and acknowledge their help in avoiding ambiguities and clarifying arguments.

Particularly is this true of Dr. Virgil Jordan, President of the National Industrial Conference Board, on whose executive committee it has been my privilege to sit for several years. I am indebted to the Conference Board's staff, too, for checking and verifying such statistics of an economic character as I have used. Also, I have received useful suggestions from Mr. Sterling Edmunds of St. Louis. However, no one has guided my pen or put into my mouth the words that appear on the following pages; nor do I mean to imply that Dr. Jordan or my other friends have any responsibility for, or even that they are in entire agreement with, the analyses, arguments or conclusions. The accountability is mine alone.

EDGAR M. QUEENY

THE SPIRIT OF ENTERPRISE

CHAPTER I

A.D.-1943

AFTER THE UNITED STATES MARINES HAD SWARMED UP THE beaches of the Solomon Islands in the summer of 1942 and the rattle of machine guns and reverberations of bursting bombs had died away, our newly-won positions were hastily consolidated; then reconnaissance parties fanned out to find any lingering Japs who might be hiding in the hot and forbidding jungles.

Flanking the archipelago on the northeast is finger-shaped Malaita Island. Marine detachments which filed up its beaches saw, offshore, small man-made islands. They proved to be dwelling places of natives—refuges of the docile salt water folk from the forays of cannibalistic Bushmen who live deep in the malarial mountains in a jungle teeming with vicious insects and venomous snakes.

These fierce and primitive savages wear bones thrust through their noses and smear ashes over their black faces and naked bodies. When the natural foods of the wilderness and their elementary agriculture fail, predatory instinct sends them down to the seashore in search of human fare. But the short stretches of water separating islands and mainland are ample protection for the salt water folk, for the Bushmen have not learned to swim, nor do they know how to build boats.

In these Bushmen one finds rudimentary man living as all men must have lived in the beginning. Yet a Bushman is of the same biological species as a Marine; both belong to the human race; both have the same kind of bodies, the same passions and the same senses. Their bloods are indistinguishable even under a microscope.

The American Marines, however, are a product of a great industrialized civilization—the highest culture attained by man. Bushmen live in primitive communal tribes.

Americans differ from Bushmen in intellect. We have greater reasoning power and understanding, and greater ability to think because of our knowledge. And knowledge grows not only through experience—it is also an accumulation of impressions that man obtains through his senses. And the more prolonged the periods of time and more vast the space over which the senses can be extended, the more opportunities are presented for varied sense stimulation and the greater knowledge can become.

The knowledge of Bushmen is limited to that which can be retained in their memory and passed down by word of mouth—woodcraft, primitive agriculture and taboos. Bushmen are unable to record thoughts or experiences for succeeding generations, so their tribal knowledge remains static.

We, however, are heirs to the accumulated knowledge of scores of preceding generations, each having left its experience, thoughts and observations in writing. For centuries our ancestors have not needed to explore and begin anew; they have built, block by block, generation by generation, upon an inherited foundation.

Our civilization took root with the invention of written language, but it bloomed and spread with the discovery of printing. Now American culture is stored in hundreds of millions of books that lie in thousands of American libraries. In America each man, woman and child reads on the average three books a year. They read the philosophy, the imaginative fiction and the recorded experience of contemporary men, as well as those of men dead for centuries. And translations leap national boundaries. The knowledge available in these books is so great that no one can learn all or even a fraction of a small part. Knowledge of history, exploration and science is so vast that even savants know generalities of one field only and specialize in and really master but a part of it.

Our newspapers, too, spread knowledge widely. Forty-eight million copies are printed daily. News from all the world, columnized editorials of popular contemporary writers, sections with radio photos of current happenings and articles of general interest—all can be purchased for the wages of a minute or two of common labor.

National thought is shaped and cemented by discussion in our magazines. Through them we learn also about the world, about things, about people, about our politicians and our artists, and become acquainted with our authors. The enormous circulation of our national magazines is sufficient to provide each family with four issues a week.

Thus our literature lays open the world, past and present, to our eyes. Knowledge is spread through all classes. It grows rapidly.

Our eyes have been helped through time and space, not only through the printed page, but in some localities through television, and at the price of an hour's work of common labor, moving pictures bring plays costing millions to produce, travel in faraway lands and important world events soon after they occur.

Shrinking the earth to Lilliputian dimension, we have produced telescopes through which man may inspect our sun of boiling elements and look into a space that exceeds our imagination to comprehend, where a hundred billion suns are burning trillions of miles away. Through the electron microscope man can now see molecules—proof that no matter is solid. It magnifies so that if a six-foot man could be seen through it, he would be a super Brobdingnagian standing two hundred and forty miles high, his outspread hands being capable of reaching over the eastern and western boundaries of Missouri.

An American's eyes are useful to him for more hours than are a Bushman's. Nature's night does not end his day. From torch through tallow, oil and gas to electricity, his eyes have been given constantly increasing scope. Now the turning of switches enables the tumbling of a distant waterfall or burning of coal miles away to give cities, towns and homes twenty-four hour days; men can read, enjoy the theatre, or travel highways even when the sun is in its nadir.

And our sight has been preserved longer than nature intended. Glasses permit one to read after nature says he is too old. Medicines and surgery preserve sight against disease and accident.

Nor is our mind extended through time and space through sight alone. Speech and hearing have been aided, too. Through the telephone one may speak to a distant city or to another nation across the sea. Sound movies enable him to hear as well as see plays and action all over the world.

Phonographs enable him to hear his favorite music when he pleases and as often as he pleases. What a pity recording came too late for us to hear Mozart playing or Patrick Henry shouting his defiant "If this be treason make the most of it!" But the generations of the future will not only be able to read such of our music and speeches as outlive our generation; they will listen to our composers and statesmen as well.

Speech also knows no bounds of time or space. Our voice is not limited to the few hundred feet of the trumpet-tongued Bushmen. Through a telephone one can summon any one of our hundred and thirty million people and speak to him. And with radio one may address the world. Only fifteen thousand people were present to hear Lincoln speak at Gettysburg. After Pearl Harbor ninety million Americans heard the President's war message; and his words, translated into eleven languages, were shortwaved to more millions scattered over the whole surface of the earth.

Our taste is pampered, also, for unlike Bushmen our diet is not limited to that which has been recently killed or that which is growing in nearby fields. Our taste is satisfied and our bodies made more healthy by a diet that knows no season nor climate. We may have oranges from Florida, bread from Kansas wheat, cheese from Wisconsin, salmon from Alaska, coffee from Brazil, tea from India, cocoa from Africa, fruits from California and beef from the plains of the Argentine. No longer is it necessary for our sailors to exist on rum and hardtack nor our explorers and Marines to attempt living off the land. For most of us, diet is not dictated by season or locale, but rather by palate and physician's recommendations for nicely-balanced proteins, carbohydrates and vitamins.

As miraculous as are all the intricate systems of collection, refrigeration, preservation and transportation, in peace times to most Americans these choices are always available. We have no famines, such as Bushmen fear. Our improved diet has made us a bigger and stronger race; soldiers of Uncle Sam's 1942 army average one inch taller and ten pounds heavier than their fathers of 1917! [1]

A Bushman's travel is limited. With his two legs he can traverse through the jungle but twenty or thirty miles in a day. In half this time our businessmen and vacationists fly across a continent or sleep in airconditioned comfort while a train moves them hundreds of miles; and our continent is checkered with highways along which we can speed ourselves.

Luxurious floating palaces, which crossed the Atlantic in a few days, are already obsolete, and before long skyliners will make the journey in as many hours. A yarn was current recently that a British pilot remarked to his companion in a New York night club, "Just about this time last night I dropped my eggs over Frankfurt, Germany." Whether or not this story is true, it is readily possible.

If we consider the sense of touch to include that of nerves, we include the workshop of medicine and surgery, in which scientific and industrial skill has made some of its greatest progress. When pain warns of a miscarriage of the function of a human organ, anesthetics and analgesics shut it off, as one might an alarm clock. Surgery then often restores health and vigor and repairs crippled faculties before they incapacitate or prove fatal.

Beginning with sanitation and sterilization, conquests have included all but a few dreaded diseases. An American baby at birth may expect to live sixty-four years! In 1850 his life expectancy was only forty years! Fifty years later it was forty-nine years. By 1930 it had grown to sixty years and by 1940 sixty-four years! Children under fifteen now have a death rate only forty per cent of that of 1920.[2]

And while Americans now live longer, they also live more easily. We have more leisure than any other nationality because machinery does most of our work. Fewer men heave heavy sledges; they pull levers. Farmers ride tractors instead of swinging scythes and beating with flails, and household drudgery has been lightened by many conveniences.

Our morals have come a long way, too. The mere thought of a feast on a loose piece of broiled human flesh, which to the Bushmen brings mouth-watering longing, is to us horrid and nauseating; and as terrible as this war is, one accusation not yet made by the Russians is that the Germans are eating them! Our mental progress has been marked by the development of a keen sense of right and wrong, increasing compassion and respect for the rights and sensibilities of others.

Standards of conduct have been established. They are for the most part manifestations of decency and behavior, and of enlightenment. Only rudimentary laws are enforced on the few not equal to the duty of respecting rights of others.

Step by step our conception of human relationships has improved. Long ago we abandoned human sacrifice; later we ended slavery, indenture of workmen, duels and ruthless imprisonment. Step by step our solicitude for our fellow human beings has grown. Fiendish entertainment afforded by the suffering of gladiators belongs to antiquity, along with the diabolical fury exhibited by the Puritans when Stafford was permitted to die without seeing his own bowels burned before him. We are moved to war not for glory or conquest but as a means to peace. Women are no longer chattels and consigned to the meanest drudgeries of existence. Indeed, in America all human beings have at least equal civil rights.

In spite of sporadic outbreaks of atavism such as the Nazi's aggravated exhibit, since the acceptance of Christianity by the western world the long-term trend has been toward application of the Golden Rule and the Ten Commandments.

We are, however, far from the ideal. The predatory instinct still lurks within us; self-interest is still the force that activates much of our thinking and behavior, and love has not yet conquered all hate. We have come a long way, but the animalistic Bushman is not yet bred out of us.

Human relationships as expressed in working conditions of industrial labor have paralleled the advance in other fields. In Florence of The Renaissance, wage rates were fixed by the employer and paid often in depreciated money or, if demand was light, in kind. Workers were forbidden to combine even in religious groups unless they had special permission. They had no political rights and if rebellious at the harsh terms of their employment, judges, who often were their employers also, sentenced them to the lash or jail.[3]

Four centuries later working conditions had shown only slight improvement. In early industrial England tiny tots toiled in cotton mills before their bones were hard. Poor law authorities turned pauper children over to factories and mills in batches of fifty or a hundred, no accounting for their welfare or survival being required. The employer was merely obliged to accept a percentage of idiots. Brutal taskmasters worked them often eighteen hours a day and beat them and clapped them into irons if they whimpered. In the dark tunnels of mines, children slaved alongside half-naked men and women. All working communities were sore-ridden, illiterate masses of rankled humanity.[4] Karl Marx tells this terrible story well. What community would tolerate this today? We have come a long way in the last century![5]

Progress to our fuller life was slow. Each step in the improvement of the human relationship of the common man—in his progressive emancipation from slavery to serfdom, to freed man and to citizenship—was a struggle. Commerce changed, too, from bartering of the caravaning traders to medieval merchant princes, to intriguing state-sponsored monopolies of Elizabethan England and the absolutist Sun King Louis XIV, to our modern corporate giants of the free enterprise system.

But more distance was covered in the past century or century and a half than in all preceding time. Little separated Napoleon's battles from Caesar's other than cannon and gunpowder. The conquest of space and time had scarcely begun. Transportation and communication of armies remained unchanged. Napoleon's wounded suffered and died, like Caesar's, without antiseptics to cleanse and heal and without ether or general anesthetics to ease the pain of surgery. Nor had the way of life changed much except for newly-won liberties and the broadening of knowledge through printing. After his Russian disaster, Napoleon's flight from Vilna to Paris took three hundred and twelve hours. With every conceivable advantage of the times, he averaged less than five miles an hour. Julius Caesar could have done as well returning to Rome from Gaul.

The tremendous change that took place in the past century or so occurred with private enterprise dominating other forms of commerce. This is particularly true of America. Railroads spanned continents; steam and electricity ushered in a power machine age; science bloomed and became a powerful force in the upsurge of production.

American private enterprise differed from earlier state monopolies and mercantilism because anyone or a group of individuals could embark on a project without state consent and without a politician's approving nod.[6] It was private venture, not political nor bureaucratic. It was called enterprise because of the element of risk in attempting the untried and difficult. With the exception of land grants to pioneering railroads, America granted no bounties, tax remissions nor monopolies. It did not protect one venture from the competition of another. America progressed faster because the government insisted on competition and prevented monopoly in all fields except public utilities.

And when the stealthy Japs awoke Pearl Harbor one Sunday dawn with their rain of death, they put the American individualist and his system of private enterprise to their supreme test. One month later President Roosevelt stood before a microphone and challenged: "We will build during 1942 60,000 airplanes and during 1943 125,000 airplanes." He then called for the building in 1942 of a merchant fleet almost as large as the pre-war fleets of Germany and Norway combined, and by the end of 1943 of additions to our fleet equalling the floating tonnage of pre-war Great Britain—more tonnage within two years than the world had built in the previous decade.

Not only were ships to be constructed but the shipyards also. Concurrently America was to build naval tonnage exceeding the combined British and Japanese fleets. He called, also, for the production of fabulous quantities of tanks and guns and innumerable camps. To equip the fighting men his program required millions, even billions, of almost everything—cots, shoes, uniforms, medicines, trucks, jeeps, parachutes, cartridges and shells.

On all sides one heard, "Fantastic! Impossible! It can't be done!"

For almost two years American industry had been at work on a defense program in a lumbering, muddling sort of way under rather confused leadership and political direction. Its production of war matériel was a mere trickle compared to the torrent required. However, before the President had finished laying out the program, industrial management was answering with an all-out conversion to war production. Draftsmen were burning midnight oil over their drawing boards; telephone and telegraph lines were choked with orders for tools and materials. Assembly lines were being revamped, factory walls were being pushed out, soon new foundations were being poured and new walls were rising.

Industry, whose organizations for the most part had authority delegated in clear-cut and unequivocal manner and whose trusted juniors were accustomed to acting directly and freely without conflicting with others, was geared to make quick decisions. Organizations which were inured to teamwork and whose efficiency had been sharpened by a keen competitive economy, were clicking as they never had before. With very few exceptions, profit was a secondary consideration; management had a patriotic duty to perform!

Many believe that conversion of plants from peacetime products to war munitions is a relatively easy matter—the stopping of automobile assembly lines, for instance, and starting them again on tanks or airplanes. But it was not that simple! A comparatively minor portion of America's peacetime plant could be employed.

T.N.T., for instance, cannot be made in a dyestuff plant. T.N.T. must be made away from habitations. New locations had to be fenced off and new plant erected. The explosives program alone called for the industrializing of more than three hundred thousand acres of countryside and woodland.

When General Motors completed its building and conversion program, less than twenty-five per cent of its wartime facilities was composed of its former plant. General Motors used some $230,000,000 of its assets, or approximately sixty per cent of its peacetime plant, mostly for trucks, and airplane and Diesel engines. In order to complete its war assignments, it spent $66,000,000 of company money for new construction, conversion and expansion of facilities, and in addition nearly $700,000,000 that was supplied by the government.

However, the part of General Motors that was completely converted from peace to war purposes was the *organization*—the management, the engineering staff and the purchasing, accounting and production men. It was the brains of General Motors—that part that doesn't appear on the balance sheet—which was wholly converted.

Soon the nation was shocked into the realization that it had been robbed of the source of a most essential raw material—rubber! We had less than enough to supply the war and normal civilian needs for a year. An entirely new industry was called for. Synthetic rubber, hitherto made in America only in the laboratory, had to bloom over night into a million ton, billion dollar industry. Chemical companies, oil companies and rubber companies were called upon to magnify relatively undeveloped laboratory processes and pilot plants into huge production.

If the goal is achieved, it will rank as one of the industrial wonders of all time, but the public seems serenely confident as to the outcome. It appears this confidence will not be misplaced.

About six months after the President outlined his war program, a group of newspaper correspondents toured war industries to report the progress. From their articles one senses an unanimous verdict that Roosevelt had rubbed Aladdin's lamp! Miracles had happened!

Ray Springle of the Pittsburgh *Post-Gazette* summarized the opinion of the group when he reported: "Industrial America is winning its share of this war—the war on the production front. Back of the production already achieved—and that is stupendous—are vast production lines from which, right now, is beginning a flood of tanks and guns and planes and ships that staggers the imagination. American industry has smashed bottlenecks. It has whipped shortages. It has so exceeded schedules that now, in the light of present production, those schedules look foolish. It has flattened every obstacle that stood between industry and the complete and efficient arming of the Navy, the Air Corps and the Army. It has built vast war production plants such as no other country in the world dared dream of. It has tooled them. It is turning armaments out of them. . . . What about aluminum forgings? The same story there, but even more dramatic. Production for April of this year up to twenty-five times the production two years ago. And a production figure absolutely certain at the end of this year, up to fifty times the production at the beginning of the war emergency—4,900 per cent! Industrial America leads the way to victory.

It is doing its job as no other nation in the world could do it. Nine long years, six peace years, three war years, Nazi Germany has labored to build a war machine that was designed to conquer the world. In a brief two years, operating under a system of free enterprise, American industry has already shattered that dream of conquest. Already we have passed Germany in war production. Some critics read the death sentence for free enterprise in this country in 1933. Today it is saving the nation. Tomorrow our fighting men of the Army and Navy, on land, at sea and in the air, will win the war—with the tools that industrial America has put into their hands." [7]

Later on we heard about shortages—a steel shortage, for instance, but there was no suggestion that the steel industry was not on schedule—a copper shortage, but no suggestion that the copper industry was not on schedule. Several things had taken place; our exports of raw materials were greater than planned. Steel billets took less vital shipping space than tanks; therefore, it was better to ship steel billets to England, which had excess tank fabricating capacity. It was better to ship copper to Russia than to add to our stock of U.S. 30-06 cartridges, which our allies could not use.

Faulty planning and routing allowed inventory to dam up—shell forgings, for instance, may have been so far ahead of their schedule that shell loading plants could not consume them fast enough thus steel accumulated in the form of shell forgings. Also, factories exceeding rated capacities chewed up raw material faster than planned—and finally, the ship sinkings lost many a valuable cargo of copper coming up from Chile, bauxite from Guiana, and tin from Bolivia.

However, this did not influence the opinion of Major C. B. Baker, a member of the British Army staff, whom one of the reporters quoted as saying: "I don't think the rest of the world really appreciates it, but the totalitarians will never beat this country." [8]—nor that of Oliver Lyttelton, the British Minister of Production, who later added: "If Hitler could see American industry at work he would quit now." [9]

CHAPTER II

The American Climate and Its Storm Clouds

JUST A CENTURY BEFORE THE UNITED STATES HAD ELECTED a president for a third term, Henry Reeves, an Englishman, who was translating de Tocqueville's "De la Democracie en Amérique," found a word which was new to him. The word was "individualism." After considering the word carefully, he wrote: "I adopt the expression of the original, however strange it may sound to the English ear—I know no English word exactly equivalent to the expression." [1]

Count de Tocqueville, a young French aristocrat, had voyaged to America to study the means by which "liberty was regulated and reconciled with the social order." He wanted to ascertain what made America "tick." He discovered "individualism!"

He described his finding in these words: "Individualism is a novel expression, to which a novel idea has given birth. Our fathers were only acquainted with egotism. Egotism is a passionate and exaggerated love of self, which leads a man to connect everything with his own person and to prefer himself to everything in the world. Individualism is a mature and calm feeling, which disposes each member of the community to sever himself from the mass of his fellow creatures; and to draw apart with his family and friends, so that, after he has thus formed a little circle of his own, he willingly leaves society at large to itself. Individualists owe nothing to any man, they expect nothing from any man; they acquire the habit of always considering themselves as standing alone, and they are apt to imagine that their whole destiny is in their own hands. Individualism is of democratic origin and threatens to spread in the same ratio as the quality of conditions."

De Tocqueville might have added that individualism was the logical human reaction to the economic and spiritual freedom enjoyed by a people who had fought for and who had gained "the inalienable right to life, liberty and the pursuit of happiness," because for the first time in history free men were working as equals, not for political masters, but for themselves.

In a century and a half these individualists conquered a continent and created a society of unparalleled material and spiritual wealth—a society whose Christian spirit was expressed in a respect and tolerance for the beliefs and ambitions of others, an almost lavish generosity, and whose material wealth in many categories exceeded that of all the rest of the world.

In three decades after the signing of the Declaration of Independence Americans gave to man many fundamental inventions of great economic significance: Fulton's steamboat, Perkins' nail machine; Newbold's cast-iron plow, Whitney's cotton gin, Whittemore's textile carding machine, and Evans' high pressure steam engine. The list is interesting because of the utilitarian nature of the inventions, reflecting the individualist's desire for emancipation from the drudgeries of common labor. The individualist's philosophy was production with the greatest economy of manpower. This was in sharp contrast to European tradition; and it bore fruit.

Between 1800 and 1850 America, with a population of less than twenty-five million, produced one-half of the world's increase in physical assets.

During the nineteenth century a long list of labor emancipatives and time- and space-conquering inventions marked America's progress. Some of them, for instance, were the mowing machine, friction match, harvester, vulcanized rubber, pneumatic tire, turret lathe, sewing machine, safety pin, electric locomotive, modern elevator, typewriter, railway refrigerator car, lawn mower, telephone, talking machine, incandescent lamp, fountain pen, turbine, trolley car, adding machine, motion picture machine, gasoline, automobile, disc plow, high speed alloy steel, radio telephone, airplane, plastics, hydroplane and cyclotron. Each development bore the characteristic element of utility and economy of manpower, or the means for learning new truths and disseminating knowledge.

Individualism produced the unique industrial machine the Englishman said Hitler could never beat!

How can one account for this? Were these American individualists supermen? On the contrary. Early settlers were for the most part of the middle and lower classes, with an admixture, in goodly proportions, of indentured workers. America's population was made up of people who had made no great mark in the old country. Most were common men or sons of common men. They knew the drudgery of common labor.

Was it due to America's abundant natural resources? No! Individualists marked substantial progress on the relatively barren hills of New England. It was not until they pushed over the mountains that they uncovered the continent's great natural resources. But even then these resources were not greater than those of Russia, or South America, or Africa, or those of Europe. Certainly, they were no greater than those of Asia.

Nor was it due to an abundance of capital, for this had

to be sought largely from European bankers and individuals, which made it more expensive than it was abroad.

Nor were these people more skilled in individual crafts. Hardly a craft can be named in which artisans of the old country were not more skilled than ours. England could be justly proud of the superior skill of her textile weavers and cabinet makers. Italians excelled in masonry and leather goods; French artisans outdid the world in pottery and all of the arts and crafts patronized by European courts; German workers excelled in making precision instruments and fine tools.

Although they worked hard, the American individualists fought drudgery. By making slaves of machines, they steadily reduced the working hours of American labor.

The answer to the marvel of individualists' accomplishments cannot be found in higher education, for although they early recognized the advantage of universal education and spread its benefits widely, it is only in recent years that we have paralleled Germany in science, and it is still the ambition of many to study art and literature in England, France and Italy.

What, then, accounted for the American phenomenon? The only difference that can be found between the American economic and spiritual climate and that of other nations of the world was the inalienable right of Americans of freedom to pursue happiness without interference from the state. This the American Constitution guaranteed the American people. By it for the first time a community set up specific safeguards of its freedom against its government.

Americans were free to pursue their ambitions, whatever they might be—to pursue happiness in the achievement of great wealth, to pursue happiness in securing great knowledge, to pursue happiness in faith and self-denial and by ministering to the spiritual or material needs of others, to have large families or none at all, to go where they pleased and do what they pleased so long as they did not interfere with another's freedom or right to pursue his happiness in his own manner. And if one did not value worldly goods he could forego them and, like Thoreau at Walden Pond, pursue happiness in leisure, contemplation and philosophy. This new freedom, protected against encroachment by the state, released for the first time the full powers of the human mind, and allowed it to dream and hope and exercise, unhampered, its full adaptability and ingenuity.

It was fortunate that our colonists had endured a long era of oppressive government, which attempted to impose monopolies and restrictions on their freedom to engage in production and commerce. They realized the repressive effect this subjection had upon them and their trade; they remembered the unhappiness caused by the frustration of their ambitions.

It is not surprising, therefore, that they were impressed with arguments of the political economist and moral philosopher, Adam Smith, whose "Inquiry into the Nature and Causes of the Wealth of Nations" was presented to the world about the time of our Declaration of Independence. His work, in which Benjamin Franklin is supposed to have had a hand, was much discussed in both England and America. By the time our Constitution was written, eleven years later, it had taken an authoritative place in the minds of intelligent and progressive men.

There is ample evidence that Adam Smith's philosophy profoundly influenced the framers of the American Constitution; that the Constitution reflects Smith's doctrine of natural liberty. Smith's tenet was that "Man's self-interest is God's providence," and that if government refrained from interfering with free competition, industrial problems would work themselves out.

Therefore, the American Constitution established a government so restricted in power and scope that individuals would have the greatest liberty of action. Recognizing that all men are mortal and that none can be wholly good, a system of checks and balances was instituted to assure the permanence of the people's liberties. Thus individualism was born!

In time, there was hardly a village in Europe that did not know about the land of opportunity, wherein no matter how humble one's origin, by the exercise of hard work and fortitude, by adventure and hardship, men became rich because they worked not for feudal lords but for themselves and their families. Farmers, fresh from continental communal farms where they had been either tenants or serfs, in America became individualists. As their minds and spirits were released, they prospered and in so doing became landowners, merchants and manufacturers.

They pushed over the Alleghenies, crossed the Mississippi, marched over the plains and climbed the Rockies to the shores of the Pacific, conquering each wilderness, leveling forests, draining swamps and bridging rivers. They found the treasures of the mountains. They established the nation.

The development of industry followed as soon as it offered greater opportunities than the exploitation of land and mine, for, unlike patrician Europe, those who engaged in trade in America were not at the bottom of the social scale. In Europe, ambition for social stature could be achieved only through art, service in the army, or the church, or as an officer of the state. The wealth of nobilities was founded on land, not business.

In those countries, social ambition could never be achieved through business alone. European prejudice against businessmen has not been overcome completely to this day. Over there business might be a means of obtaining wealth to be used in turn as a stepping stone to a title or to enjoy the reflected prestige of a daughter's marriage to a title. In America, however, the development of business did not suffer from this handicap. America had no titles, no feudal nobility. America had no family aristocracies created by a law of primogeniture. Thus if great wealth was amassed by one generation, it was broken up, then dissipated, by descendants. Here a man was judged by what he was, whether his occupation was business, science or in the service of the church or state.

But ownership of wealth brought a large measure of prestige and even power over professional politicians to whom not only businessmen but other groups gradually and unwisely delegated the duty of running the state. It is understandable, therefore, in view of the prestige wealth enjoyed in America, that many men sought wealth in their pursuit of happiness. But in so doing they confirmed the Adam Smith philosophy—the important innovation instituted by the American Constitutional Convention—that through the seeking of one's own financial advantage one increased the general welfare—for in the pursuit of their own self-interest, businessmen contributed to social progress.

The American standard of living rose faster than that of any other nation; it reached unparalleled heights. Our business and industry became supreme in scope and size; its methods became a model the world sought to copy.

However, the early ascent of businessmen and industry to positions of influence started trends which, like the appearance of inauspicious mares' tails in the sky, presaged an approaching storm.

It is but human nature for men to use their influence in their own self-interest. As early as 1802 Jefferson wrote from Monticello to Hugh Nelson, a member of Congress, "I observe Congress is loaded with petitions from manufacturing, commercial and agricultural interests, each praying you to sacrifice the others to them. This proves the egoism of the whole and happily balances their cannibal appetites to eat one another." However, as the importance of business and industry increased, particularly after the Civil War, the influence of its leaders on politicians grew. Although special rewards had previously been made to the soldiers of our wars, and protective tariffs were as old as the nation itself, businessmen became the first effective economic minority pressure group. Early western and transcontinental railroads received huge land grant subsidies. While these subsidies stimulated railroad construction, opening up the vast west to settlement and commerce, and worked to the interest of all the people in the long run, they certainly worked with greatest emphasis to the immediate interest of the railroad pioneers.

Pressure secured increasing tariff protection for growing industries. The effect of this, too, had it been maintained at moderate levels, might have been to the interest of all the people, but it always worked, certainly, to the greatest immediate benefit of the business pressure group.

And at this point America turned off the road of free and unrestricted markets pointed out by Adam Smith into that path which led to the economic and moral jungle of today.

With but few short intervals American businessmen dominated the government until after the turn of the century, but in the meantime other pressure groups emulating their example were rising to power. Labor, smoldering under what the workers deemed unfair conditions, organized its pressure groups. Then farmers, as a nation living amidst heavily-armed neighbors is itself forced to arm, organized pressure groups in their own defense.

In time, each of these groups sought and received from government special benefits for itself at the expense of the people as a whole. After the Civil War, the Spanish-American war, and the Great War, individuals who had been members of the armed services organized, sought and received substantial benefits for the veterans at the expense of the people as a whole. Other pressure groups—the silver interests, the Townsend Old Age pensionites and a myriad of minor ones flocked to the trough of special benefits in Washington.

Business is now represented in Washington by the National Association of Manufacturers, the Chamber of Commerce of the United States, the Association of American Railroads, the American Bankers Association, and trade associations by the dozen. Each group, whether manufacturers, an individual trade, railroads, bankers or merchants, seeks advantages for itself at the expense of other business pressure groups, and many seek advantage for business at the expense of the people as a whole.

The American Federation of Labor and the Congress of Industrial Organization seek special benefits for labor; the American Legion for veterans; the Townsendites for the aged; the Farm Bureau Federation, the Grange, the Farmers Union, for farmers. All these pressure groups maintain elaborate and expensive headquarters in Washington, not because Washington is the center of the farm belt or the center of union labor or the center of manufacture, but because Washington is where national legislation originates, where the members of the House of Representatives and the Senate and executive agencies, who pass legislation and administer it, live and work. This is where the special benefits for organized minorities can be pried out of a government designed to safeguard the interests of the people as a whole.

All pressure groups use the same technique—the "gang up on 'em" idea. Speakers and public relations men are engaged to create favorable public opinion. Fires are built under a Senator or Congressman back home by arousing his constituents to prod him into favorable action or overwhelm him with protests. They browbeat or cajole these representatives of all the people with implications of retaliation or promise of support at the polls; they insinuate that campaign contributions will be given or withheld if this legislation is not passed or that legislation is not rejected or repealed.

Officers of these pressure groups measure success solely by the satisfactions they are able to obtain for the self-interests of their own group. In order to demonstrate the great usefulness and continued necessity for their organizations, they frequently manufacture issues and magnify elements of danger that are supposed to be lurking in pending legislation. They never allow their members to become satisfied with the status quo because in this event the need for the existence of their organizations would cease. Therefore, they offer continual evidence of being progressive; if one goal is attained, another is set up that will provide new and additional special privileges. Or if in some aspects a status quo is satisfactory to one group and others seek to change it, Congress feels the wrath engendered by the group's officers. It is impressed with the injustice of the proposed change.

For many decades America has witnessed the growing power of these minority pressure groups. A government "of the people, by the people and for the people" has steadily given way to a government whose policies are dictated by pressure groups, and in the process the character of the people's representatives has suffered. Frequently those who have had the courage to oppose one pressure group or another have, because of such action, been defeated for re-election. Thus others become intimidated. Eminently qualified men do not become candidates for public office because they decline to grovel for the support of businessmen or labor leaders; nor will they fawn on farm leaders or officers of the American Legion.

Thus the word "politic" has gradually lost its early meaning of "wise and skillful," and politicians are no longer esteemed. We have too few statesmen in Washington. This is because our Congress is but the trunk of a tree whose roots are buried deep in the sour ground of city and county political organizations. But as local politics has deteriorated almost into a shamanistic trade wherein skill is measured by the degree of success with which lip service compromises various popular causes, and as the tree must live on the sap sent up from its roots, we are fortunate that the character of our representatives is as high as it is. There are still men who enter politics with lofty ideals of public service but most men do so for what they can get out of politics—the noisy satisfaction of a blaring limelight, a shabby prestige derived from the power of patronage, and, in most cases, because it is a way to more money than they can earn in private life.

As pressure groups corrupted the people's representatives with campaign contributions and blocks of votes, in return the people's representatives corrupted the pressure groups by voting for their special privileges. Unfortunately, most of us, as either businessmen, laborers, farmers, veterans, sportsmen or reliefers, are members of some pressure group or recipients of some special benefits, and we are influenced by the special privilege we receive in our voting. Congress lets our "cannibal appetites" feed one on another. The situation approaches the corruption of the people feared by Benjamin Franklin, which he voiced when accepting the Constitution: "There is no form of government but what may be a blessing to the people if well administered," he said, "and this Constitution is likely to be well administered for a period of years. It can lead to despotism, as other forms have done before it, when the people become so corrupted as to need despotic government, being incapable of any other."

Because of the decline in statesmanship and the lack of leadership and courage, Congress, the check on mortal ambition and absolutism provided by our Constitution, has lost its stature. There is much ominous evidence that as a body it is losing public confidence.

Another trend evidenced itself toward the end of the nineteenth century—the growth of individualism into large-scale incorporated enterprise. Today there are myriads of companies operating throughout the nation which need so much capital for operations that in each case hundreds, even hundreds of thousands, of silent partners share in the ownership.

It is human nature to believe that in size lies strength and that if two or more team up they have a better chance of survival or conquest. And so in the development of business, owners, believing their self-interests would be served by eliminating competition, merged with others or bought out weaker competitors. Gradually the monopolies, or trusts, of the nineties came into being. Then the moral force of the people expressed itself in anti-trust laws and the Clayton Act, which have had a salutary effect in maintaining our unique competitive market. These laws preserved the vigor and insured the continuing growth of American free enterprise.

However, it was possible within the framework of these laws to effect combinations which were not deemed to be monopolies. Competitors might merge so long as they did not dominate a market. One corporation might buy another which was a large consumer of its products or which was a producer of its raw materials, or it might buy or merge with any other company whose products were not identical. This became fashionable, particularly during the late twenties, when investment bankers scoured the country to see what they could put together for large fees. These combinations did not add to productive capacity but profits had to be shared or additional profits earned for the promoters' shares.

Human relationships between employer and employe altered, in direct ratio to the growth of industrial units. In small shops or mills the boss called all hands by first names; he knew their families' histories; he could help in emergencies and send candy to the babies, appear at funerals and evidence his interest in his employes. The hands knew the boss as a human being, lovable or otherwise. They were in touch with shop problems and knew of big orders, or understood, if business was poor, why they were laid off. The boss told them why. They could see him trimming his own sails.

Big business placed insurmountable obstacles to such intimate contact. The boss became a soulless corporation, represented frequently by tactless foremen. Hands became payroll numbers. Instead of doing whole jobs, in which they could take interest and pride, men were regimented to banks of machines and performed monotonous motions.

A changed worker attitude arose with the different working conditions and human relationships.

Concurrent with this development, an increasing number of people became dependent upon others for jobs. From a nation of self-sufficient and self-employing farmers and small shopkeepers, we grew through the adolescence of the employer of a small force into a nation in which a very large portion of the population were working for money wages. We became a nation of people whose permanency of employment could not be assured by their own efforts.

During depressions millions of good workmen were marooned from vital income. They wanted security against such inequitable hardship.

And during the last century our average age increased twenty-five years. We are now a nation with a large percentage of old people.

In these changes one finds the underlying causes of the

demand for labor unions and social security; a demand which simmered quietly till it boiled over in the recent past.

Another significant trend was the shifting of immigration to America from western to eastern Europe. The origin of much of our early immigration lay in the persecution of religious groups abroad. The Pilgrims and the Huguenots came not to seek wealth but to be free to worship God in the manner in which they believed rather than as a king prescribed. The impetus of much of the early migration to our shores was spiritual. Others came not to seek wealth but for adventure, to shake off the remaining yokes of English feudalism and to seek freedom of movement in the American wilderness.

Much of this same spirit of the early settlers remained in the lands from which they came—the countries of the Reformation, western Europe where people were securing progressive amounts of religious and political freedom. This was particularly true in Great Britain, the source of almost all of our early immigration, where the Magna Carta had established fundamental political rights not only for nobles but for all classes of free men.

A study of the origin of the American people shows that until 1870 Germany, Ireland, Great Britain, Canada, and the Scandinavian countries had contributed ninety per cent of our immigration; thereafter this percentage diminished steadily until after the turn of the century it fell to twenty per cent.[2]

John R. Commons, commenting on this shift of immigration from western to eastern Europe,[3] points out that a line drawn across the continent of Europe from northeast to southwest, separating the Scandinavian Peninsula, the British Isles, Germany, and France, from Russia, Austro-Hungary, Italy and Turkey, separates countries not only of distinct races, but also of distinct civilizations. He reminds us that it separates countries of representative institutions and popular government from lands which prior to the First World War were governed by absolute monarchies and in which present dictatorships arose. West of this line education is almost universal; east of it illiteracy predominates. To the west one finds most of Europe's manufacture, progressive agriculture, and skilled labor. East of it primitive hand industries and backward agriculture prevail. It separates an educated, thrifty peasantry from a peasantry scarcely a single generation removed from serfdom. As Commons points out, it separates Anglo-Saxon and Teutonic races from Latin, Slav, Semitic and Mongolian races.

The causes of this shift were many. During the seventeenth and eighteenth centuries "the colonies," to the British people, meant North America. The British Empire did not exist; it was in early processes of assembly. North America was readily accessible. Almost all British migration came to our shores. But as the empire grew and Australia, Africa and other constituent parts became accessible, venturesome youth had a wider choice of new lands. Also, after the American Revolution a Britisher could go to Africa, Canada, Australia or New Zealand and remain a loyal British subject, whereas domicile in the United States offered the prospect of forfeiting allegiance to the crown. Few men relish a change in nationality. Britain's remaining colonies, therefore, drew a steadily-increasing percentage of its surplus population.

The wave of liberalism that swept over Europe, ending in the abortive uprisings of 1848, shifted the center of discontented liberals seeking freedom eastward to Germany and a wave of German immigration supplanted what we lost from the British Isles.

Early immigrants did not stop in New York and other ports of entry; they pushed steadily westward, settling on the fertile lands of the middle west.

During the last half of the nineteenth century, the work of

the individualists bore large fruit. America was coming of age and had created great wealth. News of it spread to eastern and southern Europe. American industries were booming. They needed labor to man their machines. They wanted cheap labor. The cheapest was found in eastern Europe. Labor agencies and steamship companies saw that the growing industries got what they wanted.

The second wave of immigration from eastern Europe came not for adventure in the American wilderness but to seek wealth in the "land of milk and honey." The impetus of the second migration was material. Ellis Island became a jumbled mass of illiterate humanity and a babble of tongues that were strange to our shores—Polish, Italian, Russian, Greek, Hungarian, Yiddish and Slovakian.

The second wave came not so much from farms as from crowded industrial cities. They didn't go on to the land; they went into factories. Labor agencies herded them into the steel mills of the Monongahela Valley and stood them before the textile looms of New England. A boat load of Italians was sent to Boston to dig the subway, and another lot of Slovaks to the coal pits near Harrisburg. Carload after carload was shipped to the rising industries of Chicago and Detroit. Many remained in the ports of entry—New York and Boston. Few of the second wave settled on the land and became proprietors. Most remained labor—common labor.

The illiteracy and the low living standards of eastern Europe, to which they had been accustomed, offered opportunities to take advantage of ignorance and handicaps of language. Large groups were exploited by greedy employers. Sweat shops appeared for the first time in the garrets of polyglot New York.

No one can slough off completely the things he learns as a youth. Prejudices and class feeling, if any, of the land of birth are never forgotten. Nor could an immigrant to whom such things were strange ever completely grasp the American concept of freedom, especially if language and illiteracy stood in the way. Unconsciously the immigrant transmitted his prejudices to his children. Also, as was but natural with people who were barred from social contacts with Americans by education, language and philosophy, they settled together, forming communities in the slums of cities or on the outskirts of mill towns, and passed on to their children their language, their prejudices and philosophy, their folk dances and songs and other characteristics of the culture of their homeland.

The more progressive and able individuals soon learned our language, left these communities, shifted for themselves and gradually were assimilated into the American way of life. But on New York's Lower East Side are second and third generations of this second wave who have never left the environs of Greater New York. They know nothing of America or American life—only the noisy activity of streets, tenements and sweat shops.

In the "Encyclopedia of Social Science," [4] the growth of the sweat shop industry of New York is traced to the recent immigration. It comments: "The most extreme forms of exploitation often come through the immigrant's own countrymen who have migrated at an earlier date and who as padroni, foremen, saloon keepers or 'boarding bosses' often impose on the newcomers in ways the native employer would not know. In New York City the tailor trade, the main sweated industry, was first in the hands of the English, then the Irish, and later the Germans. Conditions, however, did not seem to have been very bad until about 1880 with the growth of the city and the overcrowding of the East Side. German, Austrian and Hungarian Jews entered the trade in 1873, and soon after the Polish and Russian Jews gradually captured the industry, till by 1890 it was almost wholly in Jewish hands, while a fierce and unrestricted competition had lowered wages, lengthened hours, and increased the speed of work to the almost inhuman degree. . . . The same conditions to a less extent developing in Boston, Rochester, Philadelphia and Chicago. About 1890, too, the Italian immigration entered the trade and increased the competition still more. . . ."

It is understandable, therefore, how, in these metropolitan centers where exploitation of labor remained unchecked by moral or legal force, even second and third generations have been unable to shake off the class prejudices and the Marxist philosophy that flourished in the eastern European cities. They have never had an opportunity to comprehend the American way of life and idea of individualism. It is understandable how these centers have incubated class unrest and class feeling; how they have given birth to our so-called "labor agitators." In them one finds advocates of the collectivism which they envisage would not only raise their miserable standards but eliminate the prejudices and distinctions which separate them from descendants of the earlier immigration.

It is largely in the big cities—the industrial centers and mill towns where these alien cultures persist—that communism has secured a substantial foothold. It is also in these centers, particularly New York, that the American conception of collectivism, the social planning concept, originated, and it is in communities of second wave race and nationality that it finds its greatest support.

Again we have come a long way since we turned off the promising road pointed out by Adam Smith, who, we must not forget, was first of all a moral philosopher. As a prominent sociologist [5] points out, the "Wealth of Nations" was not only an economic doctrine; it offered solutions to "First, a problem of religion; second, a problem of ethics; third, a problem of civil justice; and fourth, a problem of economic technique."

Can we turn back? Must we go on and confirm the fears of Benjamin Franklin? Which course will be the best for the most of our people? The nation's opinion is divided. New Dealers and businessmen are in violent disagreement! Can a common solvent be found for their conflicting ideologies?

CHAPTER III

Black and White

It is unfortunate that in some circles the words "New Deal" or "New Dealer" carry an undertone of disdain. There are, however, no satisfactory alternative words to describe a philosophy and a group of men which these words identify. My New Deal friends insist they have no objection to being called "New Dealers," provided, of course, the words are not snarled at them. They point out that this phrase was originated by them and they are proud to have it associated with them, their philosophy and their purposes.

The subconscious suggestion aroused in some minds by "New Deal" is due undoubtedly to association with those holding the opposing philosophy. The word "capitalist" probably causes an even more violent reaction in Union Square or in the little red house in Georgetown, for businessmen and New Dealers have little in common. The general principles of the two groups flow from opposing poles—the extremes of one are found in the orthodox interpretation of laissez-faire capitalism, that of the other in the communism of Lenin and Trotsky.

Not that the New Dealers as a group are Communists; they are not—they do not advocate the overthrow of our government by force, any more than businessmen as a group are complete free traders advocating total elimination of tariffs.

In each group are found individuals with all shades of opinion. Among New Dealers, for instance, there are those who are anxious to preserve private enterprise but who would safeguard the public against past violations of special privilege, as well as those who believe man's interest can be best served only by the totalitarian state. The elite of the New Deal desire what they term a "modified private enterprise" or a "mixed economy" operated by state planning.

Many businessmen are in wholehearted sympathy with what they suppose are the New Deal objectives of a fuller life for the underprivileged, but are fervently convinced New Deal methods will not obtain the objective. Other businessmen see no good in either its aims or its methods and want to return to the tooth-and-claw, anything goes, catch-as-catch-can competition.

I believe most of each group will be found in the temperate zone of their philosophy's hemispheres. And to continue the analogy further, public opinion polls indicate the public stands on the equator where both philosophies fade into neutrality, looking north, then south, seeing virtues and faults in both directions.

Why should we have such violent differences of opinion? Social caste is found on both sides. Intelligence and sincerity are found on both sides. But temperaments differ. Life's experiences and environments have been different!

Let's start with the New Dealers as a group. They have brilliant, agile minds. They pursue their convictions with a burning zeal. Many of them are sincere and aspire to great things for mankind. Their souls embody much of the noble Christian spirit. But others work silently and with settled purpose, and one wonders if they love the poor as much as they hate the rich.

Everyone's sympathy extends to the underdog, whether it is the Jew in Germany, the worker in an American factory, an individual deprived of civil liberty, a nation which is a victim of aggression, or the Negro race in America which has been denied social equality. But in New Dealers sympathy rises to fervor and their emotions control their thoughts and actions. They are impatient for results. Their temperament is that of the artist.

As social workers, many of them witnessed the hard blows which the depression of the thirties let fall upon the working classes, while businessmen were preoccupied with their own intense problems.

How much more mutual understanding there would have been if every businessman had made a day's round with a visiting nurse during cold, sleety December, 1932.

Decisions to shut down a department or a plant were not pleasant to make; they were not lightly made. But after the head of a business gave such an order, for a true understanding of its impact New Dealers feel sure that he went to the wrong home. He should have watched the expression on a woman's face that night as she heard, "I am laid off!" He should have seen the baby in the crib and the tots sprawling on the floor, perhaps an invalid, bedridden mother in a back room. He would then have realized better the problems carried into homes that night—rents, groceries, medicines, shoes, all denied to men who were willing to work and provide.

Although worried with problems of a different sort, the business head returned to a comfortable home which was free from fear there might not be life's essentials. This was fundamental injustice! The marvel is that there was so little bitterness, especially when the morning papers may have twisted a knife around in the wound by headlining Mr. Fat Wealthy's large salary!

On the other hand, the social worker, the visiting nurse, the minister, the professor and the man who was laid off should have spent the day at Mr. Wealthy's desk. They should have been given a chance to understand his problems! Much bitterness might have been avoided. It would have helped no one if Mr. Wealthy had exhausted his business making things that could not be sold! Preservation of future jobs lay in preservation of the business itself! Decisions to lay men off were never made as one determines to switch off a battery of lights, but nevertheless the human factor was weighed too lightly—much too lightly!

While the businessman's sympathy reaches to the underdog, too, his attitude may be summarized by "Let the best man win!"—a fair fight is required but he realizes that afterwards there will be a winning cock to stand up and crow while of necessity there must be another prostrate, bleeding and gasping. His life is competition. There must be a winner and loser in every race. He recognizes this and risks being the loser for a chance of winning; and as the stakes are high, the playing is hard. Occasionally someone hits below the belt. But business is an adventure. Those with zest for it are men with faith in themselves.

The ambition of a typical successful businessman is never satisfied. Keeping just beyond reach like a desert mirage, it is always ahead of his achievements. If he is producing six things and employs one thousand people, his ambition is to exceed a competitor who may be twice his size. This competitor also has ambition to exceed another or to engage in still other activities where he visions new opportunities.

Acquisition of wealth is not the sole motivating force of a businessman; he is pursuing happiness in a game in which he hopes to prove a winner. I have seen multimillionaires spend an afternoon at poker and take great delight in winning either five or fifty dollars; yet if anyone offered these men many times the amount of their possible winnings to sit at the same table all afternoon and do nothing, they would be insulted. On the other hand, if there were no stakes and no chips to be cashed in as symbols of success, the table would draw no players.

It is competition that makes any game interesting, and monetary gain, in poker and in business, is the symbol of success or accomplishment. Elements of luck, skill, risk and calculation of chances are common to both.

Every businessman has an ideal toward which his ambition drives him, and his happiness is measured by his advances. Most businessmen want a large and successful business, bigger and more profitable than their competitors. Many achieve happiness if they feel that they have contented employes, if their plants are better designed and more efficient than those of competitors, if they have the confidence and good will of their customers and the respect of their competitors—the admiration one feels for an able adversary.

Businessmen want their organizations to be loyal, harmonious and hard-working. Many take special pains to assure that their organizations are well-balanced, with young talent coming along ready for responsibility in key positions, and more talent in reserve.

In the long march toward his goal, a businessman gets as much satisfaction as an artist who sees his mental conception take form on canvas. But it is rare for a businessman to complete even one canvas to his satisfaction. He works constantly to improve this detail of organization or that imperfection in marketing procedure or financial structure.

An artist who already has sufficient material means continues to paint, not because he is bearing in mind constantly how many dollars his next canvas will bring, but because he is inspired by some new subject, because he enjoys and takes pride in his work. He is happy if his studies are admired and praised by critics. So it is with most businessmen I know.

If he builds a successful organization, each member is made to realize, to some extent at least, that his own future is linked with the future of the enterprise of which he is a part. Like a team that noses out its adversary in the ninth inning, a well-knit organization rejoices in winning a contract away from a competitor. It is happy in the successful introduction of something new and useful, which is usually achieved only after a long struggle in which many individuals or departments have cooperated.

Profits are calculated! Certainly! They are the marrow of business! But they are concomitant, not always primary!

I have always believed that if something other than dollars, such as stripes on sleeves, ribbons on breasts, and so-called "scrambled eggs" on visors, were the traditional reward for ability and unusual service in business, businessmen would work just as hard and get even more enjoyment out of their work. Wealth—their symbol of success—when it exceeds what they need, merely means being nursemaid to additional worries and responsibilities.

I believe that business would be better off, too, without the high salaries that have become the custom in recent years. These salaries, even when well-earned, instead of stimulating close application to work, tend, in many cases, to divert thought, energy and even ambition. High salaries provide the means for pursuing happiness in travel, hobbies and other fields, which often become the main interest. In such cases business suffers.

However, a scheme of gold braid and medals is infeasible, because in the enterprise economy more than 130 million people determine the winners of business competition. Their acceptance or rejection of a product means success or failure. The degree of acceptance determines the degree of success, which in the long run is calculated in money terms. Rewards for business success are necessarily monetary. Unusual individual contributions to success must be rewarded accordingly.

The different temperaments of businessmen and New Dealers account for the manner in which each group approaches conclusions. Businessmen do not think on emotional grounds. Reason dominates their thinking.

Businessmen are reconciled to the fact that commercial success is a slow and painful process. There is a saying in the chemical industry that it is ten years from production in a laboratory beaker to a tank car. Often it is longer. They know that progress is quickest after painstaking proof in pilot plant—the small-scale experimental plant—and they know that the cheapest experimenting is not even in pilot plant but in the laboratory, where mistakes are cheapest. The businessman knows that large-scale experimentation is ruinous and that haste is costly. Often the most promising laboratory products prove commercial failures. On the other hand, products for which the originator has faint hope sometimes find wide markets. Successful business never builds a commercial plant on laboratory hopes.

In contrast, New Dealers, many of whom are underpaid and underworked professors of law, economics and sociology, have theory as their forte. They deal in the abstractions and unrealities of the academic world. They have had no commercial experience and are unconvinced of the necessity of experimenting on a small scale. Rather, their scientific investigation consists of discourse. Social and economic problems are debated back and forth among themselves, and the conclusions are drawn in the manner of Plato's dialogues.

They appear so fascinated with solutions resulting from these seances that they are factious and intolerant of criticism. They seem to regard everything they touch as holy water. They ascribe any questioning of their work to the carping of mean motives. They are unwilling to await small-scale trial of their solutions; they demand national application—and—we have in prospect even world application!

Most New Dealers are a product of our big cities. In cities

one can never learn to love a rustic hillside or watch the sun play on the riffles of a trout stream. In cities children can't know lambs, ducks and calves, the age-old, wholesome toys of nature. On the contrary, cities consist of material things, and the pleasures of their inhabitants in large measure consist of the consumption of material things.

Big cities harbor life's extremes of wealth and poverty—winners and losers in capitalistic competition—which deeply offend a sensitive spirit. In the artist temperament, sympathy is given wholeheartedly to the loser. Lacking the businessman's experience of seeing society in a Horatio Alger flux, the artist temperament assumes that the big city cross-section of life is typical and static. Doubts are aroused regarding the justice of a social system that breeds such inequalities.

And in our biggest city, New York, enterprise is not that of production, which is usually shaped and hardened by competition into slow, steady growth. The most evident part, at least, is parasitic—that of the promoter, the scalper and the speculator—a type more apt to make a pretentious parade with quick winnings than a small town manufacturer whose community knows him well. The offense to the sensitive spirit, therefore, is greater. It is not surprising, that the New Deal bloomed in New York.

Whether or not due to this urban environment, the thinking of New Dealers places all emphasis on the material things of life. It ignores the moral and spiritual values of individualism, the love of liberty and adventure. They assume most Americans would willingly exchange this freedom for security; at any rate they propose to make the exchange for them by aligning themselves with the poor and working classes in their struggle to free themselves from the imagined domination of capitalists. They desire to create a classless, homogeneous society collectively controlled in the interests of all the people. This is socialism. The idea is as old as history. Its modern form was argued with much vehemence by Karl Marx a century ago. What is new about the New Deal is the recruiting to the cause of social workers, agents of capitalistic charity, intellectuals and members of the leisure class. Jan Valtin records how the Comintern, of which he was a member, was puzzled at the Communists' ability to make greater headway during the twenties among our intellectuals than among our workers.

Monopoly, if in the capitalistic system, is an anathema to New Dealers, but their tenets admit of an apparent paradox. Their sympathy for the underdog prompts the sponsorship of curbs on competition so that there will be no losers. The trade union movement, for instance, tends toward the elimination of competition between individuals in the sale of their services; it prohibits one from underselling another. Superior ability is not recognized in the equalization of union rates. A union's aim is to monopolize the labor supply.

The National Industrial Recovery Act, with its Blue Eagle, was designed to eliminate the "chiseler." Its codes restricted competition. The Guffey Act eliminated price competition in coal and fixed prices high enough so that inefficient producers had a margin. A planned economy retains no vestige of competition!

Anti-competition legislation is not a contradiction of New Deal philosophy. It is a rather logical economic expression of the New Dealers' aversion to contest. In contests one proves superiority over another. That is why one finds few students of natural history in the New Deal. Naturalists know that life is competition and that the results of contest disprove equality.

Thorstein Veblen, mentor of the New Deal, whom Stuart Chase calls "The Great Man" and "One of my idols," expresses this phobia toward competition in his "Theory of the Leisure Class," which Chase calls the "Classic of economic and social literature."[1]

Veblen wrote: "Modern competition is in large part a process of self assertion on the basis of these traits of predatory human nature . . ." Carrying the philosophy even into the realm of sports, he adds, "The culture bestowed in football gives a product of exotic ferocity and cunning.[2] . . . The spiritual traits which go with athletic sports are likewise economically advantageous to the individual as contra-distinguished from the interests of the collectivity. . . . Sports are conceived to foster a habit of mind that is serviceable for the social or industrial purpose. . . . But . . . it is these 'manly virtues' that are (economically) in need of legitimation."[3] Patriotism, he added, has the "Color of feudal allegiance."[4]

The anti-competition features of a planned economy appeal to the New Dealers. They visualize opportunities of doing away with economic casualties caused by competition and loss of jobs due to labor-saving machinery which is forced by competition. They visualize opportunities to eliminate human waste, the victims of competition. By far-sighted central economic planning, they believe the huge industrial machine can be adapted to the benefit of all; that its great potential output, properly controlled, will prove sufficient to give everyone an adequate standard of living.

This philosophy runs counter to that of the businessman, who foresees in it loss of adventure and false security. He is still true to the old American ideology taught in his country schoolroom—that America is the land of the free and unoppressed! that America provides escape for the adventurous and those who want to worship and live as they please! that it is a land free of the shackles of class and omnipotent government. He remembers learning that our Founding

Fathers received almost divine guidance in framing our Constitution; that the Supreme Court was a hallowed sanctuary of justice; and that it would guard carefully everyone's rights, property rights as well as human rights. He remembers learning that every American boy has the opportunity to become president. His boyhood heroes were created by Horatio Alger. He recalls that in his youth a boy born on the wrong side of the railroad tracks could look across to the big house on the hill and hope that, if he worked harder than others, produced something better or cheaper, or invented something new, he, too, in time could have a house as big or even bigger, for there was no limit to achievement. And if he won in life's competition, his children would have a better chance than he; they would be free of privations he had suffered and they would have a better education because he could pass his acquisitions on to them.

Businessmen still believe in this ideology—that freedom to pursue happiness, to work for one's own self-interest, made America the greatest and most powerful nation in history. They believe in the possibilities of the future and that under conditions restoring freedom to pursue happiness and freedom of enterprise, policies based on trust of these principles will prove the solvent of our social and economic difficulties to the advantage of all.

The New Dealers argue the nation has not time to wait!—that while individualists and their private enterprise have done a splendid job in the creation of agencies capable of producing abundance, they have not provided for its equitable distribution. They argue, further, that because of the greediness of those owning and managing the system, the problem will never be solved, for, in private enterprise, production is permitted only so long as it is profitable. When it is not profitable, they say production ceases, causing periodic depressions, and large bodies of men, who are idle involuntarily because they cannot find gainful work, suffer misery and distress. They cherish the ideal that state central economic planning by political officials, with state power to coerce, will emphasize consumption by providing the masses with ample means for acquisition; thus, production is to be continuous and unemployment and the other evils which they attribute to private enterprise will vanish.

CHAPTER IV
Ten Years

BUT UNEMPLOYMENT IS NOT CHARACTERISTIC OF PRIVATE enterprise; it is the growing pains that are characteristic of our liberal civilization's social order! Bushmen have no unemployment! There was never unemployment when workers were slaves!

Our civilization, however, has eliminated other even more dreaded scourges that haunted mankind for countless generations. Only when war interferes with its normal operation does thought of famine cross our minds. Even the word is almost obsolete. Nor do we think of plagues—that cycle of pestilence and black death which has visited almost all the world at one time or another, which recurred in Rome four times in one century, which in the Middle Ages robbed various parts of Europe of two-thirds of their population, then decimated and re-decimated the London of Samuel Pepys. Plagues are lost in antiquity.

Unemployment is impossible among Bushmen of the Solomons, African pigmies or Indians of the Brazilian jungle, because they are never employed in production for others. Hunting and fishing only for themselves and building their own huts, each family is self-sufficient. They have never learned to divide work, allocating to groups of their people work each can do best.

It was this division of labor which steadily permitted the production of more things for use. One making better shoes became a cobbler and provided shoes for others; another capable of building houses better and faster became a carpenter and built houses for others; and so on until individuals, groups, communities, even nations, became interdependent. Now a shoe factory's operation depends upon farmers and workers in other plants buying shoes. A farmer's employment depends upon the shoe and other workers buying farm products. None of us is sufficient unto himself alone. The satisfaction of one's needs depends upon the production of others; and the employment of each of us is dependent upon the ability and willingness of others to buy the products which we have a part in producing or distributing. In times when everyone buys from another, everyone is busy, and we have prosperity. In times when we do not or cannot buy from one another, we have depression and enforced idleness.

The misery, distress and unemployment such as we witnessed during the 1930's have recurred with regularity throughout the history of civilization, in all parts of the world, among all races and peoples and under all types of government.

The early Christian Father, Lactantius, bemoaned the difficulties and deprivations of Romans under the regimented state of the despot he termed "That author of evil," Diocletian. The Chinese people never forgave the Mongols the unhappiness and distress resulting from the Great Khan's disruption of the Chinese economy.

It was the unemployment and distress of Henry the Eighth's England that caused Sir Thomas More to vision a perfect life and write his famed "Utopia"; and the French suffered unemployment, hunger and distress under the absolutism of their Grand Monarch, Louis XIV. Unemployment accompanying the early industrialization of England caused much of the migration that sent welcome waves of settlers to our shores. Because the power loom made his father's trade obsolete, Andrew Carnegie came to America. Disrupted economies appear countless times in all ages of civilization in all countries.

Most of these unhappy periods follow wars, when economies are always dislocated, when men are drained into the non-productive work of armies, when business and commerce are diverted from their peaceful pursuit of supplying man's wants into providing for killing and destruction.

During war men destroy former production and waste current production while civilians use up their accumulated store of useful things. Whole economies are pushed backward. Nature demands retribution for such orgies, and until economies recover and are readjusted, nations have inevitably paid with periods of want, adversity and hardship.

In America we suffered such a period of distress and unemployment in 1785, as an aftermath of the Revolutionary War; others following in 1837 and 1857 were harvests of popular enthusiasm resulting in speculative land booms in the Middle West. There was a prolonged depression in the 1870's and the latter 1880's, a sequel to the Civil War. We had brief ones in 1907 and 1921.

However, from all these depressions American private enterprise regenerated itself with full vigor. It attained greater prosperity—so much so that in almost every case the vale of each depression provided greater national income, more employment and a better average standard of living than the heights of prosperity that preceded the earlier depression.

The depression beginning in 1929 and reaching its depth in 1932, however, was different—not in origin but in the fact that American enterprise could not dig out! In previous depressions groups which advocated unorthodox remedies were only vocal minorities. They agitated from without.

This time they were in control of government and in a position to enforce their theories and remedies.

The Socialist Party's 1932 platform called for "A federal appropriation of $5,000,000,000 for immediate relief of those in need, to supplement state and local appropriations; a federal appropriation of $5,000,000,000 for public works and roads, reforestation, slum clearance, and decent homes for the workers; legislation providing for the acquisition of land, buildings and equipment necessary to put the unemployed to work producing food, fuel and clothing and for the erection of housing for their own use; the six-hour day and the five-day week; a comprehensive and efficient system of free public employment agencies; a compulsory system of unemployment compensation with adequate benefits, based on contributions by the government and by employers; old-age pensions for men and women sixty years of age and over; the abolition of child labor; government aid to farmers and small home-owners to protect them against mortgage foreclosure; and adequate minimum wage laws." With some exceptions of degree, each and every one of these Socialist planks was fulfilled.

A shocked business world looked askance as these measures were inaugurated. Hindsight now tells us that in many cases businessmen were wrong but nevertheless at the time they were perplexed and confused by the appearance of such evidences of Marxism amidst their laissez-faire.

And disturbing laws in addition to those contained in the Socialist platform followed each other into the legislative mill with a constancy that Eskimos would liken not to the wind, which stops, but to a river, which is ceaseless.

Confidence in the monetary system was shocked by a series of unorthodox acts. One gave the President power to cut the gold content of the dollar in half, but he stopped at sixty per cent. Then the Gold Reserve Act provided that he could "purchase gold . . . at such rates . . . as he may deem most advantageous to the public interest, any provision of law relating to the maintenance of parity . . . to the contrary notwithstanding." Thus the gold content of the dollar remained the province of the President. The Thomas Amendment empowered the President to adopt bimetallism at the Bryan 16:1 ratio. He was empowered to issue three billion dollars of greenbacks. The issuance of Federal Reserve Bank notes was authorized, up to one hundred per cent of the face value of United States Government securities offered in exchange. The President was authorized to buy silver until it reached one-third the value of the nation's gold holdings.

Nothing can be more disturbing to business than uncertainty regarding the money in which it calculates its investment, its costs and its selling prices. No tariff has ever been as great a barrier to international trade as a fluctuating and depreciating currency. When the gold content of the dollar was cut forty per cent, for instance, an importer had to pay $1.66 for what he formerly bought for $1.00. Devaluation of the dollar acted as a new and prohibitory tariff.

Similarly, when we bought silver and inflated its price, we automatically raised the value of the currency of nations with silver monetary standards. The prices of products from the Far East rose in terms of our dollar. We could afford to buy less of them.

The Securities Act, supplying a long-needed device to put truth into the issuance of securities and to protect the purchaser, went further than business felt was justified, for the Securities Act made any issuer of a stock or bond prove his innocence if challenged. This placed businessmen in a worse position than criminals, who are innocent until proven guilty. No sooner was this out of the way than a long-needed measure to regulate the Stock Exchange was tossed at Congress.

But it went further; it also controlled many relationships of companies with their shareholders and the public.

An act providing for the regulation and dismemberment of public utility holding companies and public utilities, although to a large extent justified by the inexcusable abuses of public interest prevalent in that industry, disturbed businessmen. Who would be next to suffer the death sentence?

The Wagner Act, containing obvious faults, was brought forward to bring peace into the disturbed labor relationships and was passed over business protests. The National Labor Relations Board read new meaning after new meaning into the Act, each being sustained by the Supreme Court. Starting with understandable orders to restore employment and back pay to employes who had been dismissed on account of union activities, it progressed by ordering back pay and employment to those whose applications for employment had been refused because of suspected union activities. Then it vaulted to the ridiculous by ordering back pay to those who *had not even applied* for employment because they feared that, on account of past union activities, they would have been refused employment.[1] To lesser extent other acts, such as the Robinson-Patman Act and the Walsh-Healy Act, disturbed the business world.

The execution of many of these laws was confided to executive agencies which were empowered, like the Star Chamber, to make their own rules and regulations, to pursue their own investigations, to prosecute and sit in judgment in their own cases. These tribunals acted as shackles on business. Business had placed over it, for instance, the Securities and Exchange Commission, the National Labor Relations Board and a Wage and Hour Administrator. Government by boards and men replaced government by laws. Instead of laws with clearly-defined limits of action, which could be interpreted by lawyers, the meanings of the laws were determined by commissioners who were given considerable latitude for exercise of judgment. On the whole, these administrators were impractical idealists, knew business only in theory and at heart were unfriendly to the system of private enterprise.

Uncertainty and confusion were caused by delays and changing policies, as the personnel of commissions were constantly changing. The Securities and Exchange Commission, for instance, has had six chairmen in eight years and with but one exception none had experience as either a securities dealer, stock exchange broker or businessman. Yet they were empowered to render decisions affecting the vitals of these trades and industries.

The President was given the power to cut tariffs in half, which contributed uncertainty and hesitancy about new ventures. Every year new and additional taxes were levied, each making the risking of capital in enterprise less attractive. Some of the taxes, such as the Undistributed Profits Tax, Capital Stock Tax, and the pre-war Excess Profits Tax, were unorthodox and punitive and caused much apprehension in business circles as to the true motives of the sponsors. Some remembered Karl Marx's exhortation: "If the Democrats propose proportional taxation then the workers must demand progressive taxation; if the Democrats themselves move for moderated progressive taxation the workers must insist on a tax whose rates are so steeply graduated as to bring ruin to capital."[2] Left Wingers who confidently predicted that private enterprise could never recover, even that it would pass away, were thinking mainly of the tax poison in its food.

Perhaps business should not have been shocked into passivity at alterations in its relationships with customers, stockholders and labor. Many of the changes are now recognized as having been long overdue, and business as a whole would not desire their repeal. However, the fact remains that American economy was undergoing a violent revolution and its business organism was severely jarred by the rapid changes in climate to which it was subjected.

Biologists maintain that through the process of evolution man has evolved from a fish. However, if our fish ancestors had been yanked violently out of water and thrown onto arid land they would have perished. We would never have peopled the earth. The New Deal measures in effect yanked the business fish out of its familiar waters of traditional capitalism and it lay wiggling on an unfamiliar and hostile bank. Of course it could not recover!

The depression in which we wallowed so long was not in its beginning confined to America, like many historical antecedents; it was a world-wide aftermath of the Great War. Starting with our 1929 stock market crash and the failure of the great Credit Anstalt of Austria, it swept up through Germany and the rest of Europe and shocked England off the gold standard.

However, by 1932 all great nations of the world started a recovery which brought some back to prosperity a few years later—a few to the greatest prosperity in their history. There was one exception in Europe—France—which was also socializing and experimenting with her economy. Canada lagged, too, because she is bound so closely to us.[3]

England, however, elevated the Conservative Party to office, abandoned free trade and erected tariffs to protect manufacture; she rationalized her dole and passed legislation regulating trade unions. By 1934 England had a budget surplus and reduced taxes.[4] By 1937, prior to her rearmament program, she had practically abolished unemployment and the biggest housing boom in her history aided in her greatest post-war prosperity.

As the well being of the whole world is so dependent upon American prosperity, it may not be too far-fetched to throw out a supposition that if we, too, with our tremendous resources and vigor, had been allowed to work our way out of the depression as did England, the world, including Germany, might have been enjoying such prosperity that war might have been averted.

But our economy, struggling in its new harness, made little progress. Unemployment persisted. As mention of unemployment brings to one's mind visions of closed manufacturing plants, smokeless chimneys, and "No Help Wanted" signs on factory doors, it is on the manufacturing industry alone that the blame for unemployment is put unfairly.

However, manufacture is but one of many fields in which men are employed. Average employment during 1940 in manufacture increased two per cent over the average employment of 1929, whereas employment in agriculture increased but four-tenths of one per cent; in transportation employment decreased twenty-one per cent, in forestry and fishing it decreased more than twenty-two per cent; the decrease in mining was twenty-nine per cent and in construction more than forty-two per cent.[5]

Manufacturing, the greatest user of labor-saving machinery, actually employed more people than it did ten years earlier, whereas industries such as mining and construction made the poorest comparison. Industries subject to the greatest amount of government regulation and government competition, such as transportation and public utilities, also compared unfavorably.

Nevertheless, in January, 1940, there were more than ten million people seeking jobs.

What is needed to make jobs in our industrial civilization? Tools and machines! Therefore, the prime essential is thrift and the accumulation of savings for investment as capital. Capital and capital goods are absolute necessities in the tool kit of every industrial workman. This capital is not "sure-thing," "gilt-edge" or "quick-return" investment. It is not guaranteed by government; it is venture or risk capital. It is a long-term investment. It requires faith in the future and a readiness to lose if one's judgment is wrong.

Without venture capital behind him, a workman is without a job in our industrial civilization. In the chemical industry, for instance, over ten thousand dollars must be invested in land, buildings, machinery, raw materials and other assets for each person employed. Without that investment there would be no jobs in the chemical industry. Before a truck driver can have a job someone must invest in a truck; before a locomotive engineer can be employed someone must invest in tracks, a locomotive and cars; before a pilot can be employed someone must invest in an airplane. In 1940 there was an average investment of $5,936 for each employe in American industry.[6]

During the decade of the nineteen twenties the number of employable persons in the United States increased from about forty-one million nine hundred thousand to about forty-eight million three hundred thousand.

During this period new stock and note issues, exclusive of refunding issues and exclusive of issues for financial corporations, such as investment trusts—that is, net new capital for expansion of business—averaged about three billion eight hundred million dollars a year. This was sufficient at the rate of six thousand dollars per man to provide over six hundred thousand new jobs each year. In addition, there were surplus profits of business which were not paid out as dividends and a large part of this was reinvested and provided new jobs. Seven billion dollars of new capital was absorbed annually in the nineteen twenties, enough for one million new jobs each year. This huge sum provided jobs not only for the immigrants and the normal increase in population, but jobs in new industries to replace those eliminated by technological progress in older ones.

During the decade of the nineteen thirties the number of employable persons increased as much as during the twenties but they were added to the unemployed!

From 1931 through 1939 the volume of new industrial securities averaged only seven hundred and twenty million dollars a year, or about one-fifth of that of the previous decade, and instead of business earning more profits than were paid out in dividends, the loss of net working capital of all non-financial corporations exceeded the proceeds of new financing.

Other sources that supplied the stream of business capital dried up also. On June 1, 1926, for instance, the directors of banks now composing three of the largest St. Louis banks had borrowed from their banks and guaranteed the loans of others in the aggregate amount of $7,709,000. On June 1, 1938, however, the directors of these same banks owed and guaranteed loans of others in the amount of only $413,000. Nineteen twenty-six was a year of reasonable business activity. Speculative fever of the late twenties had not taken hold. These men were using their credit and were taking business risks. The low 1938 volume reflected the unwillingness of these same men to use their ample credit, borrow and take business risks. Taxes and uncertainties had discouraged them.

The deterring effect of increased income taxes was apparent also by an examination of large estates. In 1927 tax-exempt government securities amounted to nine per cent of the total of such estates. In 1935 this percentage had risen to forty-four per cent.[7] As tax-exempt government securities yielded on the average less than three per cent, is it not significant that capital was willing to accept such a low yield in preference to taking a risk for a higher return in business? It meant simply that risks were not worth while.

This blocking of the normal channels of industrial investment affected so-called small business enterprises even more than large corporations. In manufacturing, about sixty-five per cent of all persons employed is in companies employing less than five hundred people.[8] With less available capital in proportion to volume of production, and with less reserves to carry them through non-profit periods, such enterprises suffered severely.

Small companies afford the best outlet for individualism. They are likely to be based on new ideas, new products, or new services that might not otherwise be developed. Normally, small companies are the large corporations of the future. Small companies not only need profits that can be plowed back but, if they are to grow, they usually require, periodically, additional capital. Their need is not commercial loans nor government loans, but venture capital that enters business as a partner for profit or loss. Only in a relatively free capital market and in an economic climate favorable to risks can such needs be met.

Capital wealth engaged in the manufacturing industry is constantly being consumed: worn out by depreciation, destroyed by fire or accident, rendered obsolete by improvements in machinery or processes, or scrapped because occasion for its use has passed. The thirties saw only partial replacement of this capital wealth. Twenty per cent less capital was employed in manufacture at the end of 1939 than ten years earlier, and two billion less than at the depth of the depression in 1932.[9]

Truly, the nineteen thirties were the locust years for private enterprise; never in America's history had such a long period elapsed without it showing marked increases in both capital investment and employment.

There were other obstacles that diminished the flow of new capital into industry. As business was confused by the flood of new laws and commissions, people who by the exercise of self-denial and thrift had money available for investment were intimidated also. There was a belief that the government was that of only a part of the people, and business was not that part. Capital tended to hibernate until the storm blew over. The investing public, the possessor of the needed capital, sensed the fact which James Burnham describes in an able exposition of social and economic trends. "The truth," Burnham wrote, as he raised the mask of idealism, "is that the New Deal is in direction and tendency anti-capitalistic."[10]

In its early days the New Deal announced as one of its experiments the priming of the pump of private enterprise with governmental spending. Billions were spent. The national debt increased three billion in 1933 and over four billion in 1934. As this money went round from the WPA'er to grocer, to baker, to automobile dealer, to auto manufacturer, to auto worker and back to the grocer, business picked up! However, each time as the money passed from hand to hand a little was held back. The grocer held back his profit and banked it; the automobile dealer may have paid off a debt with his profit and the recipient banked it; the manufacturer banked his profit; the laborer saved a little and banked it. And so each time a little less was passed on, until at last it vanished. As profits and savings, it wound up in the banks or took shelter in the security of government bonds. Owners hesitated to risk it in business.

From 1933 to 1939 the Federal government debt increased eighteen billion dollars. The guaranteed debt of government agencies increased five billion.[11] During the same period bank deposits increased twenty billion—all idle money.[12] It was like taking money out of one pocket and putting it in another. Normally this money would have been withdrawn for investment in a home, in a bond or in stocks, or as capital for a small business venture. However, the composite American mental attitude advised against it. There was lack of confidence, lack of trust in the state-manufactured prosperity and uncertainty resulting from the government's attitude toward business.

The cumulative force of several years of government spending was seen in 1936, when on top of the usual deficit spending, the soldiers' bonus was paid. Believing the priming had worked, that the pump was operating at last, there was an honest effort in 1937 to balance the budget. Spending was curtailed in hopes the momentum gained would carry on. However, with shrunken capital, prohibitory restrictions and a confused management, business slumped. By midsummer 1938 it was again flat on its back.

Then high priests of the New Deal cast aside taboos and inhibitions and expounded the virtue of government spending as a permanent policy, assuring us that, as we owe the national debt to ourselves its size is of no significance. But, bowing to popular aversion to the word "spending," they called it "Government investment."

The Standard Dictionary defines investment—"To let out money or capital in business with a view to obtaining income or profit." Therefore, properly to meet the definition of investment there must be a reasonable expectation of a steady income which over a period of years will pay back the outlay.

Most government spending—C.C.C., N.Y.A., W.P.A., A.A.A.—did not meet this acid test. In a broad sense it might be argued that the nation was investing in the health of its youth, in beautification of its parks, and in monuments of which posterity could be proud. Some of these things had esthetic value; they might yield a spiritual return but they did not yield a profit in an economic sense—a profit which could be used to pay interest on government debt or which could be accumulated and used in time for its retirement.

An individual whose assets consisted solely of costly Washington Monuments and Lincoln Memorials would have a wealth of beauty but he would be bankrupt at the same time.

A government investment is the T.V.A., which with proper management could in time return its cost to the Treasury and in the meantime repay the interest the government is laying out on its obligations. It also created permanent jobs. Good roads might yield additional gasoline taxes brought about by increased use of the roads; they might be called investments, too. They create jobs.

Typical government spending, however, does not create the means of permanent jobs such as results from investment in a new factory, a new warehouse or a new department store. That is why government spending can never be a permanent cure for unemployment.

However, in 1939 Hitler solved the unemployment problem—he marched! We armed for defense! Business and government poured billions into plant extensions, conversions and new facilities. Enlistment in the Army and Navy soared and unemployment fell. Industrial tempo increased steadily. Then Pearl Harbor! Now a labor shortage!

Pointing to the "prosperity" of our planned war economy New Dealers argue that the niggardliness of our deficits was the only reason the "prosperity" was not achieved earlier. Now they say we have proof that with sufficient government spending, unemployment vanishes; that if this can be achieved in wartime, building ships to be sunk and ammunition to be shot away, why can't everyone be employed in peace time, producing things that everyone needs—and they argue with persuasion that with sufficient spending and central economic planning we need never return to the anomaly of want in the midst of plenty.

But where will spending lead us? What is "planning"? And—what is the New Deal?

CHAPTER V

The Prophet and His Works

IF THE NEW DEAL HAS ANY CHARACTERISTICS DISTINGUISHING it from a long chain of equalitarian philosophies, these characteristics can be traced in substantial measure to the incubation of the teachings of the late Thorstein Veblen.[1]

One receives the impression from Veblen's works that his humble origin, his foreign parentage and a youth spent in a colony of recent immigrants, thwarted any real comprehension of the true American mentality. Veblen's adolescence and young manhood were lived amidst the hardships and unemployment of the depression years of the 1880's. When studying at Johns Hopkins and Yale he found himself an economic and spiritual outcast from a relatively gay and wealthy American student body. For seven years after his graduation he was unsuccessful in securing a job, and it was not until he had passed his forty-sixth year that his annual salary exceeded $600.

His origin, his difficulty in finding employment and the contrast between the riches with which he was thrown and his own poverty may account for his bitter and sarcastic attitude toward the American economic system out of which the riches came.

One may have the key to Veblen's mind in the knowledge that as a student he was a failure in mathematics but excelled in philosophy and economics.[2] Mathematics, the exact science of cold, sterile figures, of irrefutable additions, equations and conclusions, is the foundation of astronomy and navigation, which made possible the voyages of adventure and discovery. Mathematics is the basis of physics, chemistry and engineering, with which, after painstaking experiment, new worlds are constantly conquered by modern adventurers.

Mathematics is also the key to business accounts. Costs, output and selling prices are calculated and expressed in figures. Business' books must mathematically balance.

Every mathematician's answer to a problem is the same. Workers in fields founded on mathematics have confidence in facts and reason. They usually have vision and faith, and seek adventure.

Philosophy and economics, on the other hand, are not exact sciences. They are sciences wherein problems are subject not to experiment but to individual observation and interpretation, wherein mutually agreeable conclusions are reached by like minds through argument. Both sciences provide opportunities for armchair mental gymnastics, individual dogmas, palaver and gush. They are not even a prelude to adventure, risk or physical exertion.

Economics is the basis of a social science dealing with human equations and human reactions which, when subject to the temperament of different personalities, will yield different answers. In economics, like law, one can start with the preferred conclusion and then select appropriate supporting data as proof. One need only recall, for instance, "The New Era" and the abundant proof offered by economists in support of their theory that 1929's booming stock market did not overvalue the boundless prosperity in prospect. Their delirious conclusion convinced banker, businessman and bootblack alike. Then the theory of the "commodity dollar," one of constant purchasing power, had its day too!

Veblen was a philosophizing economist. Personalizing the

characteristics of his profession, he shunned adventure. He was physically lazy. His character found unconscious expression in his slovenly dress and in his assertion that "man's ideal is an unrestrained consumption of goods without work." [3]

Veblen's non-comprehension of American character is illustrated by his interpretation of the relationship of men and domestic animals. Analyzing to his own satisfaction the reason men keep dogs, he concludes: "The commercial value of canine monstrosities, such as the prevailing styles of pet dogs both for men's and women's use, rests on their high cost of production, and their value to their owners lies chiefly in their utility as items of conspicuous consumption. Indirectly, through reflection upon their honorific expensiveness, a social worth is imputed to them." And: "Since any attention bestowed upon these animals is in no sense gainful or useful, it is also reputable." [4] Horses fared no better with this man.

It appears that a sense of inferiority caused him to withdraw within himself, sit on the sidelines and sneer at American life and American business. He regularly lapsed into long periods of silence which, when broken, was by speech that was muffled and almost inaudible. His advocacy of the abolition of private property, of which he failed to attain any material amount, and his antipathy toward competition, may have stemmed somewhat from his sense of inferiority.

Veblen had a deep suspicion that fraud was involved in competition of any kind and that winners achieved success only because of underhanded action. This antipathy toward competition found expression in his grading of students. Aspirants to Phi Beta Kappa avoided Veblen's courses because he did not grade anyone above "C"; on the other hand, no student was too inept to merit a "C." [5] It is quite understandable, therefore, that students dubbed him a "queer fish."

He carried his dislike of competition even to the field of athletics, terming sportsmanship a "predatory and animistic habit of man."[6] College athletics, he inveighed, were fostered by businessmen to indoctrinate students with the love of competition. He stated that the habitual employment of umpires and "the minute technical regulations governing the limits and details of permissible frauds" indicated that games tolerated fraudulent practice and "a calloused disregard of the interests of others, individually or collectively."[7]

Veblen considered the Y.M.C.A. "a bourgeois and capitalist agency" whose purpose it was "to defend the existing order."[8] However, he was not above emulating the leisure class. He speculated in the stock market. He lost. One wonders if his outlook would have been less seamy had he won! Might it even have been cheerful had he done extremely well? Although Veblen taught courses in socialism and inveighed against capitalism, like our New Dealers, he scrupulously avoided saying he was a Socialist. But six months before his death in 1929 he is reported to have said, "Naturally there will be other developments right along, but just now Communism offers the best course that I can see."[9]

Veblen's writings damn what he termed "the conscientious withdrawal of efficiency" and "capitalistic sabotage" in which he said businessmen indulged. He insisted with vehemence that depressions were due to the fact that enterprise was operated solely for maximum profit and all production that might tend to lower the maximum profit was withheld by capitalistic sabotage. Advertising, to Veblen, was merely a device "to enable a shrewdly limited output of goods to be sold at more profitable prices."[10]

He argued that this capitalistic sabotage caused periodic

recurrences of streets full of idle men and factories full of idle machines. He insisted that there was no technological reason why both men and machines should not be continually busy as there were always people who wanted and needed the goods that these men and machines were capable of producing. He argued that while the common man was periodically unemployed and in want there were "kept classes"—people who lived in leisure, contributing nothing to the pool of consumable goods; that members of these kept classes spent their lifetime vying with each other as to the most conspicuous manner of wasting their riches.

He reasoned that these kept classes were the absentee owners of enterprise; that the businessmen were their agents who performed no useful function except to practice sabotage and stop the turning of wheels whenever there was danger of production exceeding that which could be sold at the maximum profit.

He urged that the revolution, which he hoped would take place during a period of depression, should under no circumstances countenance businessmen in its ranks, as "such a movement of overturn can hope to succeed only if it excludes the businessmen from all positions of responsibility."[11] He urged those who would overthrow the system to enlist only engineers and plant managers—as they were the men responsible for operations—and that these groups, released from the restrictions of businessmen, could logically be brought into the service of the state and the system operated continuously at maximum output.

Veblen's advice to exclude businessmen from positions of responsibility seems to have been followed with consistency during the New Deal administration until the defense program required their talents. That their influence, however, is still a negligible quantity is indicated by a poll of Washington newspaper reporters conducted by Forbes magazine.[12]

Sixty key correspondents were asked: "Who are the men behind the scenes in Washington? Name the top five." The five most often mentioned included: One former social worker, Harry Hopkins; two former lawyers, Felix Frankfurter and Samuel Rosenman; and two former newspaper men, Lowell Mellet and Wayne Coy. The tabulated replies listed forty-five individuals. Of the total, business may claim only three: William Batt, Bernard Baruch and Sidney Weinberg; the latter two, however, were associated with the speculative community of the New York Stock Exchange rather than business.

Businessmen throughout the land, their plant managers and their engineers have burned midnight oil without thought of "time and a half," performing miracles to help win the war, but so far no public acknowledgment of their contribution has been made by a New Dealer.

Veblen's caustic, suspicious and trenchant attitude drew to his doorstep many owlish pupils and admirers of similar origin and like experience, or with intellectually compatible souls. And his works, his teachings and his deliberations provide the foundation of current American socialism. Veblen's philosophy dominated much of the teaching staff of Columbia University, spread to Harvard and Yale and now is felt in universities throughout the land. His admirers and disciples are now planning the future of the nation—indeed, of the world.

Veblen's psychopathic loathing of businessmen and his inability to understand the mentality of his day caused him to bemoan the American people's faith in businessmen.

"By settled habit," he wrote, "the American population are quite unable to see their way to entrust any appreciable responsibility to any other than businessmen."[13] He forecast that a revolution resulting in the utilization of the means of production in the interests of all could never be accomplished without "an intensive campaign of inquiry and publicity, such as will bring the underlying population to a reasonable understanding of what it is all about."[14]

One can recognize Veblen's advice again in the New Deal campaign of "inquiry and publicity" in which the abuses and faults of private enterprise have been exposed so glaringly; a campaign which has not ceased, in one form or another, for ten long years. It continues even in the midst of war.

This campaign inaugurated a new technique for obtaining publicity. A unique procedure was introduced into American politics—that of Congressional investigations serving as a background and argument for the need of new legislation and fundamental changes in the economy. With committees headed by Congressmen and Senators friendly to the New Deal viewpoint or dependent upon the administration for patronage, witnesses who could do the most damage to the cause of private enterprise were summoned. At the hearings, business leaders who had offended were subjected to embarrassing questions and gave damaging testimony. Often the witnesses were tricked into testimony which when taken alone was more harmful than if considered in the light of all the facts. But it was these specimens of ore that were presented to the assay office of public opinion so that businessmen as a whole were downgraded.

Beginning with Pecora's investigation of Wall Street, which brought out such shocking abuses of trust and privilege by bankers, there followed the LaFollette Committee's investigation of instances of businessmen's alleged abuses of the rights of labor, the eighteen months' investigation of the Temporary National Economic Committee, and Thurman Arnold's campaign against so-called monopoly, conspiracies in restraint of trade, alleged abuses of the patent system, and international cartels.

The public has been played upon for ten years, on the front page and over the radio, by many studied instances wherein fraud has been practiced by businessmen; wherein trust has been abused by businessmen and labor has been denied its rights by businessmen. Thus, the businessman has been portrayed as a grasping, heinously selfish, public enemy.

Through the skillful use of semantics, New Dealers carefully choose between "good" words and "bad" words in the presentation of their philosophy and argument. Hence, "spending," if indulged in by government, was a "bad" word; therefore it was called "investment," a "good" word. This study of the meaning of words and mental images and associations they raise bore fruit when the American people were led to remember and adopt in their vocabulary catchy phrases of class consciousness, such as "greedy princes of privilege," "economic royalists," "the lower third," "wage slavery," and "want in the midst of plenty." These words were good for headlines. They were repeated again and again. They stuck!

Is it any wonder now that over the morning coffee a businessman's wife looks up from her newspaper and says, "Isn't it terrible about the president of the X Corporation? I know *you* wouldn't do that, dear, but nevertheless, business certainly is rotten and the government must do *something* to control it!"

Is there any group or profession without a family skeleton? Could any group maintain the public's confidence after a decade of inquisition during which its enemies were, by reason of their position, able to parade its faults, and only its faults, before public view?

If for instance for ten years the public had been exposed to examples of the quackery in medicine; to cases where unscrupulous physicians split fees unethically; if isolated cases of unneeded operations performed in order to secure fees were made to appear common practice; if we were told how unscrupulous physicians prey upon hypochondriacs and keep them returning and returning, and paying and paying, for prescriptions of sweetened and scented water—and if the people were never told about the conscientious physician who knows no hours, who devotes half a lifetime to charity cases, who unselfishly shares his knowledge with the younger men and who, through some of the very practices that might be turned to criticism, has constantly raised the standard of his profession, steadily lengthened the list of diseases that have been conquered and increased the fields of curative surgery; if all the good in the medical profession were suppressed and for ten long years only the evils paraded, would not the public be ready to support legislation so drastic as to limit the usefulness of the medical profession?

Could lawyers, labor, politicians, the church, the press, or even the New Deal itself survive a searching inquiry untainted?

But business, the American system of private enterprise, has endured for more than a decade an inquisition by unfriendly interests. Although there have been sporadic attempts by certain groups of businessmen and trade associations, such as the National Association of Manufacturers and the Chamber of Commerce of the United States, to answer the innuendo and attacks, they have been of the "too little and too late" variety and by reason of their origin they fell upon suspicious ears.

Charges against business are sensational. They are front page news. Answers by business, if made at all, are usually factual, uninteresting, punctiliously phrased by attorneys, and if printed at all wind up as fill-ins on inside pages, often in second sections. Business has been required continually to defend itself and, as in battle, the advantage lies in attack.

Thus, from a population which Veblen described as having a "settled habit of being unable to see their way to entrust any appreciable responsibility to any other than businessmen," a large share of our population has been converted to the philosophy of the planners and much of the rest is at least suspicious.

Our youth on the whole has lost faith in business leadership and private enterprise. All of our young people under twenty-eight years of age have passed through adolescence and young manhood and womanhood during a prolonged period of depression, unemployment and scandal. In many cases, after completing education and being unable to find employment, they were frustrated in their ambitions. As a class, they do not know what it is to have a free choice of employment.

They have been subjected to a constant barrage of innuendo leveled at private enterprise and against continuing the system. They have been told that its world of chicanery, greed and unjust enrichment of the few at the expense of the many is doomed to the past, along with feudalism. It would be a miracle if they would not rejoice at its passing and willingly embrace any new economic faith that held promise of a better life.

As from the Great Beyond Veblen looks at the American scene of 1943, his shade must wear the smile of a Cheshire cat! His pupils learned well!

CHAPTER VI

The Inquisition

THE BURNING ZEAL OF THOSE VEBLEN INSPIRED MADE them guilty at times of hitting below the belt. Without doubt, the most shabby attempts to proselytize public opinion ever made by a group in possession of American political power were the work of the Temporary National Economic Committee.

In another sharp departure from precedent, this important investigating committee was composed not of members of Congress only but of representatives of the administrative departments and federal regulatory agencies as well.

Business, marking the make-up of the committee, sensed that it would be another "witch hunt." However, the chairman, Senator O'Mahoney, reassured all that it would pursue an objective study of the nation's economy; that its hearings would be fair and just and its conclusions factual and unbiased. A perusal of the hearings confirms both Senator O'Mahoney's sincerity and the relative impartiality of other Congressional members of the committee. However, the representatives of the administrative departments and federal regulatory agencies—a cabal of the New Deal—constituted a practical working majority. They planned the hearings and by executive order controlled the expenditure of four-fifths of the committee funds. They selected and summoned the witnesses.

The presidential message to Congress requesting establishment of the committee called attention to the "need for a thorough study of the concentration of economic power and its injurious effects on the American system of free enterprise." The message said: "The traditional approach to the problems I have discussed has been through the antitrust laws. That approach we do not propose to abandon. On the contrary, although we must recognize the inadequacies of the existing laws, we seek to enforce them so that the public shall not be deprived of such protection as they afford. . . . But the existing antitrust laws are inadequate—most importantly because of new financial economic conditions with which they are powerless to cope.

"The Sherman Act was passed nearly forty years ago. The Clayton and Federal Trade Commission Acts were passed over twenty years ago. We have had considerable experience under those acts. In the meantime we have had a chance to observe the practical operation of large-scale industry and to learn many things about the competitive system which we did not know in those days.

"We have witnessed the merging-out of effective competition in many fields of enterprise. We have learned that the so-called competitive system works differently in an industry where there are many independent units, from the way it works in an industry where a few large producers dominate the market. . . .

"To meet the situation I have described, there should be a thorough study of the concentration of economic power in American industry and the effect of that concentration upon the decline of competition. . . . *The study should not be confined to the traditional antitrust field. The effects of tax, patent, and other Government policies cannot be ignored.*"[1]

A later message requested that study be given also to "the anomaly of idle men and idle money."

Public hearings of the committee began December 1, 1938, and continued, with but slight interruptions, for eighteen months. More than twenty thousand pages of printed testimony and 3,300 technical exhibits were in the records of its hearings. Copies of the hearings were distributed to a free mailing list consisting of seven thousand individuals, public, university and professional libraries, foundations, research organizations, newspaper and periodical libraries.

The committee also designated several economists and sociologists to make studies of subjects raised at the hearings and make reports. These reports were published in a series of forty-three monographs.

Authors of these monographs went outside of testimony before the committee to sources and references that helped to prove their theories. Nevertheless, the monographs were given the rather curious status of "testimony before the committee." Although the committee's report states that the monographs represent "solely the views of the agency and authors and not necessarily that of the Temporary National Economic Committee," 240,000 copies of these monographs were given the committee imprint and have been broadcast. Each page on each monograph and each cover bears the heading, *"Concentration of Economic Power."*

Referring to these monographs, the committee's final report states: "We have been particularly careful to present under our imprint a body of information essential to an understanding of the operation of our economic system and which will prove most useful to the legislative and administrative branches of government, to industrialists, labor leaders, and citizens generally in their search for solutions of our economic ills. Communications received by the committee show the use to which this material is being put, indicating that the information, conclusions and recommendations *will have continuing and profound effects in shaping the thinking of individuals, and groups, leading eventually to an informed public opinion."* [2]

Note that while the "information, conclusions and recommendations" are expected to "have continuing and profound effects in shaping the thinking of individuals and groups, leading eventually to an informed public opinion," the hearings did not cover the all-important subject to businessmen—that which the presidential message said should not be ignored—*the effect of tax, and other governmental policies on unemployment, on investment and the preservation of our free competitive economy as the American way of life.*

Instead of an objective inquiry, the year and a half of hearings developed, with few exceptions, but a sequence of testimony tending to substantiate and confirm the social and economic philosophy of the members of the administrative and regulatory bodies who were conducting the hearings.

That philosophy, Veblen's New Deal philosophy, might be succinctly stated as follows: That the American system of private enterprise had resulted in vast concentrations of economic power. Patents were used to establish and maintain these concentrations of power and other unconscionable monopolies. A small percentage of the people owned a large percentage of the nation's wealth. A handful of large corporations constituted a majority of the nation's industrial assets and, by this concentration of economic power, production was restricted so that maximum profits could be earned. This power should be broken by drastic taxation and rigid federal control. As there were no more frontiers to be explored and exploited, the American economy had matured. Hence private enterprise could not absorb the unemployed and give work to the constantly-increasing population nor employ the huge sums of money lying idle in banks. Such idle capital represented savings of the upper third of our society, the excess of income over and above what they could spend for living. Such accumulations should be forestalled by taxation so that the government could "invest" the money and employ the idle men.[3]

The hearings established for the record the virtue of over-all government planning and government spending as the only solution for the dilemma. The committee served as prosecutor, judge and jury and wrote the opinions, which constitute formal charges of the failure of American free private enterprise and pseudo pragmatic conclusions of its obsolescence in a world it had itself created.

A parade of witnesses substantiated New Deal theories. For instance, Alvin Hansen, Lauchlin Currie, Adolf A. Berle and Leon Henderson—known apostles of the theory of government spending—made the record for this phase of the hearing. Each of them was or had been on the New Deal government payroll. However, Dr. Fred R. Fairchild, Dr. Willford King and Dr. Walter E. Spahr, Professors of Economics at Yale and New York Universities; Dean Neil Carothers of Lehigh; Dr. Glenn Saxon, Professor of Applied Economy at Yale; Dr. Harley L. Lutz, Professor of Economics at Princeton; Dr. Harold Moulton of the Brookings Institution; Dr. Virgil Jordan of the National Industrial Conference Board—eminent economists to whom government spending is anathema—were not called. These men, who represent the thinking of the great host of the nation's independent economists, had no opportunity to record their opposing views. They believe that a policy of public spending, which rests in large degree upon unwarranted and dangerous assumptions as to the virtues of deficit financing, had already brought a huge inflation in the supply of money, and that if there is not a reversal in this policy and a repudiation of the supporting theories the nation will be plunged into national bankruptcy, economic chaos, and political dictatorship.[4]

In this manner the biased and colored record that will have "continuing and profound effects in shaping an informed public opinion" was made. So profound has its effect been already that one of the T.N.E.C. monographs has been cited in a decision of the United States Supreme Court.[5]

The hearings fell into several phases. One with which the author is especially familiar sought to determine the cause of the anomaly of idle men and idle money.

The situation was this: Between 1930 and 1940 our population had increased 7.2%.[6] Bank deposits, which at the end of 1930 amounted to fifty-three billion dollars, had recovered from depression lows and climbed steadily until at the end of 1940 they totaled sixty-five billions, an increase of 23%. Assets of manufacturing companies, on the other hand, which amounted to sixty-two billion in 1930, had shown no substantial recovery from the depression lows. At the end of 1940 they stood at fifty-one and a half billions, still 17% below that of the earlier decade.[7]

Obviously something was wrong. The billions of dollars in the banks were idle dollars. Normally much of this money would have been invested in business, thus giving employment to the millions of idle men.

For years business had contended that governmental tax and other policies had made risk unprofitable. Public "confidence" was shaken and people were afraid to invest. Business was afraid to start something new. These were the reasons American business had been unable to recover.

But the New Dealers, unable or unwilling to comprehend the business mentality, held that governmental policies had nothing to do with the situation; that the American industrial economy was "mature," anyway, and further substantial growth was not "in the cards." Business, they held, provided for its normal expansion through internal sources such as profits and recoveries from its depreciation reserves. Hence business would never tap and put to use any substantial amount of the idle money nor be able to employ the idle men.

If the latter theory could be established, the case for governmental spending would be made! In that case it would be indicated that government should take the idle money—the so-called savings—through either taxation or issuance of bonds, and spend the proceeds to provide the necessary employment. To substantiate their contention that industry would not tap the savings—the idle money—they issued subpoenas for a number of businessmen to appear before the committee.

These men were carefully selected representatives of companies whose records were believed to confirm New Deal theories. Each of them was carefully interviewed, before his testimony was permitted, to reassure the examiners that the cases fitted. Each witness was then taken over jumps and hurdles far away from the subject, then led into a maze of questioning and cross-questioning. Analysis of the testimony reveals that several times Mr. Leon Henderson and Mr. Peter Nehemkis, who was conducting this phase of the hearings, thrust with a leading question in an effort to bring out an admission suitable to their purpose. Thus, when questioned in this manner as to whether their companies would tap savings in the near future, Mr. Edward R. Stettinius of the United States Steel Corporation, Mr. Owen D. Young of General Electric Company and Mr. Alfred P. Sloan of General Motors Corporation were caught off guard and answered in the negative.[8]

Later Mr. Nehemkis, ignoring the whole testimony which would qualify or negative these answers, and using only five words which constituted but a meager part of Mr. Young's and Mr. Stettinius' answers, summarized their testimony by stating that the electrical and steel industries—not merely the General Electric Company and the United States Steel Corporation, but the whole industries—were "mature industries."[9] And fourteen words, which constituted only a tiny fragment of the testimony of these three witnesses, were lifted out of their contexts and used by Stuart Chase to verify his conclusion that it was "established beyond reasonable dispute . . . American business enterprises have little use for the savings of the public."[10]

It is significant that no businessman whose company had secured capital testified. There were many of them even during the 1930's. In fact, one such businessman was subpoenaed, apparently by mistake; he was excused from testifying after he had been interviewed.

Throughout this phase of the hearings the committee assumed that the static 1930's indicated the permanent status of industry. The fact that the nation was wallowing in a depression was given no consideration. Nor was any allowance made for the fact that financing had been made a costly and tedious affair by the new Securities Act, terms of which made corporation officials subject to unprecedented and unreasonable liabilities.

T.N.E.C. monograph #37 entitled "Savings, Investment and National Income" made a fairly accurate summary, not of its subject but of the testimony. Its author, Dr. Oscar L. Altman, senior economist of the National Resources Planning Board, was also one of the chief witnesses before the committee in substantiation of New Deal theories.

It is not surprising, therefore, that the monograph concludes: (1) That private industry has not and is not likely to need large amounts of saved funds for investment; (2) that savings institutions have had and are likely to have no substantial private outlet for the funds which are virtually automatically made available to them; and (3) that the government can, through deficit financing, return the hoarded savings to the income stream, substitute its expenditures for industrial expansion and provide the savings institutions with the securities they need—government bonds.

And later the monograph consoles the reader that, after all, private investment is not always socially desirable; it expresses doubts that the prospect for profits can be relied upon as a satisfactory determinant for the real need of investment.

Altogether in keeping with the tenor of the hearings, it is neither candid nor honest—indeed, it borders upon turpitude—for the author of the monograph to substantiate his conclusion that "internal financing, not security issues, provides the bulk of venture capital for American industry . . ." with selected parts of case histories, when the whole histories would give lie to his statement. It is not in the interest of an informed public opinion that he use as an illustration to prove his thesis: "E. I. duPont deNemours & Co., Inc., stated that forty per cent of their sales in 1937 came from products they did not make in 1928. The Monsanto Chemical Company reported that products they began to manufacture after 1929 accounted for thirty-nine per cent of the total sales in 1939. . . . These and countless similar examples are all ventures. They were all made possible by investments using venture capital. But the bulk of venture capital came from internal sources."

No representative of the duPont Company appeared at the hearings. They tapped the public savings for $50,000,000 in 1937 by issuing that amount of new preferred stock. Monsanto Chemical Company had tapped the public savings three times for a total of $16,500,000 in the years immediately preceding the hearings. These facts, which contradict the conclusions of the author of the monograph, do not appear in the "body of information" submitted in substantiation of his conclusions that "will have a continuing and profound effect in shaping the thinking of individuals," leading "to an informed public opinion."

Shortly after the hearings, Mr. Raymond Moley, evidently

unconvinced that Mr. Young and Mr. Sloan had been given an opportunity to express themselves clearly on the causes of the anomaly of idle men and idle money and that their opinion might be at variance with the conclusions reached by Mr. Nehemkis and Dr. Chase, sent to each the following questions: "Do you agree that American savings have no place to go in private enterprise? What is the chief factor blocking the flow of savings into investment?"

Mr. Sloan replied: "I feel that American savings not only have an opportunity or place, but are essential in the promotion of private enterprise. But before that necessity or opportunity can be capitalized, we must have a different attitude of mind with respect to private enterprise as it is affected by political and economic policies. The chief influence is the lack of confidence in the long-pull position of industry and business, in general, from the standpoint of the security of the investment and the opportunity to earn and retain a reasonable reward commensurate with the risk and success of the enterprise."[11]

And Mr. Young answered: "I agree that the opportunity for American savings to go into private enterprise is at the present moment restricted. That condition, however, should only be temporary. I do not agree that our industrial establishment is so far developed that it will not have ample need for American savings in the future. The forerunner for investment is adventure. Adventurous men and adventurous dollars in combination must be encouraged to take great risks in order that some percentage of their undertakings may be shown to be sound, useful and profitable. Then and not until then can savings be properly invested in such enterprise. Broadly speaking, savings may develop and carry on for profit; but they cannot and should not adventure. Therefore, to the extent which adventurous men and adventurous dollars are discouraged or paralyzed, you will have idle dollars awaiting investment and idle men awaiting employment. Indeed, you will have more, you will have stagnation of spirit, you will have so-called realism, which for the most part, as now used, is another name for destructive cynicism, in place of productive imagination and daring action. If the success of men and dollars in productive enterprise is to be scorned, rather than honored, if it is to be penalized by taxation, other than for revenue purposes, or be blackened by suspicion, there will be no adventure and no spirit of adventure, and, consequently, restricted opportunity for savings. With the inevitable advance of technology in developed industries, there will be increasingly idle men. Exploration and research will falter and our best brains and most vital energies will be devoted to mere survival in a static economy, rather than to the extension of its boundaries and opportunities. No people could push out the frontiers of productive knowledge and successful enterprise as far as we have in the last three generations without increasing the possibilities for new research and new enterprise on the perimeter of the now known. It is for that reason that I am sure, given stimulation for adventure instead of repression, there need be no idle men and idle dollars in America."[12]

The question was posed to Mr. Stettinius. Although the United States Steel Corporation had entered the market for one hundred million dollars' worth and a United States Steel Corporation subsidiary had entered the market for one hundred and twenty-five million dollars' worth of these so-called "idle savings" but one year prior to his testimony, he declined a reply for publication. Soon after the hearings he was appointed Chairman of the War Resources Board. It is very probable that a candid reply would have proved an impediment to cordial relationships with the administration, and this was essential if he was to get the job done.

Nor did the viewpoints which Mr. Sloan and Mr. Young

expressed in their answers to Raymond Moley, although published in the *Saturday Evening Post*, find their way to the free mailing list of seven thousand individuals, professors, institutions and libraries, or appear in the monographs.

Had those who were conducting the inquiry followed presidential instructions and been willing to allow "the effect of tax, patent and other government policies" to go into the record; had they summoned discontented businessmen and asked them what the government could do in order to aid them increase employment and use the idle money in the expansion of business, it is highly probable they would have received an answer similar in vein to that given to Minister Colbert, Louis XIV's famed Secretary of State.

During a similar period of strife and unemployment, following a period of intense industrial regimentation, Colbert asked the merchants and manufacturers of Lyons in what manner the French state might assist them. It is said one of them answered, "Laissons-nous faire!"—"Let us alone!" This reply is believed to be the origin of the name "laissez faire" given to the economic doctrine of Adam Smith and his followers.

To the T.N.E.C., American businessmen would probably have said, "Stop harassing us with remedies that keep us sick! Take your inquisitional commissions and exhausting taxation off our backs and we will work this thing out!" . . . "But first there is a matter of morals we want to discuss with you. Through a long and vicious campaign of intellectual racketeering, terrorism and sabotage, you have destroyed the sanctity of our symbols of achievement. Nothing has been set up to take their place. Why should we want our business to grow if big business is evil? Why should we want to achieve wealth if wealth is immoral? Your canons of social conduct deny the moral equity of both. Yet only by growth can we employ more men; only through the creation of wealth and through its use can we give them the necessary tools. We have a sense of duty toward our fellow creatures. Most of us have always dealt equitably with our employes, but your campaigns have poisoned their minds and torn them away. We have taken pride in the confidence in which our communities held us, but you have made them suspicious.

"Some of us have trespassed grievously and all of us have done some things amiss, but we are human and so are you. The mendacity of these hearings proves it! Therefore, we cannot follow your dreams of the infallibility of the state nor of the morality of bureaucrats, for they must be human also.

"The first man born on earth was a tiller of the soil; the second a keeper of sheep; but Genesis does not say it was God's land nor the state's sheep. Both were the property of men! Man's way has always been the acquisitive way. The pressure groups of farmers, laborers and veterans prove that acquisitiveness is not limited to businessmen. Our Constitution encourages the pursuit of happiness in our manner of the past, for in its process we aided others. That 'man's self-interest is God's Providence' is evident by the marble pillars of the very building in which you conduct these hearings; these pillars are totems of the power and greatness we have helped to bring America.

"However, across the water men are building a civilization for which they will fight with the fury of a tigress at bay for her cubs, yet they own no property, nor do they have liberty, nor do they acknowledge a God; nevertheless, without them they must have achieved happiness, for they will fight for it; and they have accomplished much. Those men, therefore, must have an ideology in which they believe.

"You deny ours. You do not as yet openly admit theirs. The result is intolerable confusion. What is your game? Be frank with the people! We can seek our happiness as well as any other body of men within any canons of social and economic conduct the American people determine, but it is essential we know what they are!"

But businessmen were never asked the question! President Roosevelt's instructions were ignored.

CHAPTER VII

Monopoly Bogey

NOT ALL TESTIMONY BEFORE THE T.N.E.C. WAS ONE-SIDED, however. Life insurance companies, whose existence was threatened, ably defended and justified themselves. The Commerce Department, which administers the patent system, placed its patent commissioner on the stand in refutation of theories propounded by the Department of Justice.[1] But such organizations as the National Association of Manufacturers and the Chamber of Commerce of the United States, national representatives of business—the subject of the inquiry—although they had made extensive preparations for testimony, were not called. These associations were particularly interested in the so-called monopoly and patent phases of the hearings conducted by the Anti-Trust Division of the Department of Justice.

For the American enterprise system this division, under the vigorous leadership of Thurman Arnold, had been both a Dr. Jekyll and a Mr. Hyde.

It was Mr. Hyde who weekly paraded a file of companies and their officers across the front pages of our nation's press, with indictments for conspiring to restrain trade, for maintaining monopolies, and charges of being in league with foreign cartels to hamper American war production. More than three thousand firms and individuals [2] are now awaiting trial. This continuing crusade against business is, in effect, a prolonging of Veblen's campaign of "inquiry" and "publicity, as to what it is all about," for public suspicion of business is fanned and refueled with each fresh indictment.

However, so long as this campaign was restricted to its announced objectives—to genuine cases where new enterprise is restricted, competition stifled and fellow citizens exploited—it was Dr. Jekyll who was doing private enterprise an unwanted favor. He was then seeking to re-establish the fundamentals of Adam Smith's conception of competition—a free market—a fundamental of free enterprise which some businessmen are wont to forget and would thwart if they could. It is upon competition that the vigor of our enterprise system gets its nourishment, and competition must be restored wherever it has faded if the system is to endure.

Unfortunately, our anti-trust laws are broad, vague and antiquated. They have been enforced with indifference; they have been subject to varying interpretations by a succession of Attorney Generals. Over a long period of years many business practices have sprung up, which, even though not in violation of the previously accepted interpretation of the anti-trust and Clayton acts, did trespass on the pure conception of a free market. Two or more competitors were allowed to combine so long as they did not dominate a market, but it is certain that such combinations decreased competition. Companies were permitted to purchase large consumers of their products or buy stock interests in consumers of their products, which closed markets to competition. And practically all industries were guilty of some borderline practices, which had the effect of reducing competition.

It would seem wise to permit any one company to grow to as large a size as it is able to attain itself; the result would be merely a measure of its competitive ability to contribute to the sum of progress. But no contributions to progress were made by so-called integration when many units which were links in a natural chain of production were combined, or by mere size where strength was sought through the combination of the weaknesses of individual units.

Whatever the outcry of business against the persecutions by Thurman Arnold and however inconvenient it might be in time of war to defend anti-trust suits, the announced fundamentals of the campaign in which he was engaged were aimed at the restoration of free markets. This will intensify competition and act, in the long run, to the benefit of private enterprise and the public.

The practices that evolved have not eliminated competition; that is far from the case. Our anti-trust laws have always assured that there was ample competition in every market; that no one manufacturer or supplier was able, through combination with others or through the purchase of competing patents, to control a market. The American market has always been the most free of all national markets. It is the only one wherein trusts, combinations and cartels are prohibited. But the trend indicated by mergers of formerly competing units, even though it did not permit domination of a market, did have the effect of lessening competition.

It would seem, however, that in their zeal to make up for lost time the Anti-Trust Division is going to unreasonable lengths by indicting right and left for practices formerly thought to be within the law, and one may have just cause to wonder if the restoration of free markets is the only goal of the campaign.

The penalties provided in the statutes for violation of the anti-trust law are severe. Fines may amount to $5,000 per day for each violation, and a violation may be determined to be each shipment made during the period of violation, which may be years. Officers of companies are subject to not only fines but prison terms of one year for each violation. Further, once a firm has been convicted, its customers may sue for damages which they claim to have suffered, and they may be awarded as much as treble the damage claimed.

The penalties, when the violation runs over a period of

years, may amount to so great a sum as to bankrupt even substantial companies. Hence, as has happened in many cases, when the Attorney General offers to accept a plea of guilty and dismiss further costly proceedings with an innocuous consent decree in which the defendant agrees to desist from the practices which were alleged to be illegal, business usually accepts. But in so doing, their tacit admission of guilt is magnified in the public mind and the reputation of industry and private enterprise receives another blow.

There must be some order in marketing industrial products. Four gasoline stations, for instance, located on the four corners of an intersection, could not each have a different price for the same quality gasoline. In this case one station would eventually have all the trade and the others would fail. But such a state of affairs would seem to be the ultimate desire of some who are of the opinion that identical prices are prima facie evidence of collusion. Business is now confused as to permissible practice and fraudulent practice under the anti-trust laws. Strengthening and clarification of the laws is highly desirable.

During the T.N.E.C. hearings the Department of Justice advocated compulsory licensing of patents. Whether or not this would result to the public's interest is debatable ground. The Constitution provides the recognition of creatures of the brain as property. Copyrights and patents are to be granted "to promote the progress of science and useful arts." A strictly legal concept of compulsory licensing brands it as counter to the protection to property afforded by the Constitution.

By the same Constitutional provision, if an artist creates an etching, a composer writes a song or an author a novel, it may be copyrighted and others are prohibited from reproducing it for fifty-six years. Similarly, if the brain produces a new thing or new way of doing something, it may be patented; it becomes the originator's property and others are prohibited from using it for seventeen years. After the expiration of these periods, song, story and patent become public property.

Blackstone defined private property as "that sole and despotic dominion which one man claims and exercises over the external things of the world in total exclusion of the right of any other individual in the universe."

The suggestion, therefore, that government be able to grant compulsory patent licenses would be equivalent in theory to the government licensing infringement on any other private property. In that case, to carry the illustration to an extreme: if someone owned a large and comfortable house, he could be compelled by government to move into one corner and others could be licensed to occupy parts of the house. Or if one owned an automobile the government could compel its charter to others desiring its use. The suggestion would also have its counterpart in music and literature. A composer of some music which caught popular fancy would lose the sole right to his creation, for others would be permitted to reproduce it on license; the author of an unusual novel, such as "Gone with the Wind," would be denied the benefits of its popularity, for pulp magazines could immediately secure licenses to reprint it. All newspapers could print "Superman" comic strips and other syndicated features.

But Mr. Arnold's suggestion is limited to patents. Should patents be singled out as the one field of private property in which owners be denied exclusive rights?

Of course during their life patents create monopolies, but that is the intent of the law. All private property is a monopoly of the owner.

Mr. Arnold testified before the House Committee on Patents: "I do not feel myself competent to testify as to the purely patent aspect of the patent law." [3] But it is the "pure patent aspects" that concern business, patentees and the public. There is much in the practical operation of the patent aspects of patent law which naturally could not have been evident to Mr. Arnold when he was teaching in Yale Law School.

Even if it were in public interest to invade property rights of patents, there are other important considerations of public interest which I believe are missed by Mr. Arnold and other sponsors of compulsory licensing.

The protection afforded by patents requires that the inventor disclose his invention; therefore, the knowledge of how a product is made becomes public property. But no one is compelled to take out a patent! He may keep his invention secret! This applies with particular emphasis to foreigners.

From the viewpoint of progress in research, every encouragement should be given to inventors to take out patents, for patents form the most valuable literature of a research technician. By keeping abreast of patents as they issue, the technician knows what is going on in all the world's laboratories; and one idea stimulates another. If a certain procedure works in one case, the research technician is tempted to try it in another. It is my belief that, in the chemical industry at least, the greatest stimulus to progress is the patent literature that is available to its technicians.

If processes were kept secret, the public would not get the benefit of the application of methods disclosed in patents in other fields where they might be useful. And as the invention might even die with its originator, the public might be denied its benefits forever. Furthermore, secrecy might resurrect the old evil of industrial espionage, of which, happily, American industry is free.

From a practical point of view, it would be very difficult for any government official to evaluate properly a license. How much, for instance, would a license for the manufacture of

Nylon be worth? All the facts would have to be weighed. How long will Nylon be the top fiber? When will a new invention supersede it? It is doubtful if anyone knows the answer to this, even the duPont management.

Nylon was a successful result of years of research. Hundreds of results were failures. Should a Nylon license compensate for the failures? Nylon had a long and costly development, through pilot plant and semi works. If a patent owner is not reimbursed for costly development, why should any undertake or reveal it? Without patent protection provided by present laws, development might be retarded.

Then, too, compulsory licensing would fall more heavily on the small fellow and favor the large corporation. The latter could demand a license of the small inventor and with greater resources in research, finance and market prestige, soon out-distance him. The large corporation could reap a major part of the benefits from the small man's invention.

Voluntary licensing of patents is constantly taking place. There is a general inclination among manufacturers to license competitors and secure royalties rather than chance development of competing processes on which no royalties would accrue. But even in these cases, when a patent owner is willing to grant a license and another is anxious to have it, there is considerable difficulty in arriving at an equitable rate. If stimulus to invention is not to be discouraged, licensing rates would have to be equitable. The task of establishing such rates in hundreds of industries would be superhuman.

It is frequently charged that patents are bought up and held off the market; that they are suppressed. It is inconceivable why this charge has gained such general credence. What possible benefit could the owner of a valuable patent secure by suppressing it? It is illegal for anyone to buy a competing patent and suppress it, for this would promote a monopoly and is in conflict with our anti-trust laws.

The idea that valuable patents are suppressed is an old one. Long ago Thomas Edison remarked that he had heard and read these statements but that no one had cited specific cases. "I, myself," he said, "do not know of a single case. Before any changes in the law are made, let the objectors cite instances where injustice has been worked on the public by the alleged suppression of patents."

In 1939 the National Industrial Conference Board sought to ascertain whether there were any suppressed inventions. It inquired of hundreds of inventors, engineers and others who would be in good positions, by reason of their experience and contacts, to know of such instances and cite them. They found no cases of a useful patent being suppressed.

Inventions may be unused because there is no immediate market for them or because they are ahead of their time and have to await other developments before being useful. Edison's electric lamp, for instance, could not be used generally until electric current became cheap and readily available. The Wright Brothers invented the airplane long before they could fly it. They had to await the development of gasoline motors to provide an independent power plant.

The recommendations of the Department of Justice are before the Senate in the form of amendments to our patent law. However, President Roosevelt has appointed an excellent Patents Planning Commission, under the chairmanship of Dr. Charles F. Kettering, to study the patent system and make suggestions for its permanent improvement.

There is much that is wrong with the patent law. There is no question that some of the privileges it affords are abused. One of the abuses arises in the patent office, where an application may lie for many years. The seventeen years' protection dates from the time of issuance. If, therefore, an application is permitted to lie in the patent office for say eleven years, a monopoly is granted for twenty-eight years, not seventeen as intended.

Furthermore, patents are granted too liberally. So-called "paper patents" on mere ideas are issued by the wholesale. No proof is required that they are workable ideas or that the inventions have actually been operated or in use. So-called "improvement patents" extend the life of the basic ones. There should be some combined limit to the life of basic and improvement patents.

Business has much confidence in Dr. Kettering and his committee. The public should have. If their recommendations are followed, it is hoped existing inequities of our patent law will be removed without hindering the concept of patents—that they "promote the progress of science and useful arts."

CHAPTER VIII

Bogey II

OBVIOUSLY IT IS NOT WITHIN THE SCOPE OF THIS VOLUME to discuss all of the T.N.E.C. monographs. Their thousands of pages contain a rich mine of information and misinformation about the American economy. Some of the studies are excellent; all are worth the reading by businessmen. Had these studies been objective—had representatives of business and commerce been called in for consultation and their viewpoints been given impartial consideration—the monographs would have been invaluable to generations of economists.[1]

However, in most instances the authors limited themselves to the source material of the committee's biased hearings and partisan references. In many cases, subjects have been colored to harmonize with their philosophy. This has been accomplished by the manner of presentation and by thoughtless or Machiavellian omissions of balancing data.

Let us touch briefly, for instance, the theme which is developed with variations throughout the series—that the concentration of economic power in a relatively few hands is working to the disadvantage of the people; that two hundred corporations own almost one-half of American industries' assets and that, in turn, many of these corporations are controlled by a small group of people! This is presented as a startling development. It is presented as new to our times. And the implication is that it was one of the causes of poverty and the depression. Yet this reasoning is none other than Marx's theory of increasing misery—that the accumulation of wealth at one pole causes poverty at the others.

"Three family groups," one monograph states, "the du-Ponts, the Mellons and the Rockefellers—have shareholdings valued at nearly $1,400,000,000, which directly or indirectly give control over fifteen of the two hundred largest non-financial corporations with aggregate assets of over $8,000,000,000, or more than eleven per cent of their total assets." This presentation might prove misleading or confusing, for in a hurried reading one might overlook the distinct difference between the market value of a share and its asset value. On October 20, 1942, the market value of a share of duPont common stock was $128, but its asset value was only $46. A factual presentation would have used either asset values or market values in both cases.

"In the case of about forty per cent of the two hundred largest corporations," one reads on, "one family, or a small number of families, exercise either absolute control, by virtue of ownership of a majority of the voting securities, or working control through ownership of a substantial minority of the voting stock." Working control is arbitrarily assumed to be ten per cent of the voting stock. Obviously this is debatable ground. If a corporation is unsuccessful because its management cannot maintain a competitive position in its industry, no percentage of stock ownership assures control.

Even if management held a majority of stock, minority shareholders have the right to seek protection for their interests in court. And there are cases without number wherein, because of mismanagement, minority shareholders have had managements ousted and receivers appointed or new managements installed.

On the other hand, the Board of Directors and management of American Telephone and Telegraph Company are to all purposes secure in their "control" of the company because of their splendid operation of our telephone system and the general wisdom and excellence of their stewardship. Yet the stock owned by members of the Board of Directors of American Telephone and Telegraph is but .00033% of the whole.[2]

"Interests" remain in "control" only so long as they render good accounting, or reasonably good accounting, of their stewardships, and the security of their "control" is in the degree of the confidence established with shareholders, which in turn is measured by the company's progress in relation to competitors, its relationships with customers, employes and the public at large.

It is charged, often with a great deal of justification, that Boards of Directors are self-perpetuating. This is usually true if the directors account properly for their stewardship. When vacancies occur, the "controlling" group invites to the Board men of ability who they know will be of congenial mentality. This cannot very well be otherwise, for no group of men would willingly invite participation of a man known to be in opposition to policies they consider successful. Nothing disrupts teamwork, upon which business success depends, more than division of top authority into cliques.

It is the author's opinion that most Boards of Directors would welcome the addition to their number of a labor representative if one could be found who was truly representative of the company's own laboring force, without stirring up a hornet's nest among professional labor leaders. Representation of the interest of the public at large would also be welcomed. Many board members fall into such a classification. But men willing to spend time familiarizing themselves with a company's ramifications and take a keen interest in its problems, who have ability, recognized standing in their community and at the same time fill the specifications of representing the public's interests, are few and far between. This specification is more readily drawn than filled. There is a great demand for such men.

Using its standard definition for "control," the monograph presumes that all Standard Oil enterprises, including the Standard Oil Company of Indiana, are "controlled" by the Rockefeller family. However, in calculating this family's holdings the monograph includes stock held by the Rockefeller Foundation, the Rockefeller General Education Board and the Rockefeller Institute of Medical Research. These funds are administered by trustees and the Rockefeller family has no control over them. Nevertheless, the trustees would undoubtedly be sympathetic to any suggestion made by John Rockefeller, Jr., if it were not against public interest and did not violate other moral obligations of trusteeship.

That the Rockefeller family does not control Standard Oil Company of Indiana must have been evident in 1927 when it was revealed during the Teapot Dome scandals that its president, Colonel Robert W. Stewart, had engaged in questionable transactions with the Continental Trading Company. He was also charged with contempt by the Senate Investigating Committee. It was necessary for John Rockefeller, Jr., to undertake a public fight to oust Colonel Stewart from the presidency of the company.

The letters of Mr. Rockefeller's committee, soliciting proxies from other shareholders, said: "Mr. Rockefeller did not and does not control more than a small minority of the stock of the company." [3] It was necessary that several thousand shareholders join Mr. Rockefeller in order to give his committee a majority of the stock. If moral right had not been on Mr. Rockefeller's side, he would have been unsuccessful in controlling the company's action.

In the same monograph we read that "this study of the two hundred largest non-financial corporations has shown a high degree of concentration of ownership. The top one per cent of book shareholdings, for example, accounted for about sixty per cent of the common shares of these corporations." The inference is that book shareholders are individuals.

Yet, according to the monograph, the principal shareholders of the Continental Can Company's common stock are: King and Company, Griffin and Company, Sigler and Company, Atwell and Company, and Williams and Company —those of B. F. Goodrich Company's common stock are: E. A. Pierce and Company, J. S. Bache and Company, Elkins, Morris and Company, and Tucker, Anthony and Company. The largest shareholders of the American Telephone and Telegraph Company are: Sun Life Assurance Company of Canada, Barnes and Company, Atwell and Company, and Dominick and Dominick.

The large shareholding companies are usually brokerage houses, acting as nominees for investment trusts, bank and trust companies, their own clients, and the clients of their correspondents throughout the United States. Thus one name may represent the holdings of hundreds, even many thousands, of individuals.

The twenty leading shareholders of each of the common and preferred stocks making up the capitalization of these corporations are also tabulated. The New York Life Insurance Company was the largest shareholder of twelve of these issues; the Metropolitan Life Insurance Company was the largest shareholder of ten issues; the Sun Life Assurance Company of Canada was the largest shareholder of seven issues; and the Prudential Insurance Company was the largest shareholder of seven issues.

Since so many of the leading shareholders of these large companies are insurance companies, investment trusts, other corporations and brokers acting as nominees for clients, one can readily understand why in so many cases a large proportion of stock is owned by a small proportion of shareholders. If these large holdings were apportioned among their true owners—the policy holders of the insurance companies, the shareholders of investment trusts and the clients of brokerage houses—the tabulations would show that the ownership of these companies was not concentrated in a few individuals but was spread among a very large proportion of all our people.

In apparent contradiction to this fact, the monograph states: "Fewer than 75,000 persons, i.e., less than one-fifth of one per cent of the total number of income recipients, were necessary to account for one-half of all dividends received by individuals. This certainly represents an impressive degree of concentration of ownership." Here again the author of the monograph dips his pen in venom and mixes statistics to add vehemence to his argument. Almost everyone—certainly everyone who earns a wage or operates a farm—is a recipient of income. To take a certain number of shareholders and compare their income from dividends alone with an irrelevant number of people is flummery. It is like comparing apples and eggs. It is as though someone announced solemnly that there is more juice in one lemon than in a dozen billiard balls and implied that this was significant and a great social evil. However, to a casual reader from the pulpit, schoolroom or university library, the monograph's perverted half-truths do convey an "impressive degree of concentration," which is what the author intended.

If the purpose of the author is borne in mind, it is obvious why only a very slight reference is made to data such as appear in "Statistics of Income for 1940" issued by the United States Treasury. This study reveals that fifty-three per cent of the total dividend payments by corporations in that year was received by individuals having statutory net incomes over $5,000 and that forty-seven per cent of all dividends was received either by individuals having statutory net incomes under $5,000, or companies such as life insurance companies and non-profit institutions such as universities, churches and hospitals.[4]

The Treasury's report is in decided contrast with the impression that a casual and non-analytical reader would receive from the subtle statement that "the top one per cent of book shareholdings, for example, accounted for about sixty per cent of the common shares."

The monograph, however, makes this concession to fact: "The number of shareholders in the United States has increased since the turn of the century as follows: 1900—4,400,000; 1923—14,400,000; 1928—18,000,000; 1937—26,000,000." It must, therefore, be evident that whatever the concentration of economic power is now, it is less than it used to be; it is constantly decreasing. The author of the monograph writes this in confirmation: "For the period 1927-1937 the most important reason for the increase in the number of shareholdings by about 8,000,000 seems to have been the purchase of shares by persons not previously owning stock."

Dr. Virgil Jordan pointed out some time ago that the possession or ownership of property, which is houses, furniture, clothing, household appliances, automobiles, as well as savings, bank deposits and life insurance policies, is more widely distributed in the United States than in any other country and more so than in any other period of history. The same is true of land, which is the primary means of production, and the same is true of corporations, which own other means of production.

The extreme in the concentration of economic p... er is found in the communistic state, wherein the state o... everything and individuals own nothing except the cl... s on their backs. And in Russia absolute control of all ... nomic power is fixed in one man—Stalin!

For centuries, as common man gaine... asing amounts

of liberty he enlarged his proportion of wealth. Although we still have extremes of wealth and poverty, the so-called concentration of economic power in America is as relatively insignificant as a midget, compared to the power wielded by the giants of the Renaissance, such as the Medici family of Italy, the merchant princes of Venice, and the Augsburg Fugger family of the Holy Roman Empire.

Miriam Beard relates that Jacob Fugger not only enjoyed the right to coin money; he had a quasi-monopoly on the metal that supplied most of Europe's currency. He owned the silver of Tyrol and Carinthia and held a close grip on the Hungarian output of both silver and copper. In addition, Fugger controlled the quick-silver mines of Spain, which, together with a mortgage on the incomes of three Knightly Orders, also in Fugger's possession, were the chief sources of Spain's income. Mining, however, was but part of Fugger's enterprise. He was among the leading spice importers from Portugal to the rest of Europe; he brought cotton from Venice to the factories of South Germany, and handled silks, jewels and other luxury articles for the continental courts. On the top of this pyramid was Fugger's banking system, whose facilities were used all over Europe.[5]

Beard recites a story related by Martin Luther when he was exploding against Fugger's influence over the Catholic Church and Emperor Charles V: "Once a bishop of Brixen died in Rome," Luther said, "and when he was dead, no money was found by him, except a little piece of paper a [illegible]ger in length, that was stuck in his sleeve. When Pope Ju[illegible] sent that to the Fugger factor and asked him if he knew [illegible] writing, the latter said: 'Yes, it is the debt which Fugge[illegible]d Company owe to the Cardinal and totals three times a[illegible]red thousand gulden.' The Pope asked: 'When could yo[illegible] the money?' The servant of the Fugger replied: 'At [illegible]ur.' Then the Pope turned to the Cardinals of France and England and asked: 'Could your Kings also deliver three tons of gold in an hour?' They said: 'No.' Then he said: 'But that is what a citizen of Augsburg can do.' "[6]

In Elizabeth's Merrie England a similar concentration of economic power rested in Sir Thomas Gresham. Single-handed he built and supplied the foundations of the British Navy, which later defeated Spain's invincible Armada. He occupied the present-day position of the Bank of England, upholding the credit of the British pound in foreign lands and raising Crown loans. His statue stands before the London Stock Exchange, for which he provided an early home.[7]

In our own brief history, liberties and freedom accelerated the trend toward diffusion of economic power. What twentieth century institution could compare in relative concentration of economic power with the Massachusetts Bay Company and the Virginia Company of colonial times, and John Jacob Astor's trading empire after we had won independence? Have we any group of companies now wielding the same economic power as the railroads toward the end of the nineteenth century, and have we today any one corporation dominating the industrial scene as did the United States Steel Corporation in the early days of the twentieth century?

But is not all this beside the point? Suppose two hundred corporations and a few individuals among their shareholders do control thirty, fifty or seventy per cent of the nation's non-financial assets; are not these statistics meaningless? Is not the people's real interest whether or not these assets accrue to the benefit of the largest possible and constantly increasing number of people? Are the Ford Company and General Motors Corporation of benefit to the community at large? Are the people as a whole benefiting from their progress and development? Or would automobiles be better or cheaper if there were many small automobile companies? Would our telephone service be better or cheaper if we had several competing telephone companies? Did the so-called integration of companies and mergers result in lessening of competition and raising of prices? This is the kernel of the subject!

Mere size of industrial units has no social significance unless they are able to retain for their own use everything they produce and by the exercise of their control over a large proportion of the nation's economy leave little for other people. If General Foods Corporation were owned by a small group who consumed all its vast food output, or if a few people owned Procter and Gamble and used or wasted the great soap output, it would be a real social evil. Obviously, however, this is not the case. The production of these companies must be distributed widely for their owners to profit. Millions of housewives and families consume the product of General Foods and Procter and Gamble. Therefore, large sections of the population must benefit from their facilities for producing high quality at low cost before the owners gain.

Viewed from the perspective of a nation's lifetime, the picture presented by this monograph will soon be out of date. Individual wealth and the relative importance of companies or even whole industries are ephemeral. Our economy is changing constantly. The old adage that in America "three generations from shirt sleeves to shirt sleeves" is as true now as when it was first said. Likewise, industries hold their positions of importance for but a brief moment in history and then give way to others or become obsolete.

The Yankee Clipper Fleet, symbol of early American economic power, faded with the advent of steel and steam; railroads lost their importance with the invention of automobiles and good roads, and will certainly lose much of their remaining passenger and perhaps cargo business to air transport.

Metropolitan street car companies, the center of so much political agitation at the turn of the century, belong to the age of the cigar store Indian. Trolley car rails are being torn up to swell the nation's supply of scrap. Gas companies lost their predominance to electric power companies, which in turn will fade with the advent of atomic power.

Industries in the ascendancy today—those based on physical and chemical sciences—were midgets fifty years ago and the products of other present-day giants—automobiles and airplanes—were still dreams. With the exception of Rockefeller, the great families mentioned in the monograph—Mellon and duPont—although well-to-do, were unidentified with great wealth half a century ago. And Rockefeller was then a mere parvenu.

Likewise, many names associated with the industrial wealth of that day, such as Carnegie, Brown, Frick and Leland Stanford, would hardly be recognized by our young generation except as names of libraries and universities. And can anyone identify any vestige of the economic power once wielded by Robert Morris, the powerful banker, Robert Carter, the rich planter of our Revolution, and Jay Cooke, the great banker of the Civil War?

In the normal functioning of private enterprise the next half century would see another wave of new industries and new wealth sweep over America. They might be founded on some new and revolutionary development in aviation, an outgrowth of the cyclotron, solar or atomic power, or on an undreamed-of discovery.

If some persistent scientist succeeded in unlocking the secret of atomic power and our automobiles were given the equivalent of gasoline at one or two cents a gallon; if our airplanes were enabled to double their pay load and multiply their range; and if household power were reduced to half its present cost—would it not be a fair exchange for the people if the man or group of men responsible for these boons became extremely rich? Would the people not benefit, also, by the other new industries just as they have benefited as each wave of the past rose, made its contribution and passed either to a lesser role or into oblivion?

And the ascendancy of individual companies is ephemeral, too, for it seems inevitable that whenever a Goliath assumes command of any field, like the big man in a negro "battle royal," it becomes the target of everyone's attack.

In 1925 the Goliath Ford Company produced forty-two per cent of all the automobiles. In 1940 the Ford Company produced only nineteen per cent. It had dropped to second place in the industry, with Chrysler close on its heels. Upon its formation in 1901, the United States Steel Corporation owned sixty-six per cent of the nation's productive steel capacity; by 1940, after several small, vigorous independents had hacked away steadily for four decades, its percentage of the industry had fallen to thirty-three per cent.

No company can continue to occupy a dominant position in its industry unless it continues to provide the public with the best value—either the best product at the same price or an equivalent product at a lower price. If it provides only as good a product at the same price, it will, like the steel corporation, steadily lose ground. And so, too, with an industry. It will occupy a dominating position only so long as it fulfills a specific need of the people to their best advantage. The stagecoach thus gave way to the railroad, which in turn yielded in part to the automobile, and both will give way to the airplane.

This is the natural result when men are free to pursue their happiness; free to pursue ambitions, whether or not they make sense to others; free to engage in enterprise and risk their own money without official sanction or subsidy. The American market—the spending power of the whole people—is open to whoever offers the best value in services, amusement or articles of consumption. The opportunity to capture some of this huge market stimulates men's imagination, men's ingenuity and their willingness to risk their future in competition with others in American private enterprise. Thousands of individualists who start hopefully and risk their capital have an even chance of lasting five years; only a few succeed. This was the average Mrs. Henry Ford had against her when she handed over her life savings of $2,000 to start the Ford Motor Company, and said, "Henry, go to it!"

CHAPTER IX

The Real McCoy

ONE OF THE T.N.E.C. MONOGRAPHS[1] PROPOSES TO REVIEW competition. The author, Dr. Clair Wilcox, one of the economic experts of the committee, begins with this observation: "There is perfect competition, pure competition, imperfect competition, monopolistic competition, non-price competition, oligopolistic competition, cut-throat or destructive competition, predatory and discriminatory competition, unfair and fair competition, potential competition, and effective or workable competition. Each of these concepts will be examined in turn."

This is a very erudite summary of competition, which to a businessman means continuous struggle and rivalry—a never-ending contest in research, development, sales and management.

All of the elements of competition might be illustrated by a conversation which has taken place often:

"I'm through with that X auto! Had to put my car in the shop three times before they fixed it."

"Try the Y car! Its gas consumption is low and it has that new transmission. Their agency doesn't rob you, either, and gives good, snappy service."

If the maker of the X auto and its agency went out of business eventually, they were only two of several hundred thousand American enterprises that fail every year. Mortality averages twenty per cent a year among the two million American businesses. Grocery stores and automobile agencies fail; men with new ideas or patented products build plants and start production, only to find the public does not want or will not pay the price of their products. Doors close and capital is lost.

This is the risk element of private enterprise. Several hundred thousand such hopefuls get into this "battle royal" annually; some fade out during their first year; some last two or three years [2]—but each year some, with a new and useful product giving greater value or better service, will, with good management, grow. A few become big business. But the average life of all businesses is about five years. In times of prosperity the number of companies doing business increases because new ones outnumber the ones which fail! In times of depression there are more failures than new ventures. Thus competition continuously compels the redistribution of wealth and its control.

Look back! Remember all the good automobiles that are no more? Pierce-Arrow! Peerless! White Steamer! Rambler! Stutz! Mercer! Jewett! Chandler!—and dozens more that fell by the wayside because customers thought others gave them more for their money.

Can you recall when they used to sing "Get Out and Get Under" and the family Rambler went out, with four spare tires, two strapped pessimistically on either side of the running board? Can you remember how the auto grew up, bit by bit?

The old Rambler's finish had sixteen coats of paint and varnish and each year its face was lifted with another sixteen coats. That took thirty days, and the owner walked until the job was finished, or he put on the spare body.

After World War I, the duPont Company, searching around for uses for old smokeless powder, developed auto lacquer, "Duco." At first Duco didn't look quite as good as varnish. It was used on only cheap cars. But paint companies researched and competed in development, until lacquers had the color depth and gloss of varnish. The factory's finishing time was cut from four weeks to a matter of hours. One hundred dollars was lopped off the cost of each car and competition saw that the saving was promptly turned over to the customer in the form of a lower price. Further, lacquer was good for many years—that saved more money—and we didn't need a spare body.

Then chemical companies started to make resins, from which paint companies developed baking enamels. Automobile companies jumped at another way to improve appearance and durability. Far-sighted paint companies with the first enamels got the most business and some lacquer companies fell by the wayside. New resin companies sprang into being and there was, and still is, a scramble among chemical companies to please their customers, the paint companies, with new and better resins; and among the paint companies to please their customers, the automobile companies, with a greater variety of more beautiful, more colorful, more durable finishes. The last car off the assembly line in the Spring of 1942 had a luster that would last the car's lifetime and at that time still better finishes were being perfected and tested.

Our friends in dusters who bounced around in the Rambler did not dare leave home without a jack and tire pump, for they probably would have at least one puncture. However, tire companies worked on their compounding, put more carbon black into the rubber, and soon we began to see advertisements guaranteeing the old, whining Pennsylvania Vacuum Cups for 3500 miles! Then one company made tires out of cotton cord instead of fabric. Another added chemicals to rubber to speed the curing time. This promoted a race among chemical companies to produce the best rubber chemicals.

Do you remember how the old-time rubber bands after a

year or so cracked and gnarled to look like thin strips of alligator hide, and how easily they broke? They had become oxidized! That was before chemical companies developed rubber anti-oxidants. And so today, because of competition between chemical companies and between tire companies, 30,000 miles is the standard life of a passenger tire! Owners of transcontinental truck fleets are reporting averages of 70,000 miles on trailer tires!

Automotive engineers, always on the lookout for improvements, quickly seized upon the steel companies' new continuous processes, which cut the cost of steel sheets, and safe, cheap, noiseless steel bodies arrived—wider bodies with roomier seats. Two hundred different alloys of steel—stainless, high tensile and others—were made available and promptly adopted. Automobiles became lighter yet stronger.

When chemical companies made safety glass available, one company put it in windshields, then another company put it all around, and competition forced the rest to follow. Early safety glass soon turned yellow, cracked and split, but competition among chemical and glass companies in time made it clear, tough and good for a lifetime.

As soon as aluminum became cheap enough, engine heads were made out of it; motors ran cooler and at higher compressions, aiding speed and acceleration. Gasoline consumption was lowered.

Oil companies competed among each other to produce new and better gasolines, so octane numbers rose. Ethyl gas appeared, engine knocking stopped, and smaller, more powerful, fuel-saving engines were possible. By improving oil refining methods and by adding chemicals, new properties were created that are not found in nature's product—oil that remained fluid in cold weather and oil that functioned efficiently under high pressures. New oils permitted using cadmium bearings and engine performance stepped up again.

We have almost forgotten when the family handy man spent an hour every morning with "Solarine," polishing up the Rambler's brass. Now chromium plate needs only an occasional shower and wipe-off.

If our friends in the Rambler dared to stay out past twilight, they pulled up to the roadside and put water in the carbide generator. When the Prestolite tank appeared, messy carbide was done away with. Later electric companies competed among each other for the growing auto business and now, without moving from one's seat one switches on the lights with a finger and dims them with a foot pedal. A switch turns on the heater and the windshield defroster; another, the radio. Push a button on the dash and the motor starts. Push another one on top of the steering post and a bell-metal siren clears the road.

So, as a result of competition among auto companies and their suppliers, today's Ford or Chevrolet is ever so much better than yesterday's Pierce-Arrow or Cadillac. It is more reliable and more comfortable; and it costs only a quarter as much.

When we thought the automobile industry had settled down into rivalry between two giants—Ford and General Motors—and a handful of able companies in second rank, there appeared on the scene a new man, a new face. He gathered around him an aggressive group—men with vision and zest. Starting from scratch a quarter of a century late, but with a high compression engine that customers wanted, with a new styling that appealed to women, and with daring, advanced engineering, the Chrysler Company zoomed up through the ranks and stuck its head up where two had been company. Chrysler was able to advertise, "Look at all three!"

Such is the power of the customer in an age when some people bemoan lack of opportunities and philosophize that the time has passed when men can rise from the ranks. Walter Chrysler, who started at a locomotive shop bench, and his right-hand man and successor, self-educated K. T. Keller, son of river boat people, fought in fair fight some of the most powerful industrial units in America. It's one of the things that *can,* and still do, happen here, where men are free to pursue happiness in the field of their choice.

What has happened in the automobile industry has happened in every other industry, for directly and indirectly the products of all reach the consuming public. Radio, appliances, household gadgets, clothing, railroads, transportation companies, the telephone company, movies—all are continually improving their product or service. Companies which do not keep pace fall by the wayside and new and more aggressive ones take their place.

Not only have manufacturers whose products go directly to consumers done a good job, but so have their suppliers and their suppliers' suppliers, whose roots spread deep for nature's raw materials: oil, coal, water, air, ore; into trees and across the seas to the plantations and mines of the seven corners of the earth. Where each capillary of this industrial system's root meets the fiber, and the fiber a branch, and branches meet at the crown, there is the relation of seller and customer, and there is competition.

The hundreds of thousands of purchasing agents are the real guardians of the American people against monopoly. The purchasing agents have business sense, not political sense. It is they who are insisting on two or more sources of supply. It is they who daily insist that the prices they pay bear reasonable relationship to cost; and where necessary it is they who induce new producers to start up. Vying to produce better or cheaper products or something that will do a new and useful job, competition forces all companies to work for the ultimate consumer.

Not only do individual companies within an industry compete among each other but there is inter-industry competition for the customer's dollar. Viewed from all angles, competition has even more facets, probably, than Professor Wilcox identifies.

Excepting public utilities, where monopolies are chartered, in commercial fields the importance of monopolies shrinks to insignificance. Though a company might have a monopoly of supply of a commodity such as aluminum, this monopoly loses much of its force because of competing commodities performing similar functions.

Aluminum, for instance, competes with copper for power transmission lines, stainless steel in the production of railroad cars, magnesium alloys in airplanes, and zinc and plastics in smaller fabricated articles. There is no aluminum use that cannot be satisfied by a competing article. If the price of aluminum were raised to its old figure of two dollars a pound, very few of the articles that now use aluminum would disappear from the market. They would be made of other materials.

Our airplanes would be made out of plywood, plastics, magnesium alloys and stainless steel, and after manufacturers had time to perfect the use and application of the alternative products, the resultant airplane would eventually be as good.

The manufacturers of aluminum had a choice of selling one pound at two dollars or a carload at fifteen cents a pound. Because the large volume of business at the low price yielded so much more profit than the small volume at the higher price, the price gradually fell to the lower level.

A budget is usually established when one builds a house, and the choice of materials entering into its construction is determined by the relative contribution each makes to its beauty and utility as weighed by cost. Stone, brick, wood and tile all compete with each other for outer walls. Copper, iron, tile and now plastics compete for the piping. Plaster, wood and wallboard compete for interior surfaces, and so on. The selection in each case is governed by its cost in relation to the utility and beauty desired.

Wallboard manufacturers know that if they can bring their prices down, their product will be chosen more often. Therefore they constantly strive to reduce costs of raw materials and processing to achieve this objective. So with all other producers.

Each housewife has her budget. Naturally she allocates her expenditures to those goods or services from which she believes she gets the most enjoyment or utility. It may be a question of a trip or a new refrigerator; a chair or a new radio; a new automobile or a new and bigger apartment. And the money goes where the best value is offered. Therefore, every businessman's enlightened self-interest demands that selling prices be kept to the lowest point compatible with reasonable profit.

Who runs American enterprise? The ultimate consumers! You and I and 130 million other Americans. We spend our money where we think we get the best value or service. All American enterprise is competing for our favor. It is the people who run private enterprise.

The temptation to criticize that with which one is not familiar is always great. Never do I travel by train that I am not prompted to think I could run a railroad better than railroad men. But the faults I find are so obvious it is impossible that the management is unaware of them. It knows the reasons or conditions which would make what I believe a simple solution impractical. And the T.N.E.C. monographs consider private enterprise from a similar non-participant viewpoint.

The irony of the monographs is that not one of the authors

has made a contribution to the system of private enterprise he criticizes. Most have never left the abstract scholastic atmosphere of the social science classrooms. None of the authors has had business experience; there is room for one to doubt if many of them have seen the inside of a factory.

These men live under the suzerainty of a doctrine that business consists of chicanery, greed and disregard of the rights of others, and that the bigger a business is the worse it must be. Their prejudice reaches back for centuries. Miriam Beard[3] recalls that "even in the sixteenth century the trader and banker already found arrayed against them the scholar, the poet and artist whom they patronized. The libraries and universities they had founded nourished their detractors." It was in the deepest pit of Inferno, where sinners by fraud and treachery "with their hands kept warding off, sometimes the flames, sometimes the burning soil," that Dante placed the bankers and merchants of Florence.

As the solution to problems whose practical import they do not understand, these idealists offer the coercive power of the state over enterprise and the lives and habits of the people. They offer political central economic planning.

A succinct and lucid statement of "planning" is found in L. E. Hubbard's authoritative "Soviet Money and Finance."[4] "Planning," he explains, "is the attempt to concentrate in the hands of the Government the whole power of deciding a comprehensive programme of production, distribution and consumption, aiming at an accurate and continuous direction of production to authoritatively determine consumption and the elimination of the periodic fluctuations inherent in capitalist economy. Planning can be complete only when the State owns or entirely controls all means of production and distribution. This condition has effectually been reached in the Soviet Union. Industry as a whole may be compared to a gigantic combine in which the individual industries and individual enterprises have a considerable measure of independence, but are controlled by a central organization which determines all matters of major policy."

Suppose planning had been in effect twenty years ago. Suppose Henry Ford had been commissar of automobiles. It would have been a popular appointment. Ford had led the industry in cutting prices—in mass production. He led in high wages. He was a pioneer, proven, honest and fearless. But with his power to veto any suggestion with which he did not agree, is there not a chance we might still be riding around in something resembling Model T's? Ford believed in them so thoroughly that he refused to change his production until it was almost too late. Indeed, the Ford Company never recaptured the lead it once held. Had Ford been commissar, might not his decision have been to concentrate and standardize on Model T's—a ruling which would have been made in all sincerity?

And do you remember when he is supposed to have said that "the people can have any color car as long as it is black"?

Had Ford believed in Chrysler's engineering he would have so designed his cars. In a planned economy, Commissar Ford probably would have turned down Chrysler's petition to be allowed to make such a car. Looking at his five-year plan for the automobile industry, Ford undoubtedly would have said, "No. There is ample capacity now for all the cars this year's and next year's plan calls for. And besides, your design has no particular merit!"

This decision would have been made honestly and would have been well justified by facts as Commissar Ford saw them. In America, under the enterprise system, the public is boss. They had the opportunity to render their own decision—and did!

CHAPTER X

Whose Feet Are Clay?

AFTER THE AMERICAN PEOPLE HAD BEEN SUFFICIENTLY educated by the "campaign of inquiry and publicity" to "understand what it is all about," Veblen's suggestion for completing the revolution was simple and to the point; it was to enact a law declaring all stocks and bonds—evidences of absentee ownership—void. Thus corporations having no private owners would fall into the lap of the state.

Thomas R. Amilie, a former member of Congress from Wisconsin, once proposed a twenty-second amendment to the Constitution. The amendment provided that "the absentee ownership of any industrially useful article by any person or persons not habitually employed in the industrial use thereof is hereby disallowed in the United States." All laws in conflict were to be "declared inoperative"; Congress was to establish machinery for the "administration of said property in which absentee ownership has been canceled for the common welfare of the people of the United States."

Amilie explained that state operation of these assets and the gearing of the "productive capacity to consumptive capacity" would result in a "universal standard of living now enjoyed only by the rich."

Somewhat the same idea entered into the thinking of the Industrial Expansion Act, which Amilie introduced in Congress in 1937. Robert G. Allen of Pennsylvania, Jerry Voorhies of California and Maury Maverick of Texas joined Amilie as sponsors. The Act, which Amilie said stemmed "ideologically from the writings of the late Thorstein Veblen" and which Allen said made "a reality of the dream of plenty glimpsed by Veblen thirty years ago," provided an elaborate system of industry planning and control. Capacity operation and full employment were thus to be insured.

In his remarks to the House of Representatives, Amilie commented: "If the Industrial Expansion Act had been proposed in 1932 it would have been premature. The people of the country despite the chaos then prevailing would have cried out against this attempt at industrial regimentation. . . . Now the American people have become accustomed to the new symbols. The farmers are willing to accept regimentation if it is their kind of regimentation. Businessmen are willing to accept their kind of regimentation although with more enthusiasm in periods of depression than boom. The workmen also believe in regimentation if it will make labor a scarce commodity. . . . But in the final analysis when enough support has been built up to put the Industrial Expansion Act into operation the American people will understand that any income in the form of wages or profits that cannot be spent for consumer goods by the recipient and for which there is no need for capital goods purposes must be taken over and converted into the channels of consumption through the instrument of taxation. . . . The needs of the people will be taken care of and they in their own good time can determine how long society shall continue to pay an owning class for the performance of a function that has been released to Government."

Amilie's speech and the Industrial Expansion Act are one of the Recovery Plans put forward in a Temporary National Economic Committee monograph. Appearing under the title of "Planning for Abundance," it is introduced as having been "based on the research of Mordecai Ezekiel of the Department of Agriculture," and is included with six other "proposals for economic reform" which are said to afford "a good cross section of public opinion on these moot questions."

However, the planners who sponsor Amilie's or any other proposal for taking over the existing enterprise system by substituting the state for individual shareholders assume that the able staffs of trained executives, engineers and managers would function for the state with the same zeal and efficiency they evidence under private ownership. They assume the same pace of technological progress would continue under the new ownership as under the old.

However, the planners fail to weigh human nature!

Practice would prove their theory to be a delusion, not because managers and engineers of private enterprise have more foibles than the average man but because under a bureaucratic environment a whole new set of influences would play on the fallibilities of human nature.

Only too rarely does one meet a truly Christian spirit wherein self is sacrificed in devotion to the betterment of mankind. If this spirit were the rule, we would never have been admonished with the Ten Commandments; we would now need no laws, no courts and no police.

In life, however, we find our meaner attributes such as jealousy, laziness, envy, obstinacy, greed, viciousness and bigotry balancing or even outweighing our finer attributes of generosity, tolerance and industry. Man is still cursed with primary animalistic instincts of selfishness, or self-preservation, and we have inherited in varying degrees a predatory urge, an acquisitiveness and an ambition for power over other men.

In private enterprise these meaner attributes—this selfishness and lust for power—find an outlet in aspiration for growth of one's business or greater authority which accompanies promotion in company rank.

The finer attributes are measured by one's ability to get along with fellow workers and inspire their confidence. Hope for the rewards spurs competition on. There is no limit to ambition. Every office boy may hope to be President; at least he can and will strive to executive position with more pay. The symbol of achievement is monetary gain.

The rewards are achieved by the winners in the competitive test of individual ability to sell more than others, to be first in perfecting something new and useful, or to produce more and at less cost than others.

Competition is stimulated by fear, too, for failure to achieve a minimum performance threatens security, job, income and future. One's instinct for self-preservation, therefore, compels a minimum standard of performance.

But private enterprise is not only competition among individuals but competition between groups of individuals—company organizations against company organizations. A group of men share an adventure together; they win or lose together. The interest of an individual is blended to a large extent into that of the group. Leaders of the groups, therefore, fit subordinates into places where they seem to be best suited in research, production or sales, and train them for higher responsibilities. Nepotism and favoritism are hurtful to the team spirit and to group prospects. Leaders of the most successful groups, therefore, require a nicety of balanced vision, tenacity, integrity—and enough of the finer attributes of character to inspire loyalty in their team.

The human traits of the managing group—their selfishness, ambition and lust for power—are appeased only when the efficiency of the whole organization proves its ability to keep the pace of competition with profit. By recognized standards the amount of profit in relation to that of competitors is a measure of both the degree of public acceptance achieved and productive efficiency.

In private enterprise the satisfaction of ambition and the appeasement of selfishness are concomitant with service rendered to the public in the form of new articles, better articles and cheaper articles. The roots that feed and gratify human nature stem out to the people. The people are the sole criterion; they furnish or withhold the sustenance.

"Planners" do not understand that Civil Service examinations cannot grade men in loyalty, vision, integrity, teamwork and tenacity, which rate even higher than native ability as qualifications for industrial leadership. "Planners" do not comprehend how the touch of bureaucracy will wither organization morale and the efficiency of private enterprise, for in bureaucracy the roots are bent away from the people; they stem up to the head of the state.

In the lower ranks of bureaucracy, Civil Service leaves little to hope; it allays only fear. Advancement by seniority stills individual initiative, for the slow march of progress is up a path cleared only by death and retirement of seniors. Ability and performance above average do not hasten progress; performance below average does not retard it. Hence the pace falls back to the flaccid Civil Service cadence one can measure in any post office or city hall. Jobs are assured not by competitive measure but by methodical adherence to minimum standards of attendance and obedience to regulations. Ambition is thwarted but in compensation the instinct for self-preservation is appeased with a sense of security.

In bureaucracy's upper ranks, the so-called policy-making positions, the result is not happier. The positions are not won by competition in the lower ranks nor measured by public service of a group as in private enterprise. These positions are appointive; service to the party is the chief qualification. This is true in Fascist Berlin, Communistic Moscow, Constitutional Monarchial London and Republican or Democratic Washington. It has been true as long as history. It will be true as long as there are politics and bureaucracy.

In bureaucracy, hope for the reward of a high position results in competition for the favor of the superior officer or head of the party. Personal ambition can be satisfied only by pleasing superior officers, by doing nothing that might discredit them or the party, by agreeing with them. Fear is of displeasing them or the party. Selfishness becomes a matter of taking no chances of such displeasure and no risk that might bring criticism on one's self or one's superior. Hence buck-passing—the fear of assuming authority belonging to a superior, the fear of making a wrong decision, the fear of violating some regulation—results in delay as the responsibility for making decisions is passed along.

In these human reactions lies the origin of bureaucratic red tape and inaction. Public officials can't lose by delay and inaction. They operate monopolies; they are not in competition!

These same forces would operate in private enterprise except for competition. In private enterprise, delay and inaction would cause loss of markets to another organization that risked prompt action; hence buck-passing is minimized and authority is delegated down the line. A junior of promise is given responsibility. If he makes too many errors of judgment he is removed; but if he uses his authority wisely and proves his judgment good, he is promoted to greater responsibility. There are "political" appointments in enterprise, some nepotism and some favoritism, but when these qualities govern the appointment of men to positions of responsibility, in spite of lack of ability and other necessary qualifications, the penalties are automatic. The efficiency of the organization decreases and it loses ground in competition.

In bureaucracy, however, there is no way of establishing standards of performance or measuring results. No interbureau competition measures the efficiency of those who control various bureaus or the extent of public service each performs. Each bureau or department is a monopoly unto itself. The Navy can't compete with the Post Office, for instance, the Army with the Labor Department, nor the Treasury Department with the Social Security Department.

Ambition and lust for power are expressed in rivalry among bureau heads for large appropriations for their departments and new fields over which to extend their sway. Emulation and self-aggrandizement are expressed in the ostentation of offices, numerous secretaries, large staffs, marble buildings, private cars and special privileges. Vanity and selfishness are satisfied by publicity and public acclaim.

Not for one moment is this criticism of bureaucracy meant to impute that government officials are not of as high character as those engaged in private enterprise—such an interpretation would be incorrect. Nowhere, for instance, can one find finer men than our Army and Navy officers. Chosen initially by intense competition as youths and passing vigorous training, their loyalty to their service, their honesty, their patriotism and their ability are unquestioned. Nor is any slur intended on the character or ability of any other government official.

We are merely comparing how two alternative systems, private enterprise and state control or bureaucratic operation, vary in the different responses obtained from distinguishing qualities of human character. We are considering whether fields now subject to bureaucratic control afford indications of what might be looked for if bureaucratic control extended to those fields now served by private enterprise.

Thus, no criticism of any particular administration is implied. Republicans, Democrats and New Dealers are all of the human race, all cursed and blessed by the same traits and characteristics. All respond to bureaucratic influence in about the same way, and if managers of private enterprise entered bureaucracy their response to its influences would parallel that of our present officials.

In fact, businessmen often remark the change that comes over one of their number who "goes to Washington." Suddenly he is standing before microphones parrotting ghost-written speeches, occasionally uttering philosophies that seem in fundamental disagreement with his former convictions. He takes pride in being quoted, poses willingly for photographers, becomes interested in his public following and measures the publicity he receives in the public press. Gradually he cuts adrift his old, hard-boiled sense of orthodox efficiency, because his ambitions and symbols of success are changing. His old friends say he has "the political bug." Later he loses zest for short-cutting red tape. He becomes weary of the battle—and accepts the "what's the use" philosophy.

Noah Webster describes red tape as a scrupulous adherence to prescribed routine, especially when the result is delay or inaction. He implies that its origin lay in the tape formerly used in public offices for tying up official documents. Red tape is typical of officialdom, or bureaucracy. But why is it necessary to have delay or inaction when it is the people's business that is involved, the people's money that is wasted? Why does it continue with us in wartime, when the very life of the nation is at stake?

Bureaucracy assumes no one is to be trusted, and itself has a chronic dread of responsibility! Therefore, certain elaborate but perfunctory motions are prescribed which in the ordinary course of events will prevent fraud or bad judgment which, if committed, would reflect discredit upon the superior's judgment and caution. A painstaking routine establishes an automatic alibi of precautions taken. Red tape is the luxurious insurance of self-preservation indulged in by bureaucracy. Each official retains a protection enjoyed by his predecessor and adds to it if an occasion exposes an incident of fraud or a new opportunity for fraud or exercise of bad judgment.

A friend of mine, a businessman, related a minor but symptomatic incident of the ridiculous lengths to which red tape may be drawn. He had just accepted a position in the St. Louis Office of Price Administration. On arrival at his desk he found a letter from an acquaintance volunteering his services. My friend tossed the letter to his new secretary, saying, "Write that I can't use him now. Say I'll let him know if something turns up later."

The secretary opened her desk, took out a letterhead and began making a twelve-decker sandwich of carbon paper and copy tissue.

My friend promptly inquired, "Why in the world are you putting that fat stack together?"

"I have to make eleven copies," she replied.

"Why?" he asked.

"It's regulations! We have to make eleven copies of every letter that goes out in franked mail. I suppose it is to keep people from using the privilege for personal mail."

"Where do the eleven copies go?"

"Oh," she explained, "we have to send three copies to Kansas City, our state office, three to Dallas, our regional office, and one to Washington, and we keep four here."

"What do you do with four copies here?" he asked.

"Well, one goes in the reading file, one in the central file and two in the cross-index division file."

"The devil!" my businessman friend exclaimed impatiently. "Get him on the 'phone!"

But unconsciously my friend saved the government money. The eleven copies would have cost more than the telephone call, for although the government pays no postage, clerks' time to file eleven copies, preparational cost of files and the rent of file space mount rapidly.

A recent regulation has cut this requirement to four copies—one to each office—but this is still four times the number business would require in such cases and four times business' cost.

Competition not only forces enterprise to trust its juniors and allow them freedom of action; it forces companies to trust each other and the public. Business is done on credit! Individuals buy from retail stores on credit, often paying long after the goods have been consumed. As businesses buy and sell to one another, billions of credit are extended annually; and, considering the extent of the transactions, bad debts are very small.

Bureaucracy, however, trusts no one. The Post Office, for instance, does not trust the judgment of its postmasters. Even the T.N.E.C. moguls of wealth—the Rockefeller, Mellon and du Pont families—can't buy a two-cent stamp on credit! The Cunard Steamship Line must pay Panama Canal tolls in cash before its ships are allowed to proceed.

Business, however, has always been done on trust. Trade was well established in Mesopotamia in 2500 B.C. when caravans and sailing ships plied between ancient centers of commerce.

A letter to a trader in Kanish, uncovered in one of the Asian colonies, proves that the fundamentals of credit in business are as old as business itself: "Two talents of lead are with Hura-Sanum. Two talents with Amur-Assur, son of Shu-Ishtar, and one hundred pieces of stuff are on hand. Insist upon good lead. Take the lead and cloth on short term credits. If you intend to send this money here to buy goods and your written order arrrives before the money comes, *I will buy the wares you designate from my own means and send them to you.*"[1]

Another instance—a personal experience—also of a minor nature but symptomatic of the distrustful red tape burden on the people, concerned a routine purchase of automobiles. Presumably at some time or another an individual or firm doing work for the government was extravagant. Thereupon, to prevent a repetition, no future individual was to be trusted to act in good faith. The Treasury issued an order requiring contractors for government work, when buying automobiles, to take the lowest of three bids, but in any event not more than $750 was to be paid for a car.

In some localities automobiles cannot be purchased for $750. Within War Department regulations, however, it was permissible to lease a car, from the dealer making the lowest bid, until the money paid under lease and applied to the quoted price brought the balance within $750. Then the purchase could be effected according to Treasury regulations.

By leasing instead of buying outright, state license plates and state tax, not required under government ownership, were necessary and interest had to be paid on unpaid balances. Therefore, five Plymouths cost the government $497.65 more than the cash price—the price private business would have paid—the price government would have paid except for red tape.

Our Army and Navy officers represent our highest type of manhood; they give ample evidence of it in time of war. However, as it is only during war that they are in competition, it is only during war that the best in them is brought out. If measured by the standards prevailing in private enterprise, these officers fail in the development of their "business."

The purchase of munitions, for instance, involves archaic and costly systems of inspection. Each plant supplying munitions to the Army has Ordnance Department observers and checkers stationed in the plant. No company is trusted to carry out its obligations. In one powder plant, for example, the Army stations four hundred and fifty officers and civilian employes; it has another host of officers and employes at the shell loading plant where the powder is packed into shells.

I asked a high-ranking Ordnance officer why these elaborate precautions were necessary, particularly as the checking and red tape often retarded needed production. I asked why in the case of reputable contractors a semi-annual audit of accounts would not suffice. He replied that, in his opinion, such a check would be ample but that obsolete regulations required the elaborate precautions.

The Navy follows a similar system. For example, in the manufacture of shell hoists, the Navy maintains inspectors where castings originate; it maintains inspectors at plants where Diesel engines for the hoists are fabricated; it maintains inspectors at plants where Diesel engines and castings are assembled into shell hoists; and it maintains inspectors at shipyards where shell hoists are installed in ships.

In business each manufacturer is responsible for the quality of his finished product. Therefore, it is incumbent upon him to test his raw materials. Naturally, he can be relied upon to reject faulty supplies. Surely one inspection—the final one—should suffice for the Navy.

If Sears-Roebuck or Montgomery-Ward used the Army and Navy red tape and extravagant routine of purchasing—if they employed inspectors and checkers in the plants of each of their suppliers and each of the suppliers of raw materials to their suppliers—their costs would be too high to be competitive. They would fail!

The first weakness of our military aviation was startlingly brought to public notice when the Army Air Corps was aroused in 1934 and told to fly the mail which private enterprise had been carrying safely and regularly. Major Alexander de Seversky relates that the President "could not possibly suspect that our air forces were dismally unprepared for the task."[2] For years, he said, the Army had considered radio other than that necessary for communication with ground forces as a luxury; that Army air service radios were adaptations of the standardized types used on the ground. "To Army minds the standardization of equipment in all branches seemed to be the paramount consideration." Seven army pilots died in crashes. Seversky insists that they "died as martyrs to bureaucracy and illogical procurement methods."[3]

Regarding the inadequacy of our military aircraft at the outbreak of war, Seversky commented: "The war startlingly disclosed that while we possessed many airplanes with first-rate flying characteristics, we had practically no military airplanes in the real sense of the word. It would be an insult to the dictionary to designate as 'military,' craft so deficient in the basic qualities necessary for combat."[4] He describes the military deficiencies as: woeful lack of fire power, lack of bullet-proofing of gasoline tanks, and lack of armor, all of which had been incorporated in British and German craft and of which developments our Army officials had been aware. The P-40 fighters which we sent to England in 1940 were not even uncrated, in spite of England's desperate need for fighter craft during the German raids on London.

After American fighters had been armored and leak-proof gasoline tanks and increased fire power had been installed, they proved effective against the Japs, but still they were not a match for Germany's and Britain's best.

The Army bought military aircraft from the same industry, and in many cases from the same companies, from which domestic airlines bought commercial transports.

When private enterprise worked with aircraft manufacturers, however, transport development was rapid.

At the outbreak of the war, American commercial aircraft were the best in the world. They were flying the seven seas—not even attempted by other nations, except England, and by England rather unsuccessfully, as one is reminded by the tragedy of the Cavalier. American commercial transports were setting unprecedented records in speed and safety. Air transport companies of small European states, such as Holland and Switzerland, which were free to choose from all the world's aircraft, standardized on the American Douglas DC-3. Although the military aircraft of Germany and England were superior to ours, their commercial craft were used solely by their own state-subsidized airlines. They did not gain a foothold in world markets.

It is untimely to dwell on the Army's neglect and backwardness in other fields. Undoubtedly the facts will be brought before the people when the necessity for war morale is past.

Let us review briefly the government's biggest enterprise—one in which it has had a monopoly since inception. The Post Office Department is an enterprise of magnitude. It employs 291,000 persons; its annual payroll is nearly 600 million dollars; it has 44,000 post offices, 33,000 rural routes; it operates a savings bank with deposits of one and a quarter billion dollars. Annually it transfers over two billion dollars in money orders; delivers twenty-eight trillion pieces of mail and collects three-quarters of a billion in revenue.[5]

First-class mail, however, is its only profitable operation; it loses money on second- and third-class mail, on parcel post, on its insurance charges, on its registered mail service, on its special delivery service, on its money order business. Several of these services, such as money orders, parcel post and insurance, are to some extent in competition with private business, which makes a profit.

Nor does the deficit of the Post Office Department tell the whole story. Hundreds of millions of dollars have been appropriated out of general revenue for its plant. No depreciation is taken on this plant; all new facilities are built with special Congressional appropriations. It does not provide for insurance; reconstruction of buildings because of fire or other damage is provided out of general appropriations. It does not provide on its accounts for the pensioning of its employes; this, too, is provided by special appropriations in the Civil Service. And it makes no provision for taxes. All these items are charges business must include in its costs.

The Post Office's system of internal accounting is antiquated. A uniform method of reporting cash receipts and disbursements, without which no successful business has been run since the advent of modern accounting, was adopted only after a Congressional investigation in 1908.

However, postmasters still keep stamp sales, money order transactions and postal savings in separate funds and more or less juggle these funds when reporting. Bureaucratic resistance to improvement leaves post offices without modern loose-leaf accounting and machine posting. The statement of department assets carries amounts known to have disappeared with certain southern postmasters prior to the outbreak of the Civil War! [6]

The largest customers of the Post Office, impatient to receive their mail, go themselves to collect it. Post Office superintendents seldom if ever call on large mail users to see how the service could be improved or what new facilities are needed. The Post Office does not try to adapt other new inventions that might be employed to the advantage of the users of mail service. Innovations such as automatic mailing machines and stamping machines used by large commercial firms were developed by and must be bought or leased from private firms.

Mail creeps among city traffic in trucks, although steam, power, gas, telephone and telegraph lines, and even in some cases refrigeration, move in pipes under the streets. Airmail spends as much time trailing behind heavy road traffic between the post offices in St. Louis and Chicago and their respective airports as it does flying between the two cities. Certainly in similar circumstances, competition would force private enterprise to experiment with possibilities of reducing this waste of time promised by helicopters and autogyros. and aid in their development.

The three-cent first-class mail charge is fifty per cent higher than prior to the first World War, yet the charges of the competing telegram are only twenty per cent higher and long distance telephone charges average one-half the prewar rates. The Post Office maintains no research department that would seek better ways and new services for its customers—the public. Why?

The managerial class of the Post Office Department are bureaucrats. They are chosen not for skill nor aptitude but because of their political influence in their local community. Even if these appointees apply themselves diligently, there can be no reward. The postmaster at Shelbyville, Tennessee, for example, can never hope to be postmaster at Memphis; the postmaster at Memphis can never hope to rise to be postmaster of St. Louis or New York. He can never hope to be postmaster-general except through extraordinary service, not to the public or his customers but to his party.

Therefore, incentive, the zest for work and accomplishment, is lacking, and as a result our daily mail is delivered by a man with a leather sack on his back, just as it was fifty or a hundred years ago.

In bureaucracy, big and little bureaucrats have vested interests—their jobs. Like most businessmen, they resist any change that would alter a routine with which they are familiar. But since they are not in competition, changes are not forced by competition; therefore their functions and routine become stabilized and static.

There can be no need to illustrate with instance after instance how bureaucrats seek to protect their vested interests in their jobs by seeking increased appropriations for their departments and by bringing pressure to resist public demands to reduce appropriations or eliminate their functions.

It must be evident that the political sub-division of our states into counties is archaic, inefficient and expensive. Local county seats which were established when they were a day's ride away from each other are now no more than an hour apart by motor car. However, the vested interests of little county bureaucrats in their jobs have successfully prevented more efficient and less costly political organization.

The lethargy of the United States Weather Bureau is another case in point. Hardly a greater peacetime or war service could be rendered to the people than accurate weather forecasting.

To the farmer, even accurate short-range forecasts are of immense importance for planting in time to receive the beneficent stimulus of rain and harvesting at the proper time to avoid it; for the orchardists, to prepare for frost, high wind and ice storms. There would be tremendous boon if through long-range forecasting the farmer could be told whether it would be a dry or a wet season.

In the communications industry, it would be of great advantage to know the imminence of ice storms or high winds, in order to safeguard against the icing of tracks and switches and to avoid marooning trucks on snow-bound highways; for the fuel industry to know when to expect peak demands for coal, gas and oil and how long and how severe the winter is likely to be; for the retailer to know whether the Easter season will be cold and rainy or warm and sunny; for the construction industry if it could know when to excavate without fear of rain and when to pour foundations without fear of frost.

To the construction worker it would be a boon if he could know the days that would permit outdoor work and those on which there would be forced lay-offs; to baseball if night games could be scheduled with certainty that the weather would permit playing; to vacationists and tourists if they could plan on the weather and know the kind of clothing to take with them.

Of greatest importance to the very life of the nation is accurate long-range forecasting. Campaigns have been won or lost depending on a turn of the weather. There is ample reason to believe that the Germans long ago developed weather forecasting to a high degree. Was it luck that not a drop of rain dropped during the Polish campaign? Was it luck that the battleships *Gneisenau* and *Scharnhorst* were brought from Brest to Heligoland under the protecting umbrella of thick, low-lying clouds and fog?

And yet the Weather Bureau, in whose hands weather forecasting has rested since its establishment in 1871, sat complacently behind its established red tape and cumbersome routine and not only failed to indulge in any fundamental research of its own but allowed an entirely new science of weather forecasting to develop in other countries, and even in our own universities, unheeded.

Because forecasting became a science and our bureaucrats in the Weather Bureau were not scientists, they sought to protect their vested interests in their jobs by scorning and belittling scientific advances. If the government adopted this new-fangled system the bureaucrats would be out of jobs, or they would have to go back to school! University experimentation was resented by the Weather Bureau, one high official going so far as to tell Father Macelwane, Director of St. Louis University's Department of Geophysics, that universities had no business in meteorology because the Weather Bureau preferred to train its own men. They preferred to inbreed in their archaic Civil Service!

The new science arose in Norway during the last war. When weather reports from belligerent nations were denied to them, Norwegian meteorologists turned to the third dimension and sought information from the upper air. The new idea was quickly seized upon and developed in Germany. The Massachusetts Institute of Technology and the California Institute of Technology became interested and engaged Norwegians to teach it.

Soon the airlines, which had long been dissatisfied with government weather reports, engaged the professors as advisers and graduates of these courses to establish their own weather service. Instead of inaccurate forecasts limited to some twelve hours, forecasts were extended to thirty-six hours. Airlines were informed with reasonable accuracy of icing conditions and winds at various flying altitudes. They could plan their flights with great assurance. Had the Weather Bureau been abreast of these developments, the Navy dirigible "Akron" could have avoided the storm that broke her up in 1927.

Complaints of the engineering profession and the airlines caused President Roosevelt to appoint a committee of scientists to investigate the Weather Bureau. As a result of their report [7] the department was reorganized and the new science was pushed down the bureaucratic throats—twenty years late!

T.V.A. has too short a history to permit of any conclusion, but it may be noted that, in a confession of hopelessness of ever earning an adequate return on all the people's money invested, fifty-eight per cent of the investment is charged to navigation and flood control. Up to June 30, 1941, T.V.A. had been the recipient of $550,000,000 from the government, not one cent of which has been repaid. Since that date further appropriations will raise the national investment to $776,000,000.

It has been argued against T.V.A. that if power is what is wanted, it can be provided more cheaply from modern high-pressure steam plants; that the $550,000,000 or $776,000,000 can hardly be justified to provide navigation on a river on which only a few thousand tons of shipping move a year. Furthermore, instead of being an aid to navigation, the large lakes created by the T.V.A. provide storm hazards that paddle wheel river steamers are unable to weather. If flood control is the object, one answers that the area flooded permanently by T.V.A.'s dams is larger than the biggest area ever flooded temporarily by the river itself.

On the credit side, cheaper power is available to consumers in the Tennessee Valley and they are using more of it. Cheaper power has attracted new industries, but the industrial immigration to the Tennessee Valley has been, in most cases, at the expense of other regions.

As a social enterprise, the benefits conferred upon the Tennessee Valley should be weighed alongside the costs to the people as a whole. Assuming that 1941 is a representative year, the enterprise balances out as follows:

If T.V.A. power in 1941 had been sold at the rates which would have been charged by the Tennessee Electric Power Company, the consumers would have paid an extra	$ 7,947,000
The T.V.A. received a net income from its power operations	6,990,000
	$14,937,000

On the other hand, the taxpayers of the United States have had to forego, in taxes, and pay interest on money given T.V.A.	$18,220,000
Leaving a net loss to the national economy of	$ 3,283,000 [8]

In this tabulation it is assumed that if T.V.A. were a private corporation it would pay the same income taxes on its gross revenue as other public utilities, and that the United States Treasury paid two and one-half per cent annual interest on the June 30, 1941, investment in T.V.A.

In view of the crowded condition of housing and the lack of office accommodations in Washington, D. C., the United States Senate empowered the Appropriations Committee to make an investigation of the executive departments and government agencies not engaged in war work. The purpose was to determine if some of their employes and facilities could be released to war agencies.

As the agencies investigated were those officered and staffed in most cases by advocates of state planning, even state operation of enterprise, the report of the subcommittee is pertinent. The following sentences—quotations from the report issued in 1942—are not lifted out of their contexts. They are truly indicative of the tenor of the whole report and the findings of the committee.

The report [9] states: "It stretches a well-reasoning mind to find justification for the continuance of such activities under existing conditions. . . . Another illustration of this similar lack of proper co-ordination. . . . This latter undertaking is a complete duplication. . . . It developed that although extensive duplication does not exist in the objectives of the various departments and agencies, nevertheless it does exist to an alarming and serious degree in the modus operandi by which the objectives of the agencies are reached.

. . . The committee is of the opinion that conscientious effort on the part of the executive offices would result in a material reduction of informational and statistical activities with corresponding reductions in Federal expenditures and at the same time make available several thousand employes, space and equipment direly needed. . . . Inquiries have brought out the unmistakable fact that at the beginning of this committee's operations the Civil Service Commission was in a highly chaotic state of organization. . . . The committee has found the existence of nonessential functions, some of which are overlapping, duplicating and paralleling others, inflated administrative staffs, wasteful use of office and other space, and lack of full utilization of equipment and materials. . . . A survey of this equipment and its use has revealed, in general, a gross disregard for economy and, in some instances, an abuse of the highest order. . . . The foregoing are only a few examples of the many cases which could be cited to illustrate the extent to which the various departments and agencies of the federal government are overstocked with duplicating equipment. . . . This condition not only exists in those agencies which were the subject of the illustrations, but exists generally throughout the government service. . . . An analysis of the function being prosecuted by the so-called war agencies of the Office of ———— reveals that duplication, overlapping and paralleling of functions, already being prosecuted in the regular departments and agencies, exists to an unbelievable degree. . . . The use of a properly modified system of index or punch cards is one of the more elementary methods by which control can be maintained over functions performed by the many departments and agencies. . . . The committee, in developing its study of the departments and agencies, utilized an index system, to a limited extent, in drawing together like functions and found that should the system be fully developed, undoubtedly the results obtained thereby would be astounding. . . . Inquiry of the Bureau of the Budget revealed that even this simple method of control is not maintained by that agency."

Referring to war agencies, the subcommittee concluded: "In excluding these agencies, the committee does not by any means intend to impute that they are operated more efficiently than any other."

As an illustration of duplication, the report relates: "There is within the War Production Board a so-called Labor Division which, at March 31, 1942, employed 460 persons. Yet there exists in the normal executive departments and establishments the following organizations which are interested, in whole or in part, in similar operations:

The National Labor Relations Board
Federal Security Agency:
  United States Employment Service
  Social Security Board
  National Youth Administration
Labor Department:
  Conciliation Service
  Bureau of Labor Standards
  Bureau of Labor Statistics
  Wage and Hour Division
  Women's Bureau
National Resources Planning Board
Works Projects Administration

"It is interesting to note that though the War Production Board has this superlabor organization, it was apparently found insufficient since there was set up an additional organization in this same field known as the War Labor Board. The foregoing illustration is only one of many which the committee could bring forth. . . ."

The author cannot resist the temptation to repeat that the bureaus investigated are under the direction of individuals who would plan the operation of business, some desiring government to own and operate all business.

Another indication of the efficiency the public might expect if the latter came to pass is illustrated by government purchasing methods. An author of one of the T.N.E.C. monographs [10] attempts a study of government purchasing. Government agencies' purchases approximated one billion dollars in 1938!

The first section of the monograph apologizes for the lack of adequate statistics and information concerning buying activity. It was pointed out that, as many departments did not keep purchasing records, *it was necessary to obtain some of the data from manufacturers.* Could any enterprise remain in competitive business without knowing what it purchased?

Extravagance, which is always characteristic of government operations, is the result of a human reaction which has traveled through the ages. Adam Smith, in his quaint, Quakerish way, sensed the reason. "Princes," he wrote, "have frequently engaged in many mercantile projects. . . . They have scarce ever succeeded. The profusion with which the affairs of princes are always managed renders it almost impossible that they should." Then he proceeds with his analysis: "The agents of a prince regard the wealth of their master as inexhaustible, are careless at which price they buy and are careless at which expense they transport his goods." [11] It is bureaucracy's attitude that the "prince," the United States government, has inexhaustible means. There is no need for economy. It is the little savings, however, that in business add up to constant cost reduction. Competition eliminates any business whose affairs are administered in "profusion."

European governments have civil services with traditions

of several centuries. These governments to a greater or lesser degree have always engaged in fields of enterprise that in America have been left to private hands. In most European countries, for instance, the Post Office Departments operate telephone and telegraph systems. The resulting standards of service bring profuse expressions of disgust from American tourists.

Elliot Paul, in his exposé, "The Last Time I saw Paris," paints this accurate and amusing thumbnail sketch of the operation of Parisian telephones: "One might have thought that with this huge swarm of public employes drawing pay, however inadequate, the public services in France would be passable. However," he sighs, "nothing could be further from the truth." In his little Parisian quarter containing 2,500 people there were less than half a dozen phones and "if one wished to speak with some not too far distant person, usually he saved time and trouble by taking a bus, the subway or even a train."

A defender of private enterprise might be prompted to suggest that European services, bad as they are, might be worse still had it not been for their willingness to adopt equipment and methods developed in America. He might also point to the significance of the fact that Spain and Rumania, in desperation, contracted for the operation of their telephone systems by American private enterprise.

That the inefficiency and red tape of bureaucracy is as old as government itself—at least, as old as the American government—is indicated by Washington Irving. Telling of the early efforts of our government to combat the growing influence of British fur trading companies in our own northwest, he related how in 1796 the government sent agents to establish competitive trading posts, supply the needs of the Indians, divert their trade into American channels, and, incidentally, "link their interest and feelings to the people of the

United States." The expedition, however, was not successful and Irving philosophizes that its outcome was "as most commercial expedients are prone to be when the dull patronage of government is counted upon to outview the keen activity of private enterprise. What government failed to effect, however, with all its patronage and all its agents was at length brought about by the enterprise and perseverance of a single merchant." Irving referred to John Jacob Astor.[12]

But there is no need to cite instances without end. The operating conditions of our federal government, although shockingly inefficient by the standards of private enterprise, are not peculiar to any administration, Republican or Democratic. They are not peculiar to any government, American or European, democratic or despotic. They are the inevitable result whenever influences of bureaucracy prey upon human nature, whenever happiness cannot be achieved by the free exercise of one's abilities. They are the outcome of Civil Service, politics and absence of competition. They are the end product when man's self-preservation is achieved with red tape, when his effectiveness is measured by the publicity he receives from political palaver and when his self-interest and his ambition are served, not by the amount and extent of his public service but by pleasing his political superior.

Who would gain by consummation of the goal of the planners to socialize industry? They seem to believe that if what they regard as the evils of private enterprise are removed, the excellent, proper and advantageous attributes of the system will remain. To planners, the evils of private enterprise are absentee ownership, wealth and high-salaried executives. These evil weeds sprang from the seeds of human ambitions and selfishness. Under their planned economy these particular weeds would disappear. But the seeds of these characteristic human attributes remain in the ground; they float in the air; and they will sprout a new crop of real social evils under a planned economy.

Would planning give the consumer lower prices? The average yearly earnings of all manufacturing enterprise from 1924 through 1939, after payment of taxes, amounted to $1,689,748,000 or 3.3% of their sales. All corporations, including transportation, manufacturing, distribution, communications and amusement—even including the little corner drug store, which is probably incorporated—earned in the same years, after taxes, but three billion dollars. In 1929, the biggest boom year in all American history, all these corporations earned seven billion dollars.[13]

Income taxes paid by the owners of enterprise on their dividends must be deducted to determine the true net margin if the profit motive is eliminated.

Peter Drucker writes that Germany pays heavily for "wasteful and useless red tape." [14] These visible and invisible costs he estimates amount to *twenty-five per cent* of industrial costs. "Since nobody has any decisive authority save the planning board at the top," he adds, "every small detail has to be referred to countless conflicting authorities. An everyday matter such as permission to accept an export order requires up to one hundred and twenty different permits and forms."

Fifteen per cent of all the people employed in the Nazi planned economy, Drucker adds, are non-military government employes or employes of industry doing paper and other work required by the government! [15] Germany is smaller than the United States. Because of cartels, German industry consists of relatively larger units than American industry, which has operated under anti-trust laws. Industrial planning and control, therefore, should be more easily administered in Germany than in the United States.

However, if we use Drucker's figure and apply it to a fully-employed post-war America of 56,000,000 workers, it would appear that a government force of 8,400,000 people would be necessary to supervise and control an American planned economy. These millions would not add one thumbtack to the sum of things available for consumption. They would be parasites feeding on the production of others, affronting and domineering those who provided the means of their support.

It is production, however, that makes national income, pays salaries, wages and taxes and provides for new investment. The very existence of this host of big and little bureaucrats and their sniveling red tape would retard production, reduce real national income, lower living standards and restrict progress.

Eight million four hundred thousand people working directly and indirectly for government is staggering. But "planning" requires each plant to be organized, with inspectors, similar to those now required by Army Ordnance in munitions plants, paid by industry but reporting to the state. The host of forms and reports to innumerable commissions requires additional office and factory help. Much of the work now done by local civilian rationing boards is taken over by the state. Further, as trust is nonexistent in bureaucracy, an army of spies checks inspectors, and super spies spy on the spies.

Even if the efficiency of enterprise were not lowered under planning, the administrative costs would require more than twice the profits of all enterprise in our best year. A balanced budget would necessitate either that prices were increased or that the administrative costs were made up in other taxes on the consumer. In either case, the standard of living would decrease.

As William Graham Sumner wrote some time ago: "One of the worst features of the existing system is that the employes have a constant risk in their employer. If he is not competent to manage the business with success they suffer with him." Will the worker benefit from a planned economy? He must use the same tools and operate the same machines and work in the same plants! Unless prices are to be increased to consumers, wages and working hours can be bettered only if labor increases its own productiveness, only if technological improvements decrease the amount of labor necessary for a given output. With the incentive of profit removed and red tape substituted for a free exercise of initiative, is much technological improvement likely? Will not the worker suffer from government incompetence?

CHAPTER XI

Sugar Daddy

In the office of war information's "The United Nations Fight for the Four Freedoms, the Rights of All Men —Everywhere," these inspiring words sketch plans for America's future, and, indeed, the world's future:

"Already, in this country and abroad, agencies are at work making preliminary studies and designing machinery to stabilize the peacetime world which will follow the war. They are preparing to re-employ the returning soldier, to maintain buying power at a high level, to stand behind industry while it is changing back to peaceable products, to guarantee a certain security to the groups which need such guarantees. . . . In the short space of a few decades we have changed scarcity to abundance and are now engaged in the experiment of trying to live with our new and as yet unmanageable riches. The problem becomes one not of production but of distribution and of consumption; and since buying power must be earned, freedom from want becomes freedom from mass unemployment, plus freedom from penury for those individuals unable to work. . . . But there has never been a time, since the world began, when the hope of providing the essentials of life to every living man and woman and child has been so good, or when the necessity has been so great. . . . Fighting men, coming back from the war, will not be satisfied with a mere guarantee of dull security—they will expect to find useful work and a vigorous life. Already moves are being made to meet this inescapable challenge."

Such is the essence of freedom from want—the third of the four freedoms. But why four freedoms, whereas it has been well said that venerable Patrick Henry would die for one freedom—Liberty! Was he unimaginative? Is not one freedom all-inclusive?

By defining freedom have they not limited freedom and liberty? If we tell a child, for instance, that he may play with his bicycle, his train, his plane and his swing, he is limited in his play. But if we tell him that he may play, he is not only at liberty to amuse himself with his bicycle, train, plane and swing, but he may climb trees and play games with others; he is unrestricted; he may indulge in any activity that comes within the scope of play.

So, too, with the freedoms. They are defined and restricted freedoms; and we search in vain for the freedom stated with such emphasis in the Declaration of Independence—*freedom to pursue happiness.* This guarantees the right to seek happiness through creative effort in private enterprise. Freedom of private enterprise is absent from the enumerated freedoms for sound reason—it cannot endure in the scheme.

If the architects of this new and better world could literally transform into reality freedom from want, it would be a tragedy. It would mean the end of ambition. We would be like a nation of contented cows grazing peacefully in an evergreen meadow. Wanting nothing, everyone would be completely satisfied with his manner of living. There would be no desire to work for something better; there would be no inspiration to devise new conveniences requiring less of man's labor, or new amusements. We would be satisfied with our working hours—would not seek means that would provide more leisure. We would not be inquisitive; knowledge would remain static.

We cannot, however, take "freedom from want" too literally. The phrase, while a platitude, is also a very definite goal! The authors hope not to free men from want but to satisfy mass man's minimum material wants. They mean to achieve a world society wherein adequate diet, clothing, housing, medical assistance and other necessaries of life will ameliorate the present economic status of the unfortunate. The goal is one to which almost all of us subscribe. It is in the method of achievement that we differ.

Although the Office of War Information's Freedom from Want is set forth in generalities only, it is possible to embroider its pattern from the writings of its proponents, both here and abroad.[1]

There is a common philosophy linking the dominant group in the New Deal and its British counterpart. Of the latter group, Edward Hallett Carr, Professor of International Politics at the University College of Wales, is an author much quoted by prominent New Dealers. He returns the compliment often. Thus each side gains influence and respect by commanding international authority for its pronouncements. Obviously there is a strong bond of common thinking. Carr's "Conditions of Peace," which Stuart Chase has praised unreservedly, outlines specifically the operation of a planned economy for post-war England and Europe. Carr's plan first restores order to Europe, supplies relief and aids in reconstruction; then a European planning authority takes over and rebuilds Europe, not as a group of nations but as an economic unit. Political control would be returned to the various peoples not as Germans, Frenchmen, Belgians and other nationalities but as Europeans. There would be one continental economic and political whole.

The writings and speeches of the New Deal aristocracy indicate that we would not be far from the mark by assuming that the fabric being woven for America. and, indeed, the whole world, is of similar woof and warp.

Chase defines it this way: "Every able-bodied citizen must

have work. He must receive food, clothing, shelter, care and public education. The prime motive of industry should now be to supply the community with the goods it needs, men first, money second. That is what the revolution seems to be all about."[2]

We may also glean some essentials of the plans from the reports of the National Resources Planning Board and speeches of those in influence, and more particularly from pamphlets of the National Planning Association, which has been cooperating with federal agencies.

It is noteworthy that in no speech nor pamphlet nor article is there any suggestion that the nation will return to "normalcy," which was the cry after the last war when the economy of the world was more or less turned over to itself without superstates to work out problems of demobilization, rehabilitation and re-employment. The National Resources Planning Board prophesies instead an era of "modified private enterprise."[3]

The basic tenet of this post-war program is maintenance during peace of the prosperity of war by continuing full employment and directing the output of agriculture and industry into useful articles and needed foods for all the people of the world.

The plan can readily be carried out by the federal government retaining powers now exercised and acting through agencies already established and functioning in our war economy. In confirmation, Stuart Chase says of the specific methods of achieving the goals: "Many of them are now being worked out in the trial and effort of war controls. Many of them were in effect, or had been suggested, before the war began."[4] And: "Centralization of government; the overhead planning and control of economic activity. . . . The United States and Canada in one regional frame; similarly most of Europe. Economically supreme over these frames must sit an industrial general staff with *dictatorial powers* covering the smooth technical operation of all the major sources of raw material and supply." [5]

But let us take America first. Over all would be the National Resources Planning Board to continue appraisals of the needs of the people and ascertain how much of each manufactured article and agricultural commodity the nation needs and can consume. The National Resources Planning Board has made extensive surveys of national needs and much additional information is already in the census files.

As the planned requirements would in most cases exceed existing and even potential productive capacity, the Planning Board would have to decide by a system of priorities how much of each product would be produced. That this will be a not inconsiderable task will be evident by walking through a large metropolitan department store and looking at the variety of items displayed, or by thumbing through a Sears-Roebuck catalogue.

Under the Planning Board would be a National Production Authority, continuing the functions of the War Production Board, allocating production, deciding the when and where of new capacities and who would operate them. There were approximately eight hundred N.R.A. industry codes; there would necessarily be sub-planning and production authority for each industry.

The Department of Agriculture's A.A.A. would determine and allocate production of agricultural products as it is doing now. It is indicated, for instance, that a minimum national diet will necessitate increasing our number of milk cows from twenty-four to thirty-two million. This will require twenty-one million more acres devoted to pasture and growing of feed grains. The number of laying hens is to be increased from three hundred sixty-nine million to three hundred eighty-eight million. On the other hand, after the job of feeding Europe is over, our national requirements of cereal crops could be met by taking thirteen million acres out of wheat production.[6]

Prices of raw materials and retail prices would be controlled by the Office of Price Administration; labor supply by the United States Employment Agency or the Manpower Commission; labor rates and working conditions by a Labor Board.

As industrial capacity for civilian goods would be less than that demanded by the new potential, R.F.C. would supply most of the new capital needed for conversions of war plants, extensions to existing facilities, and new plants. The N.Y.A. would be available to train youth in trades required by the program.

All those under the age of eighteen would be maintained in school; all over the age of sixty-five retired on more generous pensions. There would also be adequate mothers' pensions, disability pensions and dependent children and funeral allowances.

The minimum balanced diet would be assured by an expanded Food Stamp Plan, which might also be used for the distribution of manufactured articles deemed necessary for the minimum standard of living. Medical services would be provided by the United States Health Service, either free or on a cooperative contributory basis.

The present A.A.A. program for conservation of land and forest would be continued; in addition, farm housing and health, country schools and libraries, would be supplemented and improved to enhance the fullness of rural living. Family-sized farms would be re-established by aiding tenants to purchase either the land they work or new locations made available by irrigation and breaking up large holdings. The Farm Resettlement Administration would have this project in hand.

The Farm Resettlement Administration would also grant

aid to youth, enabling them to start farming for themselves under conditions that would permit them to marry and have families when they want to. Farm cooperatives would be established with federal aid, and local medical care associations would function in hospitals built with federal funds. One authority estimates that if each rural family contributed six per cent of its net cash income, but not to exceed $48 per year, the federal government would need add only two-thirds the amount of the family contributions in order to supply complete medical care.[7]

The W.P.A. would provide work for those unemployed in industry. A large bank of projects has been catalogued by the National Resources Planning Board. Among those prominently mentioned is the rebuilding of our cities, with federal government participation in the planning and financing. Presumably, the new municipalities would follow the pattern of Norman Bel Geddes' City of the Future which appeared in the New York World's Fair cyclorama. Slums and blighted areas, narrow streets and inadequate parking facilities would disappear and make way for arterial highways, new recreational and educational facilities, community health and shopping centers. The Federal Housing Administration would make low-cost housing available to the needy.

In this urban rebuilding, future transportation would be planned and provided for—not only railroads and airlines but express highways, bridges and tunnels. Terminals would be relocated for ease of access. All transportation would be modernized with facilities that would be both economical and carefully integrated. It is pointed out, also, that most railroads now need new, light-weight cars, more efficient locomotives, grade revisions, heavier rails and modern signal installations.[8]

In addition, many multiple-purpose river developments, similar to T.V.A., are proposed in one post-war work sheet.

Thirty or forty of the nation's major river basins are being considered for the construction of dams to regularize their flow, improve navigation and control floods; the water stored by the dams would be used for irrigation and the reservoirs for recreation facilities. And finally, the dams would make possible the generation of hydroelectric power, so that many, now deprived, would realize the blessings of cheap electricity and know alleviation from the drudgeries of home and farm.[9]

But freedom from want is a world-wide goal. Planning is to be extended internationally and world prosperity underwritten. The world would be divided into economic units such as Europe, within which there would be free trade and a single currency; nations remaining as subsidiary political units in the same manner that our individual states are part of an economic unit—United States.

Agencies similar to those outlined for America, with like functions, would be established in each geographical economic unit; the capital for international R.F.C. and branch R.F.C.s in each nation would be supplied by United States and the remaining "have" countries.[10] Control of foreign trade would lodge in the economic unit governments and multilateral trade arranged by a superimposed international trade planning and allocation authority with Chase's "dictatorial powers."

It is suggested that international trade might be continued by agencies similar to the Lease-Lend.[11] It is pointed out that as it is now operating, the British Air Commission, the British Purchasing Commission, the British Petroleum Commission, the British Food Commission and other commissions all requisition through the Lease-Lend Administration, which in turn does the purchasing. Similar two- or three-way agencies could be established with all the economic unit governments, the international R.F.C. acting as a clearing house for inter-economic unit balances.[12]

It is stated without confirmation that British industrialists are becoming accustomed to the possibility that they will have to operate through government boards or industry-wide boards under government regulation for the overseas marketing of their products, as well as for the procurement of their raw materials, and that some of these industrialists have indicated that they welcome the orderly flow of materials that such procedure induces.[13]

It is also suggested that machinery be set up for so-called "preclusive buying" whereby the output of the chief commodities of other nations is purchased for redistribution through the international multilateral lease-lend and barter agency, the International Planning and Allocating Authority.[14] Anticipating its operation, for instance, Peruvian cotton and Brazilian coffee have been purchased to insure the stability of the Peruvian and Brazilian economies. This preclusive buying would be conditioned upon the producing country agreeing to crop restriction devices of the A.A.A.[15] The ever-normal granary would be applied to the world. Milo Perkins, Executive Director of the Bureau of Economic Warfare, admitted recently to members of the Senate Banking and Currency Committee that existing contracts for the purchase of Latin American products included a clause requiring that their production conform to certain standards of minimum pay and maximum hours.

When help is needed by the planned economy of friendly and needy nations purchases would be made by the International Authority for storage. On the other hand, recalcitrant nations, unwilling to cooperate and unwilling to accept certain standards of behavior, would be blacklisted and refused the benefits of preclusive buying or access to the markets of cooperating nations.[16]

An International Development Authority would be a subsidiary of the International R.F.C. This authority would grant development loans to industrially backward nations, such as China and the Balkans, enabling them to build roads and railroads, improve harbors and establish their own industries.[17] In anticipation, the State Department suggested last year that the Export-Import Bank buy some of our manufacturing plants that have been closed by the war and ship them, complete, to South America. Ford Motor Company's tire plant has already gone to Russia. The government is paying half the cost of a large steel mill being erected in Brazil. Our industry itself, instead of its products, is thus to be exported.

The United States Treasury would supply the operating deficits of domestic operations and, through the R.F.C., America's share of the amounts the "have" nations supply to international pools.

This is the blueprint of the "Century of the Common Man." This is the peace which Vice-President Wallace said, "Must mean a better standard of living for the common man, not merely in the United States and England but also in India, Russia, China and Latin America—not merely in the United Nations but also in Germany and Japan."[18]

Considering the magnitude and daring character of the "Century of the Common Man," we may understand why Attorney General Biddle characterized the New Deal as "more dynamic than Fascism and more revolutionary than Communism." The whole scheme is dynamic! revolutionary! and alluring! Compared with a laissez-faire alternative deflation and depression, it is, indeed, almost irresistible. A debonair Utopia is to be created on earth!

Although control of private corporations under the scheme remains with stockholders in theory, actual control rests in the state. With its power to grant or withhold loans, to favor one against another in permission for new construction and manufacture of new products, or to withhold raw material or lower selling prices, the production authority could impose a death sentence on any recalcitrant company or industry.

Moreover, even for businessmen a planned economy has appeal. One dream is realized immediately—market problems vanish! Capacity operation is assured! There are no raw material problems—no labor problems! Negotiations for wages, hours and working conditions of labor are absorbed by the benevolent state! Competition vanishes, for the state fixes prices. Executives will have more leisure. During the modified private enterprise phase of planning, there will be a return, presumably—only a nominal return—on capital. But even a nominal return would be a satisfactory alternative to the recent uncertainty of any profit at all. And if capital is to be compensated, the profit would hardly be less than 3.15% annually, the average pre-war return to all manufacturing enterprise on its invested capital.[19]

There will still be luxuries for the more fortunate groups. "Jewels, country estates, custom-built motor cars. . . . No civilization," writes Stuart Chase, "not even Soviet Russia, has failed to provide a modicum of such luxuries for those at the top, whether they be kings, priests, tycoons or commissars."[20]

But in post-war America, according to plan, those "at the top" will not be business tycoons. In such an economy those "at the top" will be individuals in charge of planning priorities, industrial and agricultural controls, multilateral trade operations, and other functions of the state.

New Dealers have reasoned properly that high industrial salaries have attracted the best brains away from government; and as a result the government has been staffed with mediocre men. New Dealers have striven to correct this inequality but as a Congressman's salary is $10,000 annually, this sum is a practical maximum for any but the highest posts. Under this ceiling, however, increased standards are evident.

Press relations men, for instance, formerly paid approximately $4,000 a year, now receive as much as $9,000. Government salaries, formerly below the standard for good newspaper reporters, now offer inducement for good men to leave the newspaper industry. This is particularly true of expert propagandists.

So in the new economy it is planned to attract the best brains in the country to the posts of greatest responsibility, to form an intellectual aristocracy to plan and guide the nation and rule the world. Hence the material rewards of "jewels, country estates and custom-built motor cars" will be symbolic of achievement, not in private enterprise, but in high offices of the state.

High salaries would disappear in the new world. With limitation of profit there would be little competition for the best men; mediocre and cheaper men would suffice. High-salaried men would, therefore, find it necessary to accept lower compensation, enter state service or go without employment. True, planning calls for businessmen to sacrifice salary and independence, but in exchange there are advantages gained. Responsibilities are lighter and routine; the state assumes all former problems of moment. Businessmen would no longer have a near monopoly on gastric ulcers and bad hearts.

Like one who has looked over the attractive literature and alluring photographs of a summer resort, we have now seen the prospectus of freedom from want in the "Century of the Common Man." What will it be like, if and when we get there? Will it be an era of pure materialism? How will the mind and spirit fare? What about freedom of the press? of religion? of thought? Will the spirit be free?

Will there be Freedom?

CHAPTER XII

Speck in the Milk

When nations are suffering periods of adversity, people become disillusioned with the crassness and futility of their world. Their poets and philosophers are then often inspired to picture an escape in the form of an ideal society in which the wrongs from which they suffer are eliminated, and in these fantasies troubled minds find refuge and comfort and hope.

After the disastrous Peloponnesian War which left his Attica a mass of rubble and ashes, Plato wrote "The Republic."

Sir Thomas E. More's "Utopia" was inspired by the chaos accompanying Europe's emergence out of the Renaissance. Then soldiers returning from the wars could not find employment. The rich were fattening on the poor as land, gathered into big parcels, concentrated the economic power of that time in the nobles. The destitute, who were thrown off the land, resorted to theft and were hanged by the dozen on market place gibbets.

During our depression of 1887, Edward Bellamy, in the midst of poverty, want and distress, for which the blame was placed on the then current concentration of economic power in growing trusts, encouraged the people by writing "Looking Backward," which painted the enchanted era to exist by the year 2000.

Bellamy's character, Mr. West, returning in a bad dream to the world of 1887 from which he had escaped, glanced at a newspaper. He read of epidemics of fraud going unchecked; misappropriation of a trust fund by executors; coal barons deciding to advance the price of coal; speculators engineering a great wheat corner at Chicago; enormous land-grabs of western syndicates; shocking corruption among Chicago officials; fears of a business crisis; a woman murdered in cold blood for her money at New Haven; a man shoots himself in Worcester because he could not get work; an aged couple in New Jersey commit suicide rather than go to the poorhouse; more insane asylums wanted; and many other headlines characteristic of any modern period of adversity.

Bellamy's mental escape rose to great popularity, evidencing the desire of people to be rid of the morbid cruelties and injustices and difficulties of the times in which they lived. Over one million copies of "Looking Backward" were sold, a record for its time. More's work, written in Latin, had been translated into almost every European language; and Plato's "Republic" has lived and provoked thought through all the ages.

In the ideal societies portrayed by these authors, good fairies are permitted to revel in economics and human character. They evolve social systems in which people with admirable moral and spiritual characteristics share a community of goods. They are, in essence, communistic states. In Plato's "Republic" no one retains private property unless there be a great necessity for it. In Bellamy's state of 2000 A.D., money is abolished and each individual receives a ration book entitling him to his proportion of the community's goods. All retire at forty-five but there is plenty for everyone, supposedly because there is no competition. Churches are formed by groups willing to share their allotted goods with a minister whose intellect and theology appeal to them. The capitalistic press is abolished and special privilege is no longer able to dominate the thought of communities. Instead, groups support and provide for themselves newspapers with editorial content to their own liking.

Each of the ideal states pictures society with an abundance of the necessaries of life, particularly food, and attempts are made to forecast conveniencсs impossible of realization in their day. The efficiency of Utopian chickens, for instance, is increased, as eggs are laid in warm atmospheres and hatched without further attention from the hen. Our incubators have realized this dream. In Bellamy's state it is unnecessary to go to church because sermons are wired into homes. Radio, of course, has brought this dream into reality—even doing away with wires.

All Utopias are pictured with an extravagant amount of leisure, measured by the standards of their day. Our forty-hour week meets, in most cases, their ideals.

At least one hundred million out of the one hundred thirty million Americans now live by material standards of life exceeding those of the Utopian worlds. Even during the depression years, two-thirds to three-fourths of our people had an abundance of food, ample clothing, an amount of leisure approaching the standards of the Utopias, and, in addition, gadgets, or conveniences, amusements, access to knowledge, and control over time and space, which the authors of the past were unable to visualize even in their dreams.

However, all the ideal states are populated logically with divine people—people with human virtues but without human vices—people who have lost their animalistic, predatory instincts.

The rulers of Plato's "Republic" are endowed with wisdom, its defenders with valor. All its people are temperate and just. The community is not large. "The city may be increased to any size which is consistent with unity." Five thousand is the limit, this being the maximum number who can be within the range of a human voice. Precautions are to be observed so that the perfect strain will be maintained and the unfit eliminated, in the Spartan manner. Silver and gold are not to be used, as all silver and gold are to be in the people's souls.

In Sir Thomas More's community, acquisitiveness is nonexistent; fine clothes are disdained; men do not seek pleasure at the expense of another.

In Bellamy's state, morals have been purified so that the number of police in Massachusetts in 1887 is adequate for the A.D. 2000 nation. The abolition of property rights has almost eliminated need for the courts. Professional lawyers have disappeared. The people are truthful, unacquisitive and happy. An occasional transgressor against morals is not a criminal but an atavist; he is regarded as an unfortunate throwback to an ancestral type.

None of these societies would have tolerated the bootlegger of the twenties; none of their individuals would have been sugar and coffee hoarders. Their farmers would not have rushed unfatted cattle to market because beef prices were high. Their public officials would not have used W.P.A. as an instrument of political power. A Manpower Commission would have been unnecessary because all would have been anxious to do their duty.

These authors took logical precautions to eliminate from the human race those traits which caused St. Thomas Aquinas to conclude that although Communism is undoubtedly the ideal state for society, it is in fact unworkable owing to the sinfulness of man.[1] The characteristics of man have remained unchanged since St. Thomas' time; man's cardinal weakness remains corrosive selfishness.

The philosophies of all these idealistic states and the society they depict served a useful purpose, not only as a mental escape from the age for which they were written but as goals toward which society aspired. The economy of Bellamy's state bears a marked resemblance, in its conception of foreign trade, rationing of consumption, and many other aspects, to the new "Century of the Common Man." Heywood Broun said that "Looking Backward" aroused his first interest in socialism.[2]

However, all these ideal societies were fantasy. Until now, with the exception of a few communities such as New Harmony, which ended in failure because of human nature, there has never been a serious attempt to create a Utopian state. Now, however, the plans of the New Deal superimpose such an ideal society on the whole world!

When the guns have fired for the last time, the American people will have passed through a decade and a half of trying times—a period of unemployment, hardship, disillusionment, war and sacrifice. They will face the prospect of another long period of painful reconstruction. It would be understandable, therefore, if they grasped even more eagerly at an opportunity to try out schemes that promised security and plenty than did past generations, who sought mere mental escape from their hardships into the fantasy of their contemporary writers.

And we might all be sanguine if we were certain that present and future rulers of our state were endowed, like those of "The Republic," with "wisdom, temperance and justice"—if all the "gold and silver were in the people's souls"—if all the people were "truthful, unacquisitive and happy"—if they preferred "the public good to their own desires"—and if each one avoided the injustice of seeking "his own pleasure at the expense of another."

But our politicians are mortal; as human beings they are not devoid of ambition and lust for power. And our people are selfish; we remain organized in pressure groups.

This being the case, central economic planning will fail!

Our two-party political system, for instance, is impossible

in a peacetime economy wherein the government fixes prices of agricultural products, prices of industrial products, and wages and working hours of labor. In wartime, patriotism supplants, in large measure, self-interest. There is but one supreme national objective. Labor has given up the right to strike for the duration but no one suggests that this be continued after victory. Business has willingly accepted allocation of strategic materials, and many plants have closed in national interest. But no one has publicly said that after victory a businessman could not engage in any legitimate activity in which he thought he could make a profit and buy whatever raw materials he needed. Similarly, farmers accept price ceilings for their wheat, beef and mutton solely as a war contribution.

In peacetime operation of central economic planning, Republicans lusting for power would promise labor higher rates, the farmer higher agricultural prices, and businessmen higher prices and higher tariffs, only to be outbid by Democrats lusting for power. Such a never-ending spiral could have but one end—the seizure of despotic power by one group.

Planners deny this. They assure us that we can operate a mixed economy or modified enterprise system in a democratic way. But this is either tinseled wrapping for their package or thinking clouded by idealism. Those to whom the latter reasoning applies assume that by their skill and ingenuity we can avoid economic planning's historical course. But examples of all times prove that economic planning is undertaken by or ends in a dictatorship, whether under the name of Diocletian, Louis XIV, Il Duce, Der Fuehrer, or plain Joe Stalin.

One of the advocates of planning, Professor Jacob Viner, summarizes the situation clearly: "It is, unfortunately, equally difficult to see how either central economic planning or free trade can withstand the activities of a freely elected, freely legislating Congress."[3] Congress might exist in name, as does the Reichstag, but the latter consists of Nazis. The Soviet Constitution provides an elaborate mechanism for their national assembly, but only Communists may be members.

Planning, therefore, as contemplated by New Dealers, is incompatible with our traditional concept of representative democracy. To be operative it is essential that the planning authority have what Stuart Chase defines as "dictatorial powers," as we have witnessed in Russia, Germany and Italy.

There is a large segment of our people who would willingly trade their liberties for security, for, as has often been said, all they know of liberty is freedom to eke out existence on the cold flange of hunger in anguished tenements and putrid hovels. Gauged in worldly goods, they can hardly sink lower. Central economic planning would bring them more of life's material essentials.

But without a "freely elected and freely legislating Congress," will we not have lost our "government of the people, by the people and for the people"? Production for consumption was the medieval way—an economy of force and coercion. The centuries of struggle by the middle class for political freedom were inspired by the desire for economic freedom—and the two are inseparable.

CHAPTER XIII

The Speck Grows

THE PRODUCTIVE FACILITIES OF PRIVATE ENTERPRISE cannot satisfy the potential requirements of national or international economic planning. Therefore, government-owned war plants will not remain idle while huge, non-productive W.P.A. and public works programs employ a large portion of our people. And as the National Resources Planning Board has said, "The government has a large stake in many of these plants, and, in prudence for its investment as well as with concern over employment, after the Defense Program, it must make plans for their conversion to constructive peacetime uses." [1]

They will make butter instead of guns—not T.N.T., tanks, machine guns, cartridges and uniforms, but automobiles, washing machines, clothing and plastics. If we use the General Motors factor, the cost of converting these plants will equal seventy-five per cent of the original outlay.

They may be managed and operated by government corporations similar to the T.V.A. or under contract with established companies. In the latter case, however, management might be tempted by conflicting interests involved with two or more identical operations—one owned by the state and others by their stockholders. Human failings might prompt favoring, in one way or another, the plant still owned by the shareholders. This foreshadows a source of continuing friction. The state may forestall this friction by taking over the staffs now operating the government-owned units and establishing state enterprises. It would be the clean-cut way.

Full employment of a growing population calls for constantly increasing capital investment in enterprise. The rebuilding of cities, damming of the nation's water basins, relocation of terminals and other projects contemplated by the National Resources Planning Board will provide employment only during construction. The new Cincinnati of Norman Bel Geddes will provide no more permanent jobs than does Cincinnati of today. Permanent employment can be provided only by investment in new facilities for production and distribution—new products, new factories, warehouses, railroads, airlines and stores.

However, central economic planning contemplates continuance of individual income taxes at high rates, and, in the upper brackets, at wartime levels. There may be a ceiling on incomes. Therefore, individuals cannot save and invest. Inheritance taxes will gradually confiscate most of the accumulated wealth. Private sources of new capital for investment, therefore, will steadily diminish. If the government encroaches upon the field of life insurance, with more adequate old age pensions, allowances for widowed mothers and dependent children, the need for private life insurance will decrease and the huge funds of life insurance companies will not be available for investment.

Furthermore, few individuals would venture their money in competition with the state or in any undertaking in which there is likelihood of state encroachment. This is particularly true if large profits are not in prospect because of taxes or the state's price-fixing power.

Therefore, in a system where enterprise is partly state and partly free, that of the state will grow and dominate. The conflict between the Tennessee Valley Authority and the Tennessee Electric Power Company resulted in state domination.

The T.V.A. bought the power company's assets. Similarly, state or state-financed enterprise would virtually pre-empt all industrial expansion.

As there is always a heavy normal mortality of private enterprise, which would in this situation find no replacement, the prospect would be for an acceleration of the 1930 decade's trend, when the assets of private enterprise decreased twenty per cent. Private enterprise would pale and lose strength like constantly-watered wine. In its last stages it would retain but a grasp on merchandising. In the ultimate, however, this field, too, might be pre-empted by state-sponsored cooperatives.

This throttling of individualism would not only end man's freedom to seek happiness through the pursuit of wealth; it would choke freedom of mind and spirit as well, for all these freedoms go hand in hand.

Without the spur of competition in free enterprise, what would become of advertising? Most planners share Veblen's belief that advertising is merely an "enterprise in conspicuous waste," a device that helps "a shrewdly limited output of goods to be sold at more profitable prices." And, indeed, with prices fixed, output allocated and profits limited, there would be little reason for advertising.

We Americans pay for radio broadcasting by hearing how little tubules secreted under our armpits may frustrate an otherwise promising combination for winning friends and influencing people, or by listening to advice about our kidneys, our hair or our diet. Advertising pays for our broadcasts.

As each advertiser wants his message to reach the largest number of people, his program of entertainment is designed to please. Elaborate systems of sampling of audiences gauge popularity. Programs with wide audiences remain on the air—others do not pay and are dropped. Hence public acceptance is the only criterion. The American public now gets the kind of broadcasting it wants, good or bad.

Without advertising revenue, broadcasting stations would fall into the lap of the state. Competition between chains and stations would cease. A bureaucrat would provide the music he thought the people ought to hear and place before the microphone personalities whose views he thought would be good for the people, which, incidentally, would also serve his own vested interest. The American mind would lose its freedom of determining its own music and entertainment, and of choosing its political, economic and spiritual thought. We would lose one of our organs of freedom of speech.

We would also cease to be the best-informed nation in the world. The cost of producing our magazines and newspapers is met in most part by advertising revenue. With advertising eliminated, much higher prices would have to be charged to maintain present standards. This in turn would force drops in circulation; again prices would have to be increased, which would be followed by another drop in circulation. This descending spiral would finally end in a new balance between a lower standard, a lower circulation and a higher price.

Mr. Malcolm Muir, publisher of *Newsweek,* estimates that if advertising were eliminated, *Newsweek*'s circulation would shrink from 500,000 copies, selling at fifteen cents, to 20,000 copies, for which it would be necessary to charge one dollar. Mr. Walter Fuller, publisher of *Saturday Evening Post,* is more optimistic. He estimates that if advertising were eliminated, the *Post*'s circulation would shrink from 3,500,000 copies, selling for ten cents, to 700,000 copies, for which it would be necessary to charge fifty cents.[2]

Advertising also pays for two-thirds of the cost of our newspapers.[3] Their quality, circulation and price would follow a similar cycle. To maintain present standards, newspapers would probably cost not less than fifteen cents each. In this case, instead of each metropolitan family reading one issue a day, it is doubtful if one out of five families would be willing to pay for the privilege of reading unbiased news instead of relying on state news broadcasts.

But the state might subvene or subsidize some of the press and these organs, too, would become mouthpieces of government. And our minds, instead of being stimulated by opposing philosophies, debates, crusades, criticisms and exposés, would jog along in a dull rut of official propaganda. Then we would have lost another of our fundamental freedoms—freedom of the press.

Our habits would tend to stabilize, for advertising informs people of new products and services and stimulates their wants. We are vitamin conscious because of advertising. We are able to buy a toothbrush and toothpaste in any country store only because of advertising. The brushing of teeth is a relatively new habit—in many parts of the world it is unknown. Advertisers of toothpaste, tooth powder and toothbrushes, have taught the dangers of pyorrhea, the desirability of keeping our teeth clean; they advise us to see our dentist regularly—and as a result American teeth are the best in the world.

Quality would deteriorate also. There is no industrial advertising in Russia's planned economy. Although a dozen factories might make linen, there is no incentive for one factory to produce higher quality, for it cannot tell the consuming public about its products' superiority and stimulate demand for its own brand. This accounts in large measure for the poor quality of Russian products. Quantity is the only measure of Russian industrial efficiency. Without advertising, the American people would suffer static or deteriorating quality standards.

Private universities, private hospitals and private charities are typically American. They have been socially desirable by-products of American private enterprise. Most European institutions serving similar purposes originated with the church or state. American private hospitals so far outrank any similar service available in any other nation that it is difficult to make comparisons. They have established the standard for city, state and national hospitals, and indeed, for all the world.

Our private universities now rank with the world's best. In many fields they excel. Knowledge is dispensed by them at a fraction of its cost. Buildings were provided by individuals, chairs were endowed by individuals, operating deficits are met by gifts and revenue from endowments. Many of the basic scientific discoveries—medical, chemical and physical—were made in them. American private universities blazed the way, set the pace, and now set the standards for our newer state universities.

Washington University in St. Louis, with its affiliated Barnes Hospital, for instance, is a typical example. It is a by-product of such commonplaces as profits from frontier trading and the production of beer, boots and shoes, pharmaceuticals, rugs, chemicals, oil, railroad equipment, and real estate transactions. Hundreds of other colleges, such as Harvard, Yale, Chicago and Dartmouth, have a similar foundation. Leland Stanford, Duke, Cornell, Vanderbilt, Colgate and Brown are but a few which bear the names of individuals who contributed most to their progress, and so we can trace their source to business success in railroading, soap, tobacco and lumber.

Without a constant stream of gifts and legacies, private universities would be unable to maintain their standards. If individualism and private enterprise passed, private universities would be forced to seek support from the state.

Then education, too, would eventually fall under the regimentation of an imperious bureaucrat.

In this case, would the campus remain the free forum where ideas battle and the good are supposed to drive out the bad? Would the new regime tolerate on its teaching staff those whose views were in such fundamental disagreement with the state ideology as were Felix Frankfurter's with Harvard University's Board of Overseers'? Would a capitalistic Thurman Arnold be permitted to stay at Yale and write the Folklore of Planning? Could a Professor Harold Rugge remain at Columbia University and write invidious textbooks for school children on the "Century of the Common Man"? Could a Thorstein Veblen remain on Columbia's faculty preaching the overturn of the New Deal?

What would happen to the freedom of thought and freedom of speech that now prevail in these centers of learning? Is it necessary to recall Governor Talmadge's efforts to dominate politically the University of Georgia, which discredited college education in Georgia in the eyes of the nation? And Governor LaFollette's persecution of Glenn Frank at the University of Wisconsin?

If education were directed by a bureaucrat, is there any assurance that it would continue to progress? The dogma of scholars of old was that education consisted of the polite learning of humanities—that the only things worth knowing were languages, the ancient classics, belles-lettres, and theology.

It is only since the turn of the century that our scholars generally have admitted that applied chemistry, physics and engineering are more than base trades. England's hoary Oxford did not establish an engineering laboratory until 1914! Scholars formerly considered applied science beneath the dignity of a great university! But competition compelled one after another to place the applied sciences on a par with philosophy, to value their knowledge as highly as that of the humanities, and to place a degree in science on a par with one in arts.

Who knows what new sciences and new subjects the future holds? And is it well, for the knowledge of mankind and the progress of the world, that decision as to whether these new subjects and new sciences are good and worthy or impractical and undignified be left to one man or a group of men?

When Galileo pronounced that the earth revolves about the sun, the Roman Inquisition forced him to recant publicly and do penance. The earth was the center of the universe; the bureaucrats of Rome ruled the earth; Galileo's doctrine would have lowered the importance of their vested interests. Like our weather bureaucrats, they would have none of it. Thus, Galileo, after each forced penance, muttered his momentous discovery—"But still it moves"—to himself.

And Eve Curie, recounting the dogmatic attitude of French educational authorities, said that her parents were not so foolish as to ask for official credits to pursue their research in radium. "If two physicists on the scent of an immense discovery had asked the University of Paris or the French Government for a grant to buy pitch-blende residue they would have been laughed at. . . . Out of the traditions and principles of the French Revolution . . . the State seemed to have retained, after more than a century, only the deplorable words pronounced by Fouquier-Tinville at the trial at which Lavoisier was condemned to the guillotine: 'The Republic has no need for scientists.' "[4]

Henry Thomas Buckle sums up the history of civilization with the conclusion that civilization's advance in any nation is dependent solely on the amount of knowledge possessed by the ablest men, the manner in which that knowledge is used and the freedom with which knowledge pervades all classes of society.[5] Thus, with the passing of private enterprise, would we not also witness the closing of a brief but very creative era, when man's mind was free and his knowledge grew through space and time and civilization leaped ahead? And are not, in fact, knowledge, freedom of thought and freedom of speech tied inseparably to freedom of enterprise?

CHAPTER XIV

Disaster

THE BASIC TENET OF THE PLANNERS' "CENTURY OF THE Common Man" is that full employment be maintained by the state. To accomplish the purpose, they hold that the state must spend: that it must spend as much as necessary to give everyone a job! Planners take annual deficits for granted. Some even suggest these deficits may approach wartime totals.

This subject is involved because it involves money and money is a very involved subject. Our money is measured in dollars. Dollars are the units of our money. Alexander Hamilton wanted us to call them "units," and for a time the words "dollars" and "units" were used interchangeably.

What is a dollar? Aside from a few coins and a relatively unimportant amount of one dollar Silver Certificates, it is a rectangular piece of engraved paper. If we examine a ten dollar Federal Reserve Note, we notice a legend that it may be redeemed at the United States Treasury or any Federal Reserve Bank for ten dollars in lawful money.

But what is lawful money?

Inasmuch as the bill we are redeeming bears the legend that it is legal tender for all debts, public and private, it must also be lawful money. Therefore, it appears that the bearer has merely the privilege of exchanging one ten dollar bill for another ten dollar bill. The new piece of paper would have no more intrinsic value than the old. Inherently, both would be more valuable if they were blank, for then, like other blank paper, they would be useful for writing or typing.

True, the government has a large quantity of gold in Kentucky, and our government buys gold, paying thirty-five dollars an ounce. But individuals cannot exchange dollars for gold unless the gold is to be used in industrial arts. The arbitrary dollar value assigned to gold is merely that rate at which our federal government is willing to allow gold to be used for settling international balances. The President has the power to alter the international exchange value of gold. He raised it from about twenty dollars to thirty-five dollars. He retains specific power to revalue it up to forty-one dollars and thirty-five cents an ounce; and by reason of his broad power to purchase gold at any price he deems in public interest, the gold content or the gold value of the dollar may be fixed at any point he deems in public interest.

But even though we cannot exchange the ten dollar bill for gold, we value it because we have faith that we can exchange it for a quantity of things. We also have faith that if we do not need things now, we can put the dollars in banks and at some future time draw out the same number of dollars and exchange them for about the same quantity of the same things.

It is his faith in the stable purchasing power of dollars that prompts the worker to give his labor willingly in exchange for them, and that prompts the farmer to bring his produce to the city and exchange it willingly for them.

Our money—our dollar's value—is our faith in its stable purchasing power!

Numerous examples illustrate that the stability of the purchasing power of money—whether the money is paper or coin—depends upon the stability of the ratio of the amount of money in circulation to the volume of available things to be exchanged. Whenever the amount of money in circulation increases greatly without a corresponding increase in things, individuals compete with each other for the things. They offer more money for the things and prices rise, as long as the market for them is free.

This important balance of the amount of money and the amount of things is recognized as fundamental even by Russian planners. L. E. Hubbard,[1] the authoritative student of the Soviet economy, relates that for each Russian community, state expenditures in salaries and other payments are totaled, taxes are deducted and the balance represents the value of goods to be supplied to that community. This balancing is carried to such lengths that if the quantity of goods available is insufficient, prices are raised to an aggregate value that will absorb the community's money income. Therefore, in 1934, in preparation for the derationing of bread, its price was doubled in order to absorb what might have proved excess inflationary purchasing power.

Economists formerly pointed to years of gradually rising prices as years of prosperity, often connecting such periods with the discovery of new gold mines, which increased the world gold supply.

The sixteenth century offers a striking example. European stocks of gold and silver were being swollen as the Spaniards raided the gold and silver hoards of Mexico and Peru and exploited the rich mines in which the Indians had found the treasure. During that century, European prices trebled as the supply of money—silver and gold—became abundant in relation to things that were available.

But inflation incident to large increases in supplies of metal had automatic brakes, for the supply of metal could be increased no more rapidly than men could mine it or seize it from the Indians.

In the case of our money, however, the situation is both different and precarious. We are without the automatic brakes of a limited output of metal. The machinery that was used to finance the deficits of our pre-war budgets and is now being used to supply the government with money needed for prosecution of the war, will be used to provide for its post-war deficits. It is capable of supplying the nation with unlimited quantities of lawful paper dollars.

This is true because our great banking machine enables banks to create lawful paper dollars. If John Smith, businessman, for instance, requires $100,000 for his business, he borrows this sum from a bank in exchange for his company's note. The bank, in turn, credits John Smith's account with $100,000. The bank has, in effect, created $100,000. "Cleverer than an alchemist," Karl Marx remarked, "they create gold out of nothing!"

As businesses and most individuals pay money to each other by checks, very little currency comes into use, but banks always have the privilege of discounting John Smith's note with the Federal Reserve and securing currency—lawful paper dollars. The credit created on the bank's books is always potential money—lawful paper dollars.

Normally there is an automatic curtailment of the amount of bank deposits that can be created for business purposes, because it is not good policy for a bank to loan excessive amounts of money. Therefore, when this point approaches, banks raise interest rates or otherwise discourage borrowing. Pressure on borrowers continues until it is no longer profitable nor convenient for John Smith to continue borrowing. He pays off his loan by checking against his deposits in the same or another bank. Thus bank deposits actually decrease whenever a loan is paid off. The increase and decrease in the amount of bank-manufactured money is usually accompanied by increases and decreases in the price of commodities—the good and bad times of the "old days."

It is fundamentally different when the government sells its bonds to banks for a relatively permanent addition to their portfolios. The government, instead of giving a ninety-day note, as John Smith did, gives a government bond maturing years in the future.

If the government, therefore, borrows one billion dollars from banks, bank deposits increase one billion dollars. Again banks manufacture dollars out of nothing! As the government spends money and checks it out of banks, contractors and soldiers receive and distribute it. After passing through several hands, it winds up again in banks as deposits. The "reserve requirement" control against such unlimited expansion of deficits is now merely nominal because it is subject to discretionary change by the government.

In time of need, any individual can, of course, ask a bank for his deposits in currency; and if banks need more currency they can take government bonds to the Federal Reserve and secure their face value in currency—lawful money—in exchange for them.

The government also has the power of short-circuiting banks; it can sell its bonds directly to the Federal Reserve and use the currency received from the Federal Reserve or deposit it in banks. Thus banks have no power to stop government borrowing. Government debt is different in fundamentals from private debt. An industrial bond is secured by assets—building, machinery and materials—which theoretically can be sold, if necessary, to liquidate the debt. The proceeds of a government bond, however, have been spent. They have paid salaries and in wartime they have paid for ships and shells that are no more. A government bond has no asset behind it other than the taxing power of the government. Its worth is merely the word of the state, that it will tax its citizens enough to pay the interest and enough more to pay it off eventually.

Government has no orthodox means of reducing its debt unless its tax income exceeds its expenditures. Then, as in the 1920's, it can use the surplus to reduce its debt. However, we have in prospect for the duration of the war, and for certainly a year or so thereafter, deficits—not surpluses. A mounting government debt means mounting bank deposits, every dollar of which can be withdrawn as lawful money. In essence, therefore, when the government sells its bonds to banks, the effect on the economy is the same as printing money. Its bonds are merely interest-bearing paper money exchangeable for lawful paper dollars.

For that reason, we have a situation which by all past standards carries the most serious threat of inflation. Years ago, the British economist, J. Maynard Keynes, wrote: "It only requires a match to set alight dormant possibilities of inflation in the United States." When Keynes wrote, our bank deposits were about fifty billion; today they exceed eighty billion; and after the war they may be treble this sum. If Keynes was correct, our post-war inflationary vapor will require but the faintest spark! [2]

But the planners bank on continued deficits and they reassure us with soporific argument not to worry about inflation or where money for post-war deficits is coming from. Alvin Hansen certifies that "a government debt internally held is so completely different from an ordinary personal or business debt that it should hardly be called a debt at all." [3] He adds that only when a nation borrows abroad is there created "an honest to goodness debt." [4] The idea of paying off government debt is consigned by the planners to Limbo as an "outworn superstition." [5] Pre-war Germany is alluded to as proof that a balanced budget has lost its old-time sanctity. Hansen admits, however, that the inflationary situation might get out of hand "under inexcusable blundering and mismanagement." [6] Answering the question, "How high can the public debt go before it results in disaster?" he professes with a bookish, "It all depends on the level of national income and the knowledge and skill of those who direct fiscal policy." "Potentials of 110,000 volts are common," he reminds us, "but a current of 110 volts might play havoc if used by an ignoramus." [7] And it is implied that the planners certainly are not ignoramuses!

The major domos of planning seem to agree with the answer Stuart Chase gives to the question: "Where is the money coming from?" He replies: "Out of that one hundred million man-years of work wasted; out of that two hundred billion years of production which never was produced. It will come from the same place that the bombers, tanks and battleships are now coming from—out of the full employment of the people." [8]

However, some of these bombers and battleships are being paid for with War Savings Bonds; some of the tanks are being paid for with taxes. Daily the radio urges everyone to buy bonds for victory. I have helped sell these bonds; employes of most businesses have loyally subscribed ten per cent of their earnings. I have bought bonds; millions of Americans have done likewise. It would appear that the cost—at least a large part of the cost—of bombers and tanks and battleships is being paid for by War Savings Bonds purchased out of current income and out of capital—past savings.

On the face of these bonds it is warranted that after being held sixty days they can be exchanged for the purchase price and accrued interest. As many of the things people normally buy are no longer available and as the automobiles, refrigerators, houses, tires—in fact, everything in use—are wearing out, people will want to buy new ones when the war is over. People purchase War Savings Bonds not only to help win the war but to have money with which to buy things when they are again available.

Post-war deficit spending will not be financed by War

Bonds. The flow of income now financing the costs of bombers and battleships promises to be in a reverse direction—cashing of bonds and the use of the proceeds for the purchase of things long wanted and needed. Indeed, the government must sell more bonds to banks, even directly to the Federal Reserve Bank, in order to pay off these obligations.

Another source of payment for our bombers, our battleships and our tanks has been taxes, particularly income taxes. People of small means are paying income taxes. Even the masses pay Social Security taxes, excise taxes, gasoline taxes and cigarette taxes.

But if the fears of deficits "were never valid anyway," another billion or two a year added to the national debt should cause no concern. Thus, the planners contemplate removing taxes on low incomes and repealing sales taxes.

But if the theory is valid—if the desire to avoid national deficits is merely a fetish—why any taxes at all? Taxes are politically unpopular and no one likes to pay them. From time immemorial they have been the bane of government. Is there any ideal ratio of state expenditures that must or should be raised by taxes in the "Century of the Common Man"—one-half or one-third? Or shall we impute that taxes are to be merely an instrument for economic equalization?

Congress has already made very necessary war appropriations of two hundred and five billion. The national debt is budgeted to reach one hundred and forty billion by June 30, 1943, and by the end of 1944 it will approximate two hundred and fifty billion. If the war lasts beyond 1944, even if prices do not increase, the debt will mount not less than fifty billion a year.

We know that necessary government spending will not cease with the termination of the war. We spent more in 1919 than in 1917 or 1918. So, too, after the last shot is fired this time we will inherit heavy responsibilities that must be discharged. A starving world will need to be fed. A great army must be brought home and rehabilitated. Large forces of occupation must be maintained. All around us will be a world impoverished! We will have a surplus of food, the lion's share of the world's gold and credit, and, we hope, an unravished countryside and an unimpaired industry. It will be necessary, in our own interest, to help other nations. This will require billions of dollars and vast amounts of food and goods for either loans or grants.

After this necessary aid to world reconstruction and rehabilitation, it is certain we will have a national debt that would have been regarded not long ago as astronomical. We will have a concomitant rise in our bank deposits. As the amount of money in relation to the amount of things will be greatly increased, all orthodox elements of inflation will already be loose.

How much more, then, can we pile on top of this huge beginning to finance a planned economy without a ruinous inflation? Estimates of its cost range from five to fifty billions a year. Can America stand a debt of five hundred billion, one thousand billion, or two thousand billion? Our national wealth, the value of all our farms, factories, buildings—everything everybody owns—amounts to only four hundred billion. Somewhere, certainly, there must be a point beyond which we cannot go.

At one thousand billion, for instance, interest on the debt alone would amount to twenty-five billion a year—more than twice the pre-war average value of all our farm products—or eight times the pre-war average net income of all our corporations—or more than the annual pre-war total of all salaries, all wages, and all dividends paid by all our manufacturing industries!

Does this not indicate that at this point, even though planning raised our national income very materially, we would no longer be speaking in terms of a dollar with the same purchasing power we now know? It is axiomatic that at this point at least we would have passed the tolerable debt limit. Inflation would not have waited that long!

If the solution to an unbalanced budget was as simple as is stated by the planners, would it not have been thought of long ago? "Is there anything whereof it may be said, 'See, this is new'?" Then the author of Ecclesiastes continued, "There is no new thing under the sun!" Although his conclusion is challenged by the records of our patent office, it holds valid in the fields of human relationships, including fundamental economic laws.

History records many attempts by governments to operate unbalanced budgets. Circumstances varied. Governments varied from dictatorship to democracy. Causes inducing the experiments varied. The theories under which they were tried varied. We would face different circumstances than those existing when such attempts were tried before. A highly industrialized civilization operating as a planned economy—particularly if the whole world were operating under a centralized planned economy—is different from any historical examples in all but one essential—the basic principle of a government spending in excess of its revenue.

Marco Polo was probably the first to introduce into Europe the idea of an unbalanced budget financed with paper money. He was fascinated with the legerdemain of "pao chao"—the precious paper issued by the great Kublai Khan, who needed beyond his fiscal revenues vast sums to support his wars, the splendor of his court, his extravagant tastes, public works and public benefactions.

"I shall tell you," he recounts in his quaint and picturesque style, "of the Mint which the Emperor hath in his city. Tell it how I may, you will never be convinced that it is actually true. The Emperor's Mint is so wrought that you would say he hath found the Philosopher's stone, and you would be right.

"For he makes his money after this fashion. From the bark of a tree, the mulberry tree, the leaves of which feed silkworms, the fine inner skin is taken. This is made into something like sheets of paper. These sheets, which are blank, are cut up into different sizes—the largest being worth ten Venetian bezants. All these pieces of paper are painted with as much care as if they were actually pure gold or silver. On every piece officials write their names; then the chief officer of the Khan puts red vermillion on the State seal and stamps it upon the paper. The money is then authorized. And anyone forging it may be put to death.

"And the Khan causes such a vast amount of this paper money—which costs him nothing—to be made every year that it must equal the other treasures of the world." [9]

Harold Lamb relates that without doubt, Kublai paid no attention to the working of his financial scheme—so long as things could be bought with his precious paper. The country was being flooded with increasing amounts of it. Not any law—not even the death penalty—could maintain the value of paper money. Sellers continued to ask more paper money for goods. Kublai's ministers found an old solution of this difficulty. The paper currency was devalued! The new price was set at one-fifth the old.

Still the problem remained an uncured, running sore. Growing expenditures had to be met by growing revenues. Lamb continues: "It is doubtful if he could have reduced his expenditures even if he had been willing to do so. He demanded only that the mass of the common people be protected against poverty; that relief be given to the peasants impoverished by drought or locusts; and that the necessary revenues be raised by the minister." The issue of 1269 was rated the equivalent of 228,960 ounces of silver, while in

1290 it rose to the amazing figure of 50,002,500 ounces.

The Chinese never forgave Kublai for the breakdown of the Mongol economy.[10]

Ogadia was Genghis-Khan's illustrious son and successor. He, too, was beset by money problems. However, he had a sage adviser. Lamb also records this conversation:

"Ogadia had a fresh idea. 'I am told,' he said to Yeliu Ch'u-tsai, 'that in Cathay they stamped money out of a worthless stuff, paper. They used this paper instead of coins. Why cannot we print money in this fashion?'

"The Cathayan smiled, 'True—it was done once. And they called the minister who did it Lord Scrap-paper. After a while, with this same precious paper, it took ten thousand taels to buy one cake. Do you wish that to happen to us?'

"Paper money, he explained, had one peculiarity. If you printed a little of it, it was indeed 'precious paper'—as the Chinese called it—but if you printed overmuch, the paper would be worth nothing at all."[11]

The story of post-revolutionary France re-illustrates the deficit fallacy. Andrew White[12] traced its course clearly for us. In 1789 the National Assembly was composed of some of the ablest Frenchmen of the day—Sieyès, Bailly, Necker, Mirabeau, Talleyrand, duPont deNemours. The nation was weighted with heavy debt and a serious deficit.

However, because of the recent trials and tribulations, there was a demand for a short-cut to prosperity. The state had acquired, as a result of the Revolution, the vast estates of the church and emigrant nobles, which were valued at the then large sum of one billion dollars.

It was proposed that these estates be mortgaged and notes issued against the values so acquired. Necker, the Minister of Finance, fought against the issue, as did others, pointing out the disastrous consequences of similar previous attempts to inflate a nation into prosperity. It was argued, however, that the state possessed productive real estate of vastly greater value than the issue, and finally four hundred million dollars of three per cent assignats were issued.

The results of the first issue met fondest expectations. The embarrassment of the Treasury was alleviated. Payments were made on the public debt and as the paper money passed through the hands of the people, trade increased. The anxieties of Necker seemed unfounded. However, within five months the government had spent the issue and was again in need. Trade slumped. The old difficulties reappeared. So resort was taken in another issue, this time eight hundred millions.

Prosperity bloomed again and people began to believe that inflation was synonymous with prosperity. However, as the effect of each issue of paper money wore off, new and larger issues were resorted to and the intervals between their issuance grew shorter. France was in the position of a drunkard refusing to suffer the reality of a hangover by constant resort to the bottle. When inflation had run its course, the farmers refused to bring their produce to the cities; thousands of laborers escaped starvation only by army draft. Suffering was acute. It required almost half a century for the French economy to recover its pre-Revolution position.

Andrew White concludes his account of this planned deficit financing with: "Such . . . is the history of the most skillful, vigorous and persistent attempt ever made to substitute for natural laws in finance the ability of legislative bodies, and, for a standard of value recognized throughout the world, a national standard devised by theorists and manipulated by schemers. Every other attempt of the same kind in human history, under whatever circumstances, has reached similar results in kind if not in degree; all of them show the existence of financial laws as real in their operation as those which hold the planets in their courses."

Years later, when Napoleon was hard pressed for money, he sold Louisiana Territory to us. "While I live," he declared, "I will never resort to irredeemable paper." And in confirmation he wrote to his prefects, "The Emperor considers paper money the greatest curse of nations, as fatal to their morale as the plague is to their well being."

German inflation of the early nineteen twenties had its origin in a faulty wartime fiscal policy. Instead of taxing heavily, as did Britain and America, Germany financed with planned deficits; taxes paid only five per cent of its war cost. So confident of victory were the German leaders that they financed the war with the proceeds of bonds, anticipating that the allied nations would pay for their liquidation. The bonds were sold directly to the Reichsbank, which occupied a relationship to the government of Germany not dissimilar to that of our own Federal Reserve Bank to our federal government.

While such a step can be justified in a war emergency, as a policy it carries grave danger, for it is but one step removed from outright paper money. The government turned the bonds over to a bank whose policies the government indirectly controlled, and this bank printed the money.

At the war's conclusion Germany's indebtedness to the Reichsbank was more than forty billion marks. The result was a great increase of currency and the elements of inflation were on the loose.

However, inflation was not thought to be the great problem of the moment. Defeated armies were returning to a war-torn countryside. Bolshevism was spreading and a new government was striving desperately to bring order to a country suffering the pangs of defeat, disorder and revolution. Conditions were aggravated further by the blockade maintained by the allies. Foodstuff was short. Mortality was great and the population, on the verge of starvation, was resentful and discouraged. An abortive attempt was made in 1919 by taxation to check the course of inflation; however, about the same time the unwise Treaty of Versailles imposed impossible reparations payments. Deficit financing through the route of the Reichsbank's paper currency continued.

By the middle of 1922 the international value of the mark had fallen to one one-hundredth of its pre-war rate. There was false prosperity. Demand swallowed everything for sale. Disbanded soldiers had been quickly absorbed by an industry busy computing its paper profits. However, each month saw the mark's value sink to a new low. Reparations payments became but a book obligation. Yet the internal demand for more and more paper continued and history repeated itself. The purchasing value of the mark sank lower and lower as each new wave of paper money fell upon the country. Finally the mark almost ceased to have value; it had fallen to one-trillionth of its original worth. If a comparable fall in the value of American money had taken place, thirty million dollars would have been required to buy a three-cent newspaper. By this time, prosperity had long since vanished. Hunger riots broke out and a process of dismemberment threatened the nation. In September, 1923, a state of siege was declared.

Dr. Peter Reinhold, formerly Finance Minister of the German Reich, sums up the horrors of the final days of the German inflation as follows: "It is only natural that this nonsensical process sucked all purchasing power out of the mark. The most terrible thing occurred that can happen to a civilized state, namely, its legal tender ceased to be recognized by its own nationals; the repudiation of the mark began; only those who have experienced it can appreciate what that means. It means that the agricultural districts refuse to furnish the towns and cities with food supplies, that the retail shops decline to part with their goods against payment in the national currency, that no standard can be found to decide the amount of wages, that 'those living on their means' have ceased to have any means, that they are reduced to the bitterest penury and unable to purchase a morsel of food to stay their hunger." [13]

The experience of Germany was paralleled by that of her defeated partner, Austria. And in Russia, Lenin's theory—that debauching the currency is the surest way to end capitalism—was put to work. The Bolshevists deliberately inflated the ruble to wipe out the last vestige of the Czarist economy. In so doing they insured that the people's last memory of it would be hunger, bloodshed and chaos.

In our case, who will buy government bonds for reconstruction and provide the government cash with which to redeem billions of War Savings Bonds and Stamps and pay for the planned deficits? According to the plans, the usual savings of the wealthy will be taxed away. Business will need its money. Will there be forced loans? Capital levies? These sources, if resorted to, will not be sufficient.

The government has a limited power to sell to the government-controlled Federal Reserve Bank, but through open market purchases of government bonds by the Federal Reserve the indirect sale process can go on indefinitely. Either of these courses parallels the Imperial German Government's sale of its bonds to the Reichsbank. The government would be, in effect, printing money. A mere face-saving bookkeeping transaction is imposed on the historical prelude to disaster.

But no one can predict when the conflagration will break out, because inflation is psychological. Not long ago economists were shocked at the prospect of a debt of fifty billion. Today our national debt is over one hundred billion, and two hundred billion and more is in prospect! Prices have risen only moderately, and this rise can be traced to causes other than increases in the national debt.

A planned economy in an industrial world is a new phenomenon but it smells like a witch's broth of false hopes. For a time, coercive methods may be effective in controlling prices. By all past experience, however, whenever the supply of money is far greater than the supply of things, prices rise. The inflation psychology grows as it feeds upon itself. People lose faith in the future value of their money. They refuse to bank it. They want to exchange it for something tangible. There is a rush to buy. Things become scarce! Prices soar! Labor refuses to work for money! Farmers refuse to sell for money! Everyone wants things! Everyone hoards!

Then the prairie is on fire! And it will rage until the national economy burns out. Verily, there is "no new thing under the sun."

After every section of a drama the curtain drops and there is an interlude during which scenery is shifted and actors change costumes.

Revolutions take place only in times of crisis when people suffer and despair. Marx foresaw clearly that the upheaval of the masses and the overthrowing of capitalism could take place only when its system had apparently failed. Then, he reasoned, the exploited classes could be driven to decisive action. Veblen thought the American overturn could take place only during one of the recurring depressions, when the American economy had apparently broken down.

Do those of the extreme left anticipate the intermission to follow the scene of inflation, blotting out, in horror, hunger and ferment, the last vestige of capitalism's money? Then the people's savings, insurance, War Savings Bonds and Social Security will have become valueless. The people will see some of their number unjustly enriched through speculation on the national disaster and others benefited through windfalls of shrunken debts payable with worthless money. Will they not then hate those who they think profited from their impoverishment?

Would America not have what Mussolini called the "benevolent neutrality of the populace," for any overt act against those who had survived with property?

If ever, the time would then be ripe for an equalitarian group in power to follow Veblen's advice and void not only worthless bonds and preferred stocks but equities speculatively acquired—and corporate stocks and other evidences of absentee ownership thrown in for good measure. In that case, the new scenery—all the fundamentals of Marxism or Veblenism—would be in place for the act to follow.

Thus, if our planners have not found the "philosopher's stone" of pao chao, if their "knowledge and skill" in directing a fiscal policy of unbalanced budgets is unequal to the "110,000 volt potential," will the curtain not likely rise with Communism as the next section of the American drama?

Economic freedom, freedom of speech, freedom of the press, political freedom and freedom of the mind and spirit would obviously have no part in it. Freedom! Patrick Henry's one freedom—Liberty—who played the ascendant role in the first act, would be but a memory, vanished in the shadows of drumhead trials and gray dawn Black Marias.

And it is doubtful, indeed, in view of contemporary and past totalitarian examples, how distinguished a part would be played by freedom from want. Dominating the scene, however, would be one character that overwhelms and crushes all others—an arrogant, implacable, red-handed brute—the state!

CHAPTER XV

The Skeleton Closet

SOME STUDENTS OF THE NEW DEAL MOVEMENT BELIEVE that the utter lack of concern about inflation exhibited by certain planners is because this group does not fear inflation, but for reasons other than those advanced by Dr. Hansen. These men believe that this group who have a psychopathic hatred of the successful and rich, intend to guide the American economy to the status of an equalitarian state through a short-cut. If war continues or if a state of war emergency can be continued for an extended period, it may be possible to avoid inflation by effectively demonetizing our economy through an extended and continuing scheme of taxation and rationing.

Today money alone has no power to buy gasoline, sugar, coffee, meat and canned foodstuffs. Each person is entitled to a ration. Soon clothing and other things will be added to the list. The war's end will see the number of rationed commodities greatly extended. There is no limit to the possible application of rationing. With rationing and effective enforcement, economic equalization of all individuals, during peace as well as war, is possible.

In this case, the rich and middle class would find their lawful money, in excess of that given purchasing power by ration cards, valueless. The underprivileged would, through doles and state employment, acquire sufficient lawful money to utilize the full purchasing privileges allowed by the standard rationing cards. But there will be "C" cards for "jewels, country estates, and custom-built motor cars" for those privileged by the new system, just as there are in Russia.

However, by rationing, money income would not determine living standards. And because property could not be exchanged for additional ration cards, past accumulations of wealth too would prove valueless. Owners of stocks, bonds, real estate and other property would be left with empty titles. Our economy would be, in effect, demonetized.

We have ration banking now! Retailers, wholesalers and dealers maintain bank accounts of ration coupons collected from customers as well as dollars collected from them. If a grocer orders a few sacks of coffee from a merchant, he sends two checks; one checks on his account of dollars, the other on his account of ration coupons. The government compensates banks for cashing ration checks at settled rates. A system of ration coupon banking is, therefore, ready for the transition. It is now rumored that retailers will soon be able to "make change" in ration coupons. If so, coupon "money" will parallel dollar money in most commodity transactions.

The United States Treasury's recently proposed spending tax to make expenditures above established levels prohibitive, would have been a step in the same equalitarian direction. This proposal would have imposed a progressive tax on all spending. A tax of eighty-five per cent was suggested on all expenditures of an individual in excess of $10,000 a year. Only payments on account of capital acquisition, such as life insurance and war bonds, were to be exempted. Thus, a person buying a meal, a book or a railroad ticket, after having spent $10,000 for rent, food, clothing, education and other living expenses, would pay eighty-five per cent more than if he were a member of the lower third of our economy. It would have been possible for subsequent tax bills to levy a tax of one hundred per cent or even a thousand per cent on all expenditures over $2,000 or $1,000. There is no limit to the application of the spending tax. It could impose a form of rationing by making the spending of more than an equalitarian maximum prohibitive.

Rationing, however, is more to the point. Until 1935, ration cards, not money, was the method used to control the distribution of life's necessaries in Russia.[1]

We have already heard suggestions from high sources that a peace should not be made for ten years after hostilities cease. The Army is training men in economics and planning, to qualify them for administering conquered and re-conquered territories. Left Wing minds may be thinking of a United States Government extended world wide, ration cards forming the basis of a world W.P.A., while agricultural nations are being industrialized and multilateral trade through barter and other plans of collectivism are effectuated.

I do not suggest that the idea of permanent rationing and demonetization of our economy is in the minds of the administration. But circumstances force a speculation if this reasoning of certain students of the New Deal might not have resulted from exploding a mental flash bulb in a dark seance of the Marxian radicals, thus capturing the image of their skeleton.

It would be logical for this group, who believe that President Roosevelt is but the Kerensky of this revolution, to encourage government spending to the limit, also. The more money spent by government the greater the need for a tight and heavy lid of rationing. Otherwise the orthodox inflationary reaction to such excesses of money would boil over.

These radicals may reason, also, that if a group gained control of government, intending to restore a free economy, inflation would be a time bomb they would leave in the house to bring about its destruction. They may reason further that a ruinous inflation taking place during the conservative regime, would assure their ability to grasp dictatorial power.

After ten years have worn the plush of idealism off the New Deal fabric, these are some of the rotten threads that become exposed. Together with the prospects and problems outlined in preceding pages, they form the basis of business' apprehension of the future.

CHAPTER XVI

Hope

Spinners of Grecian mythology related that Pandora was full of great expectations as to the contents of her box. But when she raised the lid, all manner of frightful miseries and ghastly evils flew out and plagued the earth with disease and vermin. Quickly she slammed down the lid and wept in disappointment. Then short, sharp, cheerful sounds came from the bottom of the box. Pandora peered in. She discovered that the sounds were the chirping of Hope, who had lingered there.

Similarly, for ten years a bitter Veblenian campaign of vilification, Marxian taxation and other economic miseries and evils, one after another, have flown out of America's political Pandora's box to hamper and harass business and threaten the life of American political and economic freedom. Then came war! Then the Four Freedoms! And businessmen viewed an ominous future from a threshold of frustration, if not despair.

Then the 1942 election took place!

Its effect was like that of Pandora's spirit-lifting Hope singing encouragement and cheer from the bottom of the box. Rubbing his eyes with amazement, a businessman read that Albert Hawkes, a "big businessman," formerly a director of the National Association of Manufacturers and formerly president of the Chamber of Commerce of the United States, had evidently not been considered a malefactor by society. He had been elected Senator from New Jersey. His heavy majority could not have been realized without a large labor vote! Another businessman, a Republican, was elected Senator from traditionally Democratic Oklahoma. Others with close business affiliations were elected by large majorities. Many business baiters and supporters of a planned economy were voted out.

Encouraging, too, were political analysts' reasons for the overturn. The war was not being waged in a businesslike way! The people disliked rationing—"being pushed around," they called it! They resented the government's reluctance to take them into its confidence. They thought the government had been feeding them honeyed words while withholding unfavorable war news!

Does the last-named reason carry ominous forebodings if the public is not taken into the government's confidence as to its peace aims? Might we face more than a revolt at the polls if the people do not understand clearly the portent of the Four Freedoms that the Office of War Information says we are fighting for?

A questionable precedent has been established in recent years in the form of international treaties and executive agreements not being ratified by the constitutional two-thirds of the Senate. Tragic consequences might follow if, upon the war's conclusion, our President should hastily request of Congress power to make such agreements and to incur such obligations and establish such agencies as are deemed necessary to carry out the Four Freedoms, unless the people were in complete understanding of what those freedoms were.

Is it not desirable, therefore, that plans for peace and the post-war world be freely and openly discussed now? Any discussion after the war will be too late. Furthermore, peace may come in Europe and war continue in Asia; thus the national war emergency would carry on. However, wherever war ends, peace begins. The world will not wait while we debate what we were fighting for. Nor do the planners intend to wait. Therefore, is it not imperative that we enter each peace with an informed public so that our government will approach the difficult problems with a full understanding of what the American people want?

If so, it is important that the group now engaged in planning the peace take the American people into their confidence—not with engaging, ethereal platitudes, gushing rhetoric and vague generalities, but by being specific as to their design and the methods which they propose to employ in achieving it.

In addition, their presentations should avoid the skillful use of words. They should be frank! Even though "socialism" and "spending" may be "bad" words, from the planners' point of view, people are accustomed to them. These words convey to the people an exact meaning. "Planning," like "investment," is an improper synonym when applied to the planners' purposes. "Regimentation" would be clearer than "planning"; "international socialism" would be more so!

If they believe in international socialism, they should advocate it openly. When our own Constitution was completed, Franklin commented that "there is no form of government but what can be a blessing to the people if well administered." International socialism is a way of life. The war has dissipated much of the prejudice against it. The Russians evidently believe in it. Certainly they fight for it. Harold Laski, a disciple of Veblen,[1] led the British Labor Party into declaring itself frankly as a socialist party, and into advocating the end of private ownership of the primary means of production—industry and land.

But "planning" is too plausible a word. When applied to government, it carries no precise meaning to the average mind. Business plans; everyone plans. Of course government should plan! But the people should know that New Deal "planning" means coercive control of their economy; that planned production means planned consumption; that if the state plans what farm and industry produce, it follows that the state plans, with what Stuart Chase defines as "dictatorial powers," what each individual will eat, what he will wear, and not only what he can do but what he must do; that in peace as in war an individual's duties[2] to the state supplant his former inalienable rights; and that all of this means being "pushed around" in peace as well as in war.

They should know that world planning means world equality, with our standard of living falling to the world average; that "planning" means that the world will have been set up to compete with America's industry, if the planners' plans fail. They should know what equal access to raw materials means. Italy has no oil. Can she send her men to Texas and pump out our reserves?

Through this discussion the public might identify freedom from want projected world wide as either a feverish dream of impractical, extravagant altruisms, an American version of Nazi geopolitics or Marx's world of international socialism. They might realize that if the first interpretation is correct, such a world would be founded on the quicksand of unbalanced budgets and the fallibility of mortal man. They might realize that any solution for prosperity and a better world based merely on the equal distribution of material things oversimplifies the problem. Because through discussion devoted to analysis and criticism it would be evident that such a solution would not create the machinery for permanent employment but that it would end private enterprise, private education, freedom of the press and radio, real progress, and freedom of the mind and spirit.

Further, the public might be brought to realize that it is

a fundamental fallacy to think that war can be a profitable enterprise. They might realize that men can't turn their cities into blood-soaked rubble, build ships and sink them, put the world's output of brass and steel into shells and burst them, bury the better part of a generation of men before their world's work is commenced, and then emerge with prosperity. They would be told by realists that this is nonsense! that war is waste! that prosperity can be created only by an abundance of production consumable by a nation at peace!

We will have dissipated the output of our labor for several years. It was diverted to war. It was an economic waste. But we face the payment. In addition, war takes a toll in biological waste. It is a reversal of the natural processes of selection. The flower of a generation is killed. Those unfit for military service survive! The war's waste will be paid for in one manner or another. Blood, sweat and tears will not end with the beginning of peace.

True, such a discussion will bring out into the open differences of opinion. This is the way of a democratic people. The minority has the right to speak and to attempt to convert the majority. Failing, they submit to the majority.

Such a discussion, taking place in newspapers, on the radio and on forums, cannot deter us from determination to win the war, because we know that if we don't win we will lose. The war can't be called off, and if we are not the victors we will be the vanquished—and few are there of us who can have any illusions of what it would mean to be conquered by Nazidom!

How important it is that this discussion of the post-war world be held now, for it might determine the destiny of America and, indeed, the world! Furthermore, might not failure to hold it re-enact the tragedy presented by President Wilson, with consequences of even greater domestic and international confusion, even disaster? Might it not endanger all chances of a just and durable peace, and allow the seeds of war-engendered hatreds to grow into another holocaust? And then, too, our government would be clothed with much greater moral force if it were known that its policies were backed by American public opinion.

If the New Deal plans for the post-war world were confided to the American people and freely discussed, public opinion polls could readily determine if such plans did or did not meet with popular approval. And after all, it is the people's brothers, sons and husbands who will have died. It is the people who will have denied themselves and sacrificed during the war; it is they who will have to bear the costs of the war. It is they who will have to shoulder and discharge the burdens of the peace and live in the post-war world.

If we are to continue as a democracy, the people will make the final decisions anyway. If we are to continue as a democracy, they should be consulted first!

After such discussions the American people might refuse to pay the devil with the freedom of mind and spirit which took centuries to win. They might decide that government administers things in "profusion"; that it could never run business and the whole economy in an efficient manner; that they do not want to be rationed and "pushed around" forever. They might agree to expend such blood, sweat and tears as may be necessary to have freedom to seek their own happiness even in a system that does not promise full employment all the time but which does promise that when they work they do so as free men, and work not for masters but for themselves.

To businessmen, this was the song of Hope.

CHAPTER XVII

An Alternative

IF THE HOPE OF BUSINESSMEN IS REALIZED, OUR NATIONAL policies and post-war program will be based on realism. There are alternatives to central economic planning. Cessation of hostilities will present a world teeming with such overwhelming problems that the author will approach them with utmost humility. But nevertheless, as international planning will not prove a common solvent for the difficulties, an attempt will be made to present and analyze briefly other solutions that have been suggested, to ascertain if they hold greater promise.

It is most hazardous to assume that any given set of conditions will exist when fighting ceases. All schemes assume that our cordial relations with our principal allies will not be interrupted by the zeal of any one of them or by inability to comprehend and make allowances for one another's national and internal problems. We must hope and assume that mutual understanding and common purpose will continue to prevail.

There is a truism to the effect that we learn history but that *we do not learn from history*. This observation seems apropos in regard to schemes which have been advanced wherein a supreme world authority is superimposed upon nations in the same manner in which our federal government is superimposed upon our states. History points out obstacles along this road to world peace. Our own history is one case in point.

Our original thirteen states were neighbors on one shore of one continent. Their people were homogeneous; they were all of common ancestry and held a common ideology. They spoke the same language; they were accustomed to the same political institutions; the Christian religion was common to them. They had been bound together in their great war of liberation, and there was a common desire to be united. Yet their first attempt as a Confederacy was a failure, because each state retained for itself a large measure of political and economic freedom, as well as its own means of defense. Only after a decade of depression and near anarchy had proven this arrangement to be conspicuously inadequate and a break-up of the Union seemed imminent, was our Constitution adopted. And this supreme law and the government it provided were approved only by the narrowest of margins, because small states feared the dominance of the larger ones and because there was a conflict between the economic interests of the southern agricultural slave states and the northern free mercantile states. It took, eventually, a bloody Civil War to cement our Union.

None of the conditions which were common to our original states applies to the nations of the world. They do not lie side by side on one shore of one continent; they are not even on one continent or one hemisphere; they spread all over our planet's land surface. Their tongues are polyglot, their religions legion; their political institutions range from absolutism to democracy. Their standards of living, ideologies and economic interests vary over as wide a range.

What common solvent can be found for such tremendous divergences and conflicts which would induce each nation to surrender its economic freedom and acknowledge a supreme political instrument, such as the United States Government, and a supreme law, such as the United States Constitution? For instance, what would be the basis for representation in such a supreme government? China has three times our population; Russia's population is four times that of Great Britain. Would American workers agree to unrestricted immigration of Southeastern Europeans and Asiatics? Would they even agree to free admission of products manufactured by such cheap labor? Would our people be willing to relinquish our Navy to any supreme government which we would not dominate? If not, we should learn from our own history that any half-way measure would be a hybrid pregnant with disruptive seeds of conflicting self-interests.

We can learn from history that the longest eras of world peace were those in which a great nation dominated the civilized world—the Roman peace of antiquity and the Victorian Pax Britannica. And we can learn that except while we were occupied with our Civil War there has been no aggression worth mentioning in the western hemisphere for a century and a quarter—not since President Monroe proclaimed to the world that we would not permit it and Great Britain insinuated that she would, if necessary, come to our assistance in enforcing Monroe's Doctrine.

We can learn, also, from recent history that we cannot buy our peace; nor is it manly that we should attempt to do so. Instrumentalities such as Lease-Lend are no twilight sleep to ease the pain of defending ourselves. We must be willing and prepared to do our own fighting. And apparently our frontiers of defense now lie in Europe and Asia.

This time, when the guns go silent and the bombers, tanks and invasion barges are put away, three great, powerful nations will emerge dominant over the world—Russia, Great Britain and the United States. Each of these three nations has a natural vested interest in peace. In the League of Nations, Russia's present regime was the outstanding advocate of collective action against aggression; she openly challenged France to join her in protecting Czechoslovakia against Hitler. Only in peace can she develop her vast internal resources for the benefit of her people, so it is only in peace that she can pursue the objectives of her ideology. History has proven that modern Britain has no aggressive designs. America covets nothing; we can prosper and retain our democratic way of life only in peace.

It would seem that in history's lessons one can find successful precedents which indicate that an enduring world peace is most probable through world-wide application of the principle of the Monroe Doctrine, enforced, with a velvet glove drawn over a mailed fist, by the three nations which have a vested interest in peace.

As Great Britain stood ready to help us enforce Monroe's Doctrine in this hemisphere, so Great Britain and Russia could stand by each other to enforce the new doctrine in Europe. So, too, we could stand by Russia in its enforcement in Asia. By maintaining bases in Far Eastern Pacific waters, we could act promptly. Thus, short, cheap, local wars would dispose of any aggressor overstepping any of the new international boundaries.

At this time one wonders if it was not toward such a scheme that Winston Churchill was pointing in his masterful speech of March 21, 1943. He spoke of a European council and an Asiatic council. In the western hemisphere we already have our Pan-American council and the Monroe Doctrine. That such a world might endure without another holocaust is given promise by the background painted by Professor Spykman in his "America's Strategy in World Politics," and by the analysis of the obstacles to peace made by President Hoover and Hugh Gibson in "Problems of Lasting Peace."

Under the protecting egis of such a doctrine outlawing aggression, to which China and our other allies could pledge themselves, also, a Council of Nations could be called to work out various international relationships. The Postal Union and international agreements applying to radio, cables, copyrights and patents are successful precedents. These agreements have endured because they are not in the self-interest of any nation; they are reciprocal; they benefit all alike. Such a council could also work toward freedom of world trade and international betterment in all social and economic fields. It could, in time, establish a code of international law and a world court with access to means of enforcing its decisions with economic sanctions and military action—either by its own independent military establishment or by those of the great powers acting temporarily under its orders.

We learn from history, also, that the phenomenal development of America's natural resources was due not only to freedom of the individual and freedom of opportunity but to the security of property that was guaranteed by our Constitution. Our development was rapid, too, because we were the only nation with laws which, by preventing monopolies, assured a free, competitive internal market.

There could be no greater stimulus to world prosperity and higher living standards in the so-called backward nations than if property in these nations and the sanctity of international contracts were guaranteed by international law. It would also be a boon to the world if utmost competition in all fields were assured by an international law, based on the principles of our Sherman and Clayton Acts, outlawing cartels and any other agreements to restrict output or allocate markets. Such laws would cause untold billions to flow into undeveloped nations, just as European capital flowed into our West, built railroads, established industries, provided employment for our people and raised our living standards, because property was secure. Similarly, capital flowing into China, South America and Africa would supply more gainful employment to their people and swell world production so that there would be more available, at constantly decreasing prices, for consumption by all the world's people. The outflow of men, machinery and equipment from industrial nations to these presently backward nations, and increased exports to the latter because of their new prosperity, would be reflected in the well-being of the highly industrialized nations.

But there are yet other suggestions and a profound discussion, such as seems to at last be emerging as this manuscript goes to press, may point an obvious and definite way by the time it is necessary for our statesmen to act.

And in our own country, if the people decide against a planned economy and resolve to face the future as free men, it would be unfortunate if the responsibility for satisfying them fell upon a rudderless Congress. In this case, the respite from planning might be short-lived.

The decision of the American people would be a revolt of the residual individualism of the American spirit against collectivist methods which are repugnant to it. It would mean that the principles of liberty are deeply rooted in America. But it would not mean that the people wanted to return to the spectacular twenties and Wall Street dominated mergers, or to eliminate social advance. It would mean they had decided that collectivism, regimentation and central economic planning was not the proper way to attain their objectives. It would mean that they had decided to give democracy and private enterprise another chance.

Domestic problems will be great and trying. The debit side is obvious. Millions of men will be demobilized and will need to be assisted until they find employment. War workers will be temporarily idle as munitions plants close and others shift their output from war materiel to articles of peace. Women war workers, finding no other lucrative employment, will have to return to the home. A very large proportion of our small businesses will have been liquidated. A huge national debt will hang on our shoulders. It is inevitable that with a return to a free economy, some inflation and consequent hardship will take place.

Such problems have attended the end of every war; but, as this is the greatest war in history, our dislocations will be the greatest ever experienced. Difficulties will be in proportion. In addition, we will emerge this time with an economy as thoroughly regimented for war as that of the most totalitarian state. Even if the people want to return to democratic ways and free enterprise, this regimentation can dissolve into a free economy but slowly. To attempt any other course would cause disastrous confusion! But the administration of our economy in the hands of those who believe in free enterprise would automatically remove many of the brakes now exerted on initiative and progress. They would seek not the perpetuation of rationing, priorities and other administrative controls, but their dissolution at the earliest possible moment.

On the credit side: Millions of our war workers will have attained new skills. Millions of our soldiers will be rich in experience. A goodly proportion will have enjoyed a higher standard of living than they knew before and will be satisfied no longer with a diet of sow belly and corn pone; they will have ambitions for better things. The health of those escaping casualty should be improved.

Hardship, self-denial and loss of loved ones may purify the American soul. Common sacrifice in facing grim realities may unite us in a better understanding and higher regard for our fellow men. Moral and spiritual values may rank higher than comforts and luxuries, which so often in the course of history have been the prelude to national decay.

On the material side, there will be greater demands than ever to recapture living standards to which the nation has been accustomed. For years we will have been wearing out everything from automobiles to stoves, without replacement. Every family will want to be re-equipped with both gadgets and necessities.

Even though war goes on, our population grows, and it will be necessary to provide housing for the new population and replace homes which have been destroyed by fire, windstorm and decay. As house building has been virtually dormant since 1930, we will have almost fifteen years of normal home construction to make up. This is true of commercial buildings, too. Construction of major office buildings, theatres, hotels and terminals ceased in 1930, yet depreciation and obsolescence have gone on.

It will be necessary to rebuild railroads worn out by excessive war traffic. New industries will be ready to spring into being; they will require vast amounts of equipment. Most of our manufacturing facilities will be obsolete, for technology goes on even during war. There will be enough unsatisfied needs to supply employment for all.

An abundant supply of the materials required for war will be available. Our aluminum capacity will be seven times that which it had reached in 1940 after fifty years of development; our magnesium capacity will be up a hundredfold. On a cubic foot basis, magnesium will be cheaper than aluminum. There will be vast new capacities of high tensile, stainless and alloy steels, plastics, and hundreds of other new products. Almost ten times as much industrial research is going on as during the last war, and the exigencies of war are making almost anything worth trying.

Our people will be in an unparalleled position to buy. High agricultural prices will have permitted farmers to liquidate mortgages that have hamstrung them since the last war's land boom. Factory workers will have gotten out of the clutches of loan sharks. Time loans on automobiles, refrigerators and other articles will have been paid off. Billions will have been invested in War Savings Bonds. Never have our people been as free of debt and as well supplied with both means and credit to satisfy their needs as they will be after the war.

To satisfy the potential demand would require a tremendous expansion of pre-war productive facilities of almost everything.

Banks will have the greatest deposits in history; credit will be superabundant. The issuance of industrial securities, which lagged during the thirties and has almost vanished during the war, could be awaited by an almost insatiable market.

Capital engaged in manufacture shrank during the thirties from sixty-two billion to forty-nine billion. In previous years it increased more than a billion annually! Under the stimulus of the war program, it rose to fifty-two billion in 1940. But at our former rate of increase it should amount to seventy-seven billion in 1945, or fifty per cent more than it was at the end of 1940! This is the normal growth of which manufacturing industries alone are capable if a climate is created in which private enterprise can blossom and thrive again.

However, to guide and allow this confused situation to work itself out in the long-pull best interest of the people, Congress will need a great moral awakening. Congress must recapture the confidence and respect of the people. And it must restore conditions conducive to national economic and spiritual health. But Congress can't recognize national diseases unless it knows and understands healthy national organs, such as free minds, freedom of opportunity and free markets. It can cure our diseases only by identifying and eradicating the foreign bodies that are attacking our vital organs.

All the pressure groups will have problems. There will be some politicians eager to advance their own selfish interests by offering each group money or privilege as solutions. But in the long run this will only aggravate our illness and further disrupt possibilities of returning to a healthy national economy. Congress will need courage and vision to root out one of the main causes of our illness by preventing our "cannibal appetites" from continuing to feed on one another. It should abolish government by minority pressure groups!

A long stride in this direction could be made by applying Hatch Act principles to pressure groups. Congress could forbid anyone who receives compensation from more than one individual or enterprise from exercising influence directly or indirectly on any legislation.

Such a law would not mean the abandonment of collective bargaining in individual plants and companies, but it would end the domination of Green, Murray and Lewis over Congress. It would not mean that farmers, individually or as a group, could not exercise their constitutional right to petition and seek redress for grievances as this right was originally conceived; it would mean that no well-entrenched lobby could hamstring Congress and prevent it from acting in the best interests of the people as a whole.

Such a law would mean that Congress could provide handsomely for all disabled war veterans, but under it well-paid lobbyists could not demand and obtain special appropriations and compensation for a group who had the privilege of serving their country in its time of need.

Under such a law a businessman could continue to address

his Congressman on matters that affected his business, but business pressure groups would be prevented from descending on Congress like a swarm of locusts and demanding particular favors harmful to the national and world economy. They could not thwart or retard other legislation that might be in the interest of the people as a whole. Dr. Townsend would be out!

Such an overturn of the past trend would start us back toward the road laid out by the authors of our Constitution. To continue on this road, business must give up the special privileges it enjoys in the way of excessive tariffs against nations with equivalent standard of living and be reconciled to a reduction of those against low standard nations, as fast as it can be accomplished without disrupting our economy.

Businessmen also should be willing to accept more of the classic conception of the free enterprise system. Business should recognize the justice of much well-deserved, although misdirected, criticism by New Dealers. Businessmen should correct the causes of the antipathy to their ways that has arisen in such profound and superb intellects as that of the Archbishop of Canterbury. They should be willing to have all conditions necessary to a free market restored, and to provide the people with the full advantage of competition. They should accept remedies that go all the way in destroying all obstacles to free competition and open markets.

Neither Adam Smith nor the authors of our Constitution could conceive of the development of modern corporations. Corporations of their day were colleges and schools. A few operated toll roads and bridges. Commerce was then in the hands of individuals and partnerships. Had our modern corporate colossi, operating factories in many states and selling in all of them, then existed, certainly a more specific provision for them would have been made than that which appears in the Constitution's section grouping interstate commerce with Indian trading.

It would seem that Congress should give consideration to a national incorporation law providing uniform rules of conduct for all business engaging in interstate commerce. Some form of a national incorporation law has been advocated by Charles Nagel, President Taft's Secretary of Commerce; Frederick Lehman, President Taft's Solicitor-General; and by Presidents Theodore Roosevelt, Taft, Wilson and Hoover.[1] A national incorporation law is also advocated in the final report of the T.N.E.C. The latter, however, visions a measure to control business through another and super commission. Earlier advocates of a national incorporation law recommended uniform legal regulations for all business, to be interpreted, as other federal laws were, by the federal courts. It is in the latter sense that a national incorporation law is now suggested.

Such a law could recodify and embody modernized and strengthened anti-trust provisions. It could, for instance, promote competition by prohibiting competitors from merging. It could also prohibit one business from owning stock in another. Thus, one manufacturer could not pre-empt the market offered by a consumer of its products through the ownership of a substantial amount of the consuming company's shares.

Competition could be increased by eliminating all interlocking directorates and by prohibiting any director from profiting, directly or indirectly, by a transaction between the company and any firm or other business with which that director was connected. This would apply with particular force to the position of investment bankers on company boards, for there is no doubt that investment bankers have at times used directorships as a means of controlling a company's finances by funnelling the issuance of its securities into their own firm.

Also, it was particularly fashionable in the 1920's for investment banker-directors to promote mergers and sales of one company to another, not because of special advantages to the shareholders they represented nor to the public, but because of commissions in which their firms participated.

Such a prohibition would not prevent management from having the benefit of the experience and valuable advice of investment bankers. If no investment banker were on a Board of Directors, management could seek the advice of several; if under such restrictions an investment banker were a member of the Board, management would be assured that his advice was not stimulated by self-interest.

The press should be made to clean its doorstep, too. We are a long way from the original concept of a free press. Freedom of the press was a counterpart of freedom of speech. As Buckle puts it, both stemmed from "the undoubted right of every citizen to lay his views before his fellow citizens." Anyone was free to say what he pleased, though he might be sued for slander. He was free to print what he pleased, though he might be sued for libel.

The early American press was free because no government license was required. No costly bond had to be deposited. No subsidies were granted. In these respects it differed from the European press. The amount of capital required for a publication was nominal. Horace Greeley, for instance, embarked on the *New York Morning Post* with only $200.[2]

Early American newspapers resembled a current county weekly; the editor was a personality, even though he was often abusive, intolerant or vindictive. But his viewpoint was sought; that was the only reason his paper was bought. James Truslow Adams relates that even after the Civil War "throughout the country men asked eagerly not what does the

Sun or Tribune say but what does Greeley or Dana think?"[3] William Allen White is the last of this older clan. In our early days, an editor's opinion on political and other topics was weighed against that of many others, for in proportion to population, there were many publications where now there is one. As news-gathering facilities were limited, news was secondary to editorial opinion. But this was before the upsurge of advertising made the penny press a possibility, which in turn evolved newspapers into a media for influencing the masses. In 1830, for instance, the average circulation of New York's principal newspapers was but seventeen hundred copies.[4]

Today newspaper chains network the nation. Newspaper circulation has grown so that enough copies are printed to provide every metropolitan family with at least one issue a day. The press has traveled as far from its early beginnings as industry has gone from the cobbler's bench and the smithy's forge. Today the press is big business! But it has become a business devoted largely to assembling and retailing the works of others. National and international news and photographs are bought from the Associated or United Press or other agencies. Cartoons, comic strips, feature articles and columnists' writings are purchased from syndicates. These purchases are assembled with the local news and an editorial page and retailed to the people. Sometimes parts are emphasized or colored to conform with a publisher's whim or settled approach. But in order to get news, the public must take the whole package, including editorials.

Today, millions of dollars must be invested before a metropolitan daily can start and millions lost before its circulation becomes profitable. Newspapers have remained outside of the anti-trust prohibitions governing other businesses. The Sherman Act and the Clayton Act do not apply to them. Newspapers have merged with competitors and bought out competitors, as the hyphenated names of so many metropolitan dailies bear witness. Associated Press and other franchises are often unavailable to anyone who might be willing to risk on a new and competitive adventure. Hence many metropolitan centers have been left with but one morning or one evening newspaper and in some communities one publisher owns both. There are no businesses other than public utilities that approach as close to monopoly, and as the market is public opinion, monopoly of the enveloping medium carries grave potential threats to free minds, at least to a well-informed public.

It is to the credit of the newspaper industry that, as a rule, its power to sway public opinion is used temperately and in accord with the ethics of journalism. On the whole, the American press has grown in dignity as well as in the scope of its services to the public. For the most part, editorial pages engage in useful discussion, crusades and exposés that are in public interest. Often, however, they resemble a bluejay sitting high in judgment of the world and scolding at it. On some occasions, because of faulty information or biased viewpoint, or because of a mistaken estimate of the motives of others the public is misled; on others, intemperate and unjustified attacks are made upon individuals and institutions.

In each case, however, editorial opinion is controlled by the publisher. Therefore, when the public is dependent on one newspaper, the public receives only one viewpoint—that of the publisher, who may be influenced by the effect that pandering to prejudice and ignorance has on circulation and his pocketbook, or the publisher may be influenced by prospective political reward.

The freedom of the press that Thomas Jefferson had in mind when he insisted that the Bill of Rights prevent the federal government from abridging it, was not conceived in times when one man could print hundreds of thousands, even millions, of copies of a misleading statement traducing the character of an individual or undermining the integrity of an institution and no adequate opportunity would be open to refute it. Nor was it conceived when one rich man could establish a newspaper, print propaganda, in the interest of a political philosophy or party, lose millions on the venture and charge his losses to the people as a taxable deduction from his other income.[5] Nor did Jefferson conceive of intemperate attacks, ridicule and misleading statements falling short of libel being made against politicians, other individuals, corporations and organizations, when those attacked had no means of replying except by costly advertisements which the attackers had the right to refuse, or by the purchase of radio time, which would reach a different audience.

It would seem in the interest of an informed public opinion and free minds that Congress consider how to restore free competition to enrich and purify the newspaper business, and how editorial pages could be made into forums like radio, which is required to grant both sides equal opportunity to be heard. This could be accomplished without abridging the freedom of the publisher to say what he pleased, while guaranteeing to those subject to misinterpretation or attack or to those of opposing political faith, an opportunity to freely "lay his views before his fellow citizens" also.

In recent years the greatest impostor on public opinion has not been publishers but government. The various administrative agencies, in a sharp departure from all precedent, have used their prerogative to invade all public opinion forming instrumentalities with propaganda intending not only to establish new trends of thought but by that means to perpetuate themselves in office.

In spite of a statutory prohibition against the employment of publicity experts by administrative agencies unless specifically authorized by Congress, the Budget Bureau's breakdown of executive department expenditures for the fiscal year ended June, 1941, prepared at the instance of the House Appropriations Committee, disclosed that 2,895 full-time and 31,618 part-time employes were engaged in this work. The cost of government publicity in that year was $47,769,-940. Almost 284 million copies of printed matter were produced, much of it being sent by franked mail to newspapers, libraries, individuals and institutions. If postage had been collected at regular mail rates, the cost of transmitting the literature would have been more than fifty million dollars.

When Representative Wigglesworth was discussing the Budget Bureau's report on the floor of the House, he was asked if the setup was similar to Goebbels' operations in Germany. He replied that "the objectives sought would seem to be similar."[6]

In a representative democracy, government is the servant, not the godfather, of the people. After public discussion, the people determine themselves what is in their best interest, then elect their representatives to execute their will. Even in a pious purpose, government has no warrant to use the people's own money to proselytize their opinion, and Congress should halt the current evasion of its own statute by administrative departments.

In the interest of free minds and an informed public opinion, it would seem that Congress should also consider compelling newspapers to divorce their commercial radio stations, allowing them to retain no connection of ownership or directorship. The ability of a politically-dominated Federal Communications Commission to withhold a license from a radio station or to grant special favors is too great a club for any administration to hold over the press. Even if this weapon has not been used in the past, public interest demands that the press be free from coercion by any political party in power.

And much legislation, particularly that of the last ten years, should be overhauled, retaining the features that protect public interest but releasing again the human mind and initiative in enterprise. It has remained dormant too long.[7]

Business can work more efficiently within the limits of well-defined and settled laws than when subject to the whims and constantly-changing policies of commissions. The Securities and Exchange Commission should be abolished. In its place a law similar to England's could provide the equivalent in protection to the investor, but the annoyance, delays and useless additional costs of financing would disappear. Chicanery and fraudulent practices of the Stock Exchange could be identified by the same law and prohibited.

The National Labor Relations Board should be abolished and in its place adequate safeguards to collective bargaining and other rights of labor could be defined and guaranteed by a law. Employers should be prohibited from labor spying and discrimination of any kind against labor. Lock-outs should be illegal. Responsibility and democratic rule should be forced upon unions. Petrillos should not be possible. A strike should be legal only when a majority proposing to engage therein vote for it by secret ballot. Audits of union finances should be made available to its own members, at least. Corporations are prohibited from making political campaign contributions. Unions should come under the same ban.

The elimination of national pressure groups and a revised labor law would restore the process of collective bargaining to its classical conception—that of a group of men dealing in concert directly with their employer. Labor would forfeit nothing in rights or working conditions, but fellowship would be restored to those factories wherein fair and equitable working conditions existed. Men can't be happy in their work if they suspect and hate their employer. Restoration of fellowship in factories should make for a happier labor force.

To provide millions of new jobs, billions of dollars must be invested in enterprise. Capital markets must be roused from their semi-comatose condition. Confidence must be restored in the investor and business risks made worth while. Therefore, Congress should leave no justified doubts as to the continuance of property rights.

Taxes should be reconsidered on the basis of what kind of taxes and what rates will bring in over the long pull the greatest well of potential revenue to pay normal operating costs of government and service and liquidate the national debt. Indirect taxation alone liquidated the very substantial colonial debt left by the Revolution. After a generation, the federal government was embarrassed by a large surplus. Indirect taxation liquidated the huge debt and redeemed the greenbacks of the Civil War. Later President Arthur was embarrassed by an annual hundred million surplus. It may seem fanciful to us that excess revenue was at times a major problem for both the Chief Executive and Congress. In ten years indirect taxation and moderate direct taxes had paid off more than a third of the debt left by the first World War. Those were days, however, when individualism was given more or less free reign and it took the war debts in its stride.[8]

Business lowers selling prices in order to broaden markets. The same principle holds in taxation. For several years prior to the war, taxes on both individual and corporate income satisfied Karl Marx's desire for "taxes so steeply graduated as to bring ruin to capital." A well known middle of the road economist, Sumner Slichter, remarked recently: "The tax history of the United States since 1932 makes sensational reading. One might almost suspect that the tax laws had been written by a Communist Fifth Columnist for the purpose of making private enterprise unworkable."[9]

To restore conditions that *will make private enterprise workable,* it is necessary to promote investment by making risking of capital worth while. Therefore, it is essential that income tax rates be reduced drastically. The capital gains tax should be repealed. As man is shortsighted, inheritance taxes are not as great an inhibition to initiative. They could remain reasonably graduated.

Congress should have the courage to inform the public that profits are a basic incentive to investment; that a man attains wealth in private enterprise only if he contributes something new and useful or makes something of better quality at lower cost. No longer should wealth be held unmoral, for people should be encouraged to seek it.

However, in a resurrection of a climate wherein private enterprise may again thrive, we need not abandon any of the publicly-expressed social aims of the New Deal. Because the public saw the New Deal as an idealistic movement aimed at bettering working conditions and alleviating distress, the era will leave an enduring appreciation of its moral and spiritual pronouncements.

Industrial management as a whole does not want to abandon these social objectives. Thousands of companies had pension plans before Social Security was enacted. Thousands of companies now supplement the inadequate pensions provided by the Social Security Act. Many companies had standardized on the forty-hour week, overtime payment and paid vacations for both salaried and hourly employes long before these were legal requirements or union goals. Thousands of companies make life, health and accident insurance available to their employes. Many provide group hospitalization, dismissal allowances and many other privileges and considerations still not required by law. This is part of the voluntary socialism which John W. Burgess pointed out as a characteristic of the American way of life.[10]

Managements respond to public opinion. Out of a public opinion that places high values on the social consciousness of business will arise an era of cleansed and purged private enterprise which can attain any social objective.

Some people hold that if relief for unemployed is made attractive, people will not work. While this is undoubtedly true in some cases, business has had no difficulty in tempting workers away from relief rolls. Indeed, when closed factories opened to engage in the defense program, W.P.A. workers bounded into them with the eagerness of air rushing into a vacuum.

Payment for a huge social program can be realized from improvements in technology. The progress made in some of our oldest industries in the past twenty years is indicative of the possibilities of the future.

Coal mining is a hoary ancient among industries, yet from 1919 to 1939 miners' average hourly output of bituminous coal increased over sixty-seven per cent. Steel genealogy goes back to the Dark Ages when iron was heated with charcoal for days on end; it is the earliest of modern industries. As viewed by the planners, steel is a static industry, and from the testimony of the T.N.E.C., one gathers that it is a mature industry, yet during the period of 1919-1939 technology increased the hourly output of the steel worker one hundred and sixty-eight per cent. Even in railroading, the old veteran of modern transportation, manhour productivity increased during the same years seventy-five per cent.[11]

Even greater strides have been made in other fields. The average increase in worker output in all manufacture during this period was one hundred and thirty per cent.

There is no reason to assume that with a continuation of an economy based on private enterprise the pace of progress should slacken. Indeed, with our native ingenuity aided by rapidly-advancing science, technological progress should accelerate.

In the normal course this does not mean unemployment for the workers displaced. New industries, new services, will arise to absorb them. In the decade 1919 to 1929, worker hourly output increased seventy-two per cent. Yet the increased population, as well as those displaced, found other employment.

There was a phenomenal rise in the automobile, radio, electrical refrigeration and many other new and minor industries. The increase in our population was absorbed in the selling and servicing of new articles. They opened garages on the highways, operated filling stations, sold and serviced radios and electrical refrigerators, manned our airports and airlines—and still there were enough left over to permit a fifty per cent increase in our professional people—more teachers for our schools, more physicians to treat our ills and more scientists to work on problems of the future.

Past benefits of technological progress have been shared between labor and the consumer. Labor's wage rates increased seventeen per cent from 1919-1929, and fourteen per cent in the following decade. Weekly hours of work decreased three per cent from 1919-1929 and eighteen per cent more in the following decade.[12] The public received the benefits of technological progress in the form of lower prices because competition assured that lower costs were passed on.

A huge social program for all industrial employes could be paid for if some of the benefits of future technological progress were captured at the source by an expanded social security tax and used to increase their pensions and provide an adequate minimum living standard when they are temporarily idle due to conditions beyond their control. It could include health and hospitalization insurance for them and their families.

In his monumental work, "The History of Civilization in England," Henry Thomas Buckle points out that if a philosophy is too much in advance of a nation it must bide its time until "the minds of men are ready for its reception." "Every creed," he goes on, "has its martyrs because society was not sufficiently advanced to receive the truths they communicated. According to the ordinary course of affairs, a few generations pass away and then there comes a period when these truths are looked upon as commonplace facts, and a little later comes another period in which they are looked upon to be necessary and even the dullest intellects wonder how they could ever have been denied."[13]

The "truth" of public education passed through the sequential stages enumerated by Buckle. Another truth now dawning is probably that we are in fact our brother's keepers; that there will be collective responsibility for the basic human needs of the individual. If so, America's voluntary socialism as represented by private charity belongs to the past and in one way or another those to whom God has given health, ambition, ability and a willingness to work, will be required to provide for the idle, the indigent and the unfortunate.

But it is not necessary to socialize our economy through central economic planning in order to provide adequately for the so-called lower third.

A progressively-increasing manufacturers' excise tax, so gauged as to absorb a part, even all, of the savings of technological progress, would not raise average prices to the public. It would not reduce incentives to capital, labor nor management. It would merely deny most of our people, who already enjoy a high standard of living, their normal increase until adequate provision had been made for the amelioration of the status of the less fortunate, thus helping them and their offspring capture health, gain ambition and self-respect so that they will help themselves.

Thus, over a period of years, dreams of adequate standards of diet, health and housing, and social security for all, could emerge a reality.

And private enterprise can do even more!

CHAPTER XVIII

Vision

SHORTLY AFTER GEORGE III LOST THE AMERICAN colonies, an advocate of planning alarmed England with a theory that the world's increasing population would outgrow the land's productivity. He conceived England of A.D. 1800 as mature. He believed productivity of the soil had reached its maximum. He advocated that England's future population curve should be planned. His conclusions were backed with convincing statistics; they forecast a dire future for mankind, indeed.

This early planner, Robert Thomas Malthus, a Cambridge University economist, maintained that only intensive and continuous warfare and recurrent pestilence could kill off enough human beings to enable the survivors to maintain a minimum standard of living. He condemned doles to the poor as bounties upon large families, which tended to aggravate the evil. He urged postponement of marriage and moral restraint as preventive checks upon the rising population. Melancholy intellectuals of the day embraced his conclusions; their discussions had a profound influence on the public.

But in the century following Malthus' ominous prediction, the population of England increased fivefold and that of London increased eightfold. There was relative peace after Napoleon went to St. Helena. Englishmen's expectancy of life increased from forty to sixty years.

Malthus' statistics foreshadowed starvation for such a

population. Nevertheless, England's diet increased steadily in both quantity and variety, for at the century's end Englishmen had added to their national fare beef from Argentina, mutton from Australia, wheat from Canada, fruits from Spain and Syria, dairy products from Denmark and eggs from China.

Had this been suggested to Malthus as a possibility, he would have exclaimed, "Impossible! Half of England's population would be needed to build and sail the ships! Voyages to Australia take a year; enroute the crew would consume much of the cargo; and in addition the meat would rot three days out!" One can imagine Malthus throwing his hands up in horror at the suggestion of bringing eggs from China, accompanying his gesture with a pointed suggestion regarding the discomfiture of a crew housed with aged eggs on a rolling, tropical sea.

The data available to Malthus and his contemporaries made his conclusions incontrovertible. But these intellectuals could not foresee the increase in man's productivity; they could not vision modern transport and refrigeration—creations of human ingenuity in the ensuing period of individualism and economic freedom.

One wonders what course the world would have taken had Malthus been dictator of England and had he been able to enforce his theories through a planned economy. And one wonders what America would be like today had the philosophy of the New Deal been in the ascendancy during the depression that followed the Civil War. The planners of that time would have been able to point to a statement by Henry L. Ellsworth, Commissioner of Patents, in confirmation that our economy was even then reaching maturity, for as early as 1844 Ellsworth said: "The advancement of the arts, from year to year, taxes our credulity and seems to presage the arrival of that period when human improvement must end." [1]

Undoubtedly the depression and unemployment in post-Civil War days would have been laid to excessive speculation in land, non-essential railroad building and the advent of the industrial revolution, as evidenced by cast-iron plows, cotton gins and steamboats. The intellectuals of that day were unable to vision the progress still possible. No one could. Equalitarians embracing the theories of Karl Marx, then in vogue, would have planned equal division of all the good things of life available. Our industrial production then was comparatively small. America can now make as much steel in fifteen minutes as it produced in the year 1867.[2] But the equalitarian could have planned on a farm to every family, a plow, a cow, a horse and wagon, a parcel of woodland in which to cut fuel, some tallow for candles, and enough denim and calico for two changes or so a year—all of which is reminiscent of Abraham Lincoln's generous optimism, "Forty Acres and a Mule."

The New Deal's fundamental tenet is that our economy has reached maturity. The third freedom asserts: "In the short space of a few decades we have changed scarcity to abundance and are now engaged in the experiment of trying to live with our new and as yet unmanageable riches." But we are rich in material things only by comparison with other nations and with the past. The possibilities of the future, now that industry has embraced science, are so limitless that only one forecast can be made with certainty—that the most extravagant prophecy will fall short of potential accomplishment!

Realities have already exceeded the audacity of Jules Verne. They have dwarfed the dreams of inventors! When Edison created the incandescent lamp he could not have envisioned that his toy would become a necessity in every urban home and on most farms. Alexander Bell did not dream of clear and distinct conversations between San Francisco and

London; that conversations could be held between the majority of American homes, no matter how remote; and that even children would be familiar with the telephone's use. Marconi could not have envisioned the phenomenal development of modern radio networks and television. Nor did Orville Wright dream that he would live to see his invention deciding the fate of the world.

Even after the Civil War, we had sufficient material things. We have more than enough to go around now. But forever wanting new things is a characteristic of man. The continuous pursuit of his own animal comfort and well-being is one of the traits that differentiates him from animals. Satisfying human wants is thus an unending sequence!

We are already familiar enough with relatively new tools to foresee great developments in aviation, plastics and new and light metals. We foresee the probability of flying nonstop half way around the world at the speed of sound; likewise, that high-priced, perishable cargoes will take wings.

Igor Sikorsky has perfected a helicopter—a rotating wing craft—which can ascend from a back yard or the roof of an apartment building and fly at one hundred and forty miles per hour. He writes that his helicopter is capable of ascending or descending vertically as slowly as one foot per minute; that it hovers, like a humming bird, under complete control; that even motor failure would permit gentle landing; that it will fly fifteen miles on a gallon of gasoline; and that in mass production its cost will approximate that of a medium-priced car. He assures us that "the actual teaching operation will be much simpler than with the motorcar."[3] The Cessna Aircraft Corporation is advertising, for post-war production, a four-place cabin plane that can be flown by a novice after one hour of instruction.

Perhaps these claims are exaggerated but certainly they are attainable.

Does the National Resources Planning Board, as it re-designs our cities for the future, take into account that cities may be obsolete; that with the helicopter bus the health, beauties and spiritual uplift of a countryside one hundred miles away may surround the homes of city workers; that workers will reach offices and factories with no greater expenditure of time and money than is required for a present-day bus ride through five miles of city traffic?

Impossible? Only forty years ago the Literary Digest ventured the following: "The horseless carriage is at present a luxury but it will never come into as common use as the bicycle." Yet the horseless carriage and good roads made modern suburbs possible.

Business foresees that the post-war horseless carriages, with light, tough, plastic bodies, powered by small engines using ultra high octane motor fuels, will continue the ceaseless progress of the automobile industry.

Business believes that pre-fabricated houses of the future will be warmed by sunlike, healthful, penetrating radiant heat from tiny wires buried within walls. They will be air-conditioned for summer comfort, illuminated by cool germicidal light, and equipped with built-in low-temperature refrigeration to keep food fresh for months, even years. Housewives will buy fruits and vegetables in bulk when they are abundant and cheap. And we know that research is on the way to create new fruits and vegetables—larger, without seeds—and that greatly increased yields should cheapen them. Our radios will be static-free and television in full color will be universal.

The fibres of which our clothing is made are in most cases highly accidental products of animal or vegetable origin. Man adapted to his use fibres that nature made available to him. But the synthetic cloth of the future may be extruded instead of woven, stockings molded instead of knitted. Clothing will be more pleasing and more durable because these new synthetic fabrics will be waterproof, stainproof and flameproof. Laundering them will be as simple as washing a pair of rubber boots.

These are but a few of the foreseeable things—things in which research is so far along as to point the direction in unmistakable terms. But many of the really important developments are unpredictable because they remain as visions in minds of scientists and businessmen.

Scientists are limited only by the tools with which they work, and commercial exploitation is dependent upon the availability of material suited for the task. For instance, scientific work on bacteria could not progress until the microscope became available. Skyscrapers and George Washington bridges could not be built until the availability of steel and stress and strain diagrams. Aviation had to await the internal combustion engine and modern chemical high-pressure reactions had to await new alloys.

Scientists, however, are continually creating new tools. The cyclotron, a recent important development, accomplishes that which was thought to be impossible—it turns one element into another. So recent is this revolutionary tool that the latest Standard Dictionary's definition is obsolete. "Element," it says, "is that form of matter which cannot be decomposed or formed by any means known to science." The cyclotron made the dream of the ancient alchemist come true! Its curative radioactive products are more valuable than gold! Vast, indeed, are the possibilities of this new tool. Its present status may be likened to that of electricity when Benjamin Franklin caught lightning on a key.

A few laboratories are equipped with electron microscopes which enable men to see for the first time a chemical reaction actually taking place. These microscopes enable researchers to see and photograph particles but slightly larger than a molecule. Many laboratories are equipped with spectographs and x-ray and electron diffraction units which allow photographic chemical analysis, and polariscopes which visualize stresses and strains.

We can assume justly that other revolutionary tools are in the minds of our scientists and are being developed. Whereas in the past technicians worked in the relative darkness of cut and try, in the future they can work with greater exactitude. Developments will be accelerated. Indeed, each new scientific tool is like a new and larger celestial telescope which constantly enlarges man's conception of the universe, whose periphery is always beyond his reach.

Civilization's progress is marked and measured by man's efficiency in the utilization of sunbeams. Chlorophyll, the substance that makes vegetation green, allows plants and trees to store sunbeams while converting into growth the elements and compounds found in the air and soil. Early man's physical power depended on the sun's energy because his food consisted of vegetation and animals which lived on vegetation. When man tamed horses and oxen to do work for him, he progressed in his utilization of the sun's energy because horses and oxen derived their nourishment from vegetation.

Our modern industrial era's foundation of steam depended first on the burning of wood, which released the sun's energy that had been stored in trees. Later, coal and oil, the stored energy of the sun of ancient eons, were utilized. Electricity permitted our great recent strides. The sun's energy recovered from coal or oil in efficient central stations was transmitted as electric power to the myriad points of most convenient utilization.

The sun, drawing up moisture from land and sea and dropping it on mountains, turned the waterwheels and millstones of our ancestors. Now it spins our huge hydroelectric turbines. Internal combustion engines, too, such as power airplanes, are driven by the energy stored in oil.

We know that Dr. Kettering and his chemists are working on the mysteries of chlorophyll. When the problem is solved, the vast energies of the sun can be harnessed directly. It will no longer be necessary to dig deep in the earth for coal and oil for sunlight absorbed by vegetation in bygone eras.

This problem of direct utilization of the sun's energy is also being attacked by physicists. Already an electric motor is operating with sunbeams captured by photoelectric cells. Research men allude to it as a "one flypower motor." But it runs! That is significant!

We know there are possibilities of transmitting power without wires. We may expect airplanes of the future to be powered from the earth by wireless.

But most exciting to one's imagination is the unleashing of the power locked in atoms. In 1939 physicists split atoms by a process of bombardment and released tremendous amounts of energy. Ultimately a practical solution of this problem will be found; then planes and helicopters powered with atomic fuel could stay aloft for months exploring our polar wastes.

Future developments in power production will open opportunities as vast as those revealed by steam and electricity!

Have planners of the huge housing programs considered the probability of developments that will make their homes obsolete—that the word "housewife" will in all probability lapse into antiquity? Because foods will arrive in ultra vacuum containers holding correct temperatures for weeks, tomorrow's home probably will have no kitchen—and no need for one. This divines no greater development in packaging than we have seen in recent decades. Vacuum cleaners, together with kitchen ranges, will become antiques, treasured by future generations as we do bed warmers. Air conditioning systems will collect dust in a high electro-static field, such as the Cottrell precipitators now used in chemical plants.

Television is still in its early stages of development. Full realization of its possibilities will bring changes in home and business life. No longer will it be necessary to travel to attend meetings. Instead, one may remain at home or in the office and, via radio-vision, see, hear and participate in their proceedings. Attendance at meetings may be international in scope. Sound will be faithfully reproduced. Action will be seen, in full color—in three dimensions! Participation in smaller personal or business meetings will be through multiple-way radio-vision. One will merely call Central and ask for a wave length.

Today knowledge of odor is limited. We have no scientific measurements of its values. It is entirely possible that the timorous and courageous, hostile and friendly, reactions of human beings are influenced by odors of which they are not conscious but which may have a definite effect upon attitude. A dog, whose sense of smell is acute, knows when his master is angry, or when a stranger is afraid.

Odors we cannot distinguish may influence our intuition and reasoning. A grizzly cub, although he has never seen man, runs away from his first contact with human scent. We look at a person whom we do not know and instinctively we like or dislike him. He has not spoken; we know nothing about him. We believe that only one of our senses—sight—has been stimulated, but it is possible that smell, too, has reacted.

Modern radio changes a sound wave into a radio wave and reconverts it into a sound wave again, reproducing the sound with fidelity. Therefore, when we know its fundamentals, odor may be transformed into a radio wave and sent thousands of miles away, where it will revert into a faithful reproduction of the original odor. Then we will be able to send roses in three dimensions, in full color and tone and fragrance. Odors, of which we may be unconscious but which produce agreeable and entrancing reactions as does music, will be studio-created and sent over the air to accompany radio-vision programs.

Then we will have reproduced all the senses save that of touch; but may not even touch be reproduced? Touch is a mental reaction to contact with matter. Matter simply is electric charges interpreted by our senses as hearing, sight, smell, touch and taste. The touch of mercury is different from that of gold merely because there is one more electron in mercury. And an electron simply is a charge of electricity!

A tremendous evolution in physics is going to be completed when physicists discover the nature of this physical world. Then a man or a group of men will combine all generalizations into a few simple equations, such as Mendelyeev's concept of the periodic system. And it will be possible for the researcher to solve overnight our most intricate problems.

Education will meet the challenge of the future. With color television and atmosphere transmission, all knowledge will be available to every schoolroom. Instead of children being taught by a conscientious country schoolmarm anxious to impart her meager knowledge, our greatest educators will be transmitted to the most remote schoolroom. Teachers will be merely administrators and examiners.

Geologists will teach from Alaska's glacier-scoured arms of the sea, pointing out glaciers, moraines and hanging valleys to their students. They will drop down the walls of the Grand Canyon, lecturing as they scratch the sedimentary layers that have been laid one upon the other through eons of time. History will be taught from the Acropolis and Versailles; languages from their native lands.

Night educational courses might take the place of Charlie McCarthy as some advertiser brings into reality the equality of opportunity by sending through the air the best in education. Indeed, it may become possible for one to make ready for a college degree and not leave the farm. These readily available stimuli to the human mind will bring out, to the untold benefit of mankind, great latent capabilities that remain in our backwoods.

We are making constant progress in solving the mysteries of life. Many vitamins are now freely available, hormones are on the way, and scientists are busily engaged with enzymes—those catalysts of the human body that turn one substance into another without themselves being affected. The discoverer of salvarsan, Dr. Paul Ehrlich, expressed the hope that some day science would find "the magic bullet"—a product nontoxic to humans but fatal to disease-producing germs and death-dealing viruses that take shelter and multiply in the human body. Scientists hope to realize Ehrlich's dream among the thousands of experimental products chemical manufacturers are producing for clinical tests. There will be a special bullet for each germ and virus.

The discovery of vitamins, hormones and enzymes is relatively recent. Soon the mysteries of the endocrine and other glands will unfold and it will be known what diet, supplemented by synthetic hormones, vitamins, enzymes and other yet undiscovered substances, will produce a happy, contented people. Ailing organs breed irritability and querulousness. A healthy person is usually a happy person, and when a person is in a happy mood he is most unselfish. By controlling and balancing glands, an overall healthier and happier and more unselfish race should evolve.

There are many other secrets of life of which scientists are not yet aware but which they will find, and the deeper they go the closer they come to discovering the elixir of eternal youth.

In view of past accomplishments, could one be criticized justly for forecasting that man of the future will live vigorously for a century, and that he will live without illness? Once a year he will have his blood analyzed and the prescriptions will be diet and preventive medicines. Insanity will be prevented; imbeciles will not be born.

As we have already realized so many of Bellamy's dreams of material things, we will discover what glandular defects and other secrets of life make criminals. We will bring his jailless world, with but an occasional atavist, into reality, also. Then man will be close to controlling his destiny.

Not only will man live longer in a world progressing in the abundance of material things; he will live in communities of people approaching closer and closer to the moral and spiritual ideals of the Founder of Christianity.

Even the Weather Bureau will have become as wise as frogs and will know when tomorrow will be warm; it will know, as well as fish do, when it will rain. It will be as clever as the ducks, who know when a boreal storm, sleet, ice and bleak nights are on the way. It will even outdo nature's prophets, because . . .

Another Isaac Newton will have been born. He will evolve a new mathematics. And after private researchers have applied the new tool to weather and discovered its constants, another investigation will have forced the development upon bureaucracy. Then farmer, businessman and vacationist will receive long-range forecasts and count on them with the same certainty as we do on the waxing and waning of the moon. We may even learn to control weather locally!

Economics, too, will mature. It will outgrow its alchemist status and become an exact science. Then depressions will be prevented and unemployment will no longer remain as the last scourge of civilization.

But these and many hundred other visions are but promises of great adventure which lure modern pioneers—our scientists and businessmen—just as the unexplored west, the dream of a junction of the Missouri and Columbia rivers, lured Lewis and Clark into their historic voyage. There will have to be some people with faith that these things can be done—people who are willing to risk and chance failure in hope of the kind of reward they want.

We have come a long way from our Bushmen ancestors, but that we have reached maturity is a conclusion of pessimism. We have merely wet our feet in the boundless ocean on whose shore Isaac Newton said he was gathering pebbles.

In material things, reality for most Americans exceeds the Utopian visions of Plato, More and Bellamy. If we have patience, these things can be reality for all. But we have won only one round in the conquest of nature, space and time. And in the preservation of health and in the conquest of happiness, the fight has just gotten under way.

We may continue the struggle under the lash of fear wielded by the imperious bureaucracies of a coercive state, but we can conquer with hope giving encouragement to free minds and free spirits engaged in competitive enterprise!

We all remember learning that He answered and said, "It is written man shall not live by bread alone." The planners offer us bread—the bread of an alien, malignant collectivism. It will fill our stomachs, but it will not satisfy the hunger of free minds and free spirits. We cannot live happily nor progress on a debilitating diet of their bread alone.

We need moral food, also!

We need the solid meat of enterprise, with its vitamins of thrift and competition, to build character! We need the milk of ambition and hope, with its calcium and phosphorus of adventure and risk, to make healthy bone. We need the stimulating ferments of the wine of clashing ideas for our thirsty intellects!

To realize the four freedoms, we need only one freedom—Freedom!

NOTES

CHAPTER I

1. Associated Press Release, *New York Times,* April 26, 1942.

2. "Your Life Expectancy," Louis I. Dublin, *American Mercury,* July, 1942, and Metropolitan Life Insurance Co.

3. *History of the Business Man,* Miriam Beard, New York, 1938. Page 134.

4. *Ibid.* Page 581.

5. Real wages have paralleled the advance. Macaulay wrote that "on the whole, it seems reasonable to conclude that, in the reign of Charles the Second, the ordinary wages of the peasant did not exceed four shillings a week," and that "for so miserable a recompense were the producers of wealth compelled to toil, rising early and lying down late. . . . A workman employed in the great staple manufacture of England (textiles) thought himself fairly paid if he gained six shillings a week." Out of such wages men had to feed, clothe and house themselves and their families at a time when average prices were higher, expressed in today's money, than they are now. Macaulay continues: "At present a district where a labouring man earns only seven shillings a week is thought to be in a state shocking to humanity. The average is very much higher; and, in prosperous counties, the weekly wages of husbandmen amount to twelve, fourteen, and even sixteen shillings." This was a century ago but it was progress. Although Macaulay realized that human characteristics are as constant as the human form, he was not sufficiently optimistic of material progress when he prophesied: "It is now the fashion to place the golden age of England in times when noblemen were destitute of comforts the want of which would be intolerable to a modern footman, when farmers and shopkeepers breakfasted on loaves the very sight of which would raise a riot in a modern workhouse, when to have a clean shirt once a week was a privilege reserved for the higher class of gentry, when men died faster in the purest

country air than they now die in the most pestilential lanes of our towns, and when men died faster in the lanes of our towns than they now die on the coast of Guiana. We too shall, in our turn, be outstripped, and in our turn be envied. It may well be, in the twentieth century, that the peasant of Dorsetshire may think himself miserably paid with twenty shillings a week; that the carpenter at Greenwich may receive ten shillings a day; that labouring men may be as little used to dine without meat as they now are to eat rye bread; that sanitary police and medical discoveries may have added several more years to the average length of human life; that numerous comforts and luxuries which are now unknown, or confined to a few, may be within the reach of every diligent and thrifty working man. And yet it may then be the mode to assert that the increase of wealth and the progress of science have benefited the few at the expense of the many, and to talk of the reign of Queen Victoria as the time when England was truly merry England, when all classes were bound together by brotherly sympathy, when the rich did not grind the faces of the poor, and when the poor did not envy the splendour of the rich."

(Lord Macaulay's *History of England*, Vol. I. London, 1913. Pages 410, 412, 420, 421.)

6. In "Your Stake in Capitalism," a ringing defense of business, appearing in the Reader's Digest, February, 1943, Eric Johnston, President of the Chamber of Commerce of the United States, comments:

"We fear that the word capitalism is unpopular. So we take refuge in a nebulous phrase and talk about the 'Free Enterprise System.' And we even run to cover in the folds of the flag and talk about the 'American Way of Life.'

"Such language disastrously obscures the main issue. You cannot take a whiff of 'free enterprise' or a stretch of a 'way of life' and start a factory with it. To start a factory, and to start the jobs inside that factory, you have to have money. You have to have capital. . . .

"People will never understand this point unless we say capitalism."

After pondering these remarks carefully, I have concluded that free or private enterprise is the truer and more expressive name for the American business system. This is not because of any fear that the word capitalism has ugly connotations, but because capitalism is too broad and too inclusive. In its pure sense capitalism is any economic process in which society uses tools in the production of things to be consumed. Even Russian communism is state capitalism.

In its generally understood sense, capitalism is "money" capitalism—an economic order based on the profit motive. Hilaire Belloc dates the beginning of this system in England about the eleventh century. Capitalism, he points out, arose as soon as men were free to work for others for money wages. Capitalism continued throughout the period of the old mercantile system, of partnerships and individual banking, as well as when manufacture was confined to private homes. In the latter case a capitalist advanced raw materials and supplied a living to workers, or paid for their conversion into finished products—the "putting out system" of our early history. Capitalism extends over the periods of state enterprise, as well as when manufacturing monopolies were granted to favorites by the Crown and when the state fostered business by paying bounties and remitting taxes. It extends over the years of state-chartered exploration and trading monopolies, such as the Hudson Bay Company, the East India Company, and even our own Virginia Company.

The system of free private enterprise, however, is the most recent epoch of the era of capitalism. It is characterized by the freedom of opportunity available to any individual or group of individuals to acquire and risk their capital in a business venture. It is characterized by its private and unofficial nature, because the state is neither partner nor Guardian Angel. It is typical, therefore, of a competitive economy, instead of one dominated by monopolies. It is the epoch of modern corporations, wherein a great many individuals can risk their capital together in one venture, yet limit their individual liabilities.

Of all great nations, England's economy most closely approximates our own, yet even in England the State has always owned interests in enterprises. It owns interests in the Bank of England, in public utilities and transportation systems, such as the Imperial Airways, as well as in enterprises which own means of production, such as the Anglo Iranian Oil Company. Only in the United States have all the conditions of free and private enterprise been common to all manufacture and trade and services. The free enterprise system is, therefore, an *American* mutant of age-old capitalism.

Until the recent, and it is hoped temporary, advent of R.F.C. and government-financed war facilities, our federal government has not participated directly or indirectly in enterprise. Therefore, we do not "run to cover in the folds of the flag" when we talk about "free enterprise" as the "American way of life." It is one of its most distinctive characteristics!

7. *Industry's War Production,* New York, 1942. Page 6.

8. *Ibid.* Page 36.

9. Lyttelton's statement appeared in the *New York Times,* June 7, 1942, as follows: "I would have liked to have had Hitler and Goering with us. If they had been with us they would have thrown up their hands and given up."

CHAPTER II

1. *Democracy in America,* Alexis deTocqueville, published by Edward Walker, London, 1847. Page 104.

2. *Labor Problems,* Thomas Sewall Adams and Helen L. Sumner, New York, 1915. Page 73.

Proportion of the Total Number of Immigrants Furnished by Each of the Principal European Countries and by All Other Countries

Countries	*1901-1903*	*1891-1900*	*1881-1890*	*1871-1880*	*1861-1870*	*1851-1860*	*1821-1850*
Aggregate	100.0	100.0	100.0	100.0	100.0	100.0	100.0
Canada and Newfoundland	0.1	0.1	7.5	13.6	6.7	2.3	2.3
Germany	4.5	13.7	27.7	25.6	34.0	36.6	24.2
Great Britain	3.3	7.3	15.4	19.5	26.2	16.3	15.0
Ireland	4.8	10.6	12.5	15.5	18.8	35.2	42.3
Norway, Sweden and Denmark	8.6	10.1	12.5	8.6	5.4	0.9	0.7
Total	21.3	41.8	75.6	82.8	91.1	91.3	84.5
Austria-Hungary	24.7	16.1	6.7	2.6	0.4	....	....
Italy	27.3	17.7	5.9	2.0	0.5	0.3	0.2
Russia and Poland	16.5	16.3	5.0	1.8	0.2	0.1	0.1
Total	68.5	50.1	17.6	6.4	1.1	0.4	0.3
All other countries	10.2	8.1	6.8	10.8	7.8	8.3	15.2

3. *Races and Immigrants in America,* John R. Commons, New York, 1920. Page 69.

4. Edited by Professor Edwin A. R. Seligman, New York, 1932, Volume VII. Page 589.

5. *Adam Smith and Modern Sociology,* Albion Woodbury Small, Chicago, 1907. Page 9.

CHAPTER III

1. Foreword to *The Theory of the Leisure Class,* Thorstein Veblen, Modern Library Edition, 1934. Page III.

2. *The Theory of the Leisure Class,* Thorstein Veblen, Modern Library Edition, 1934. Page 262.

3. *Ibid.* Page 269.

4. *What Veblen Taught,* (Veblen's essay on *The State and Its Relation to War and Peace*) Wesley C. Mitchell, New York, 1936.

CHAPTER IV

1. "In a case brought by the International Union of Mine, Mill and Smelter Workers (CIO), the NLRB in August, 1940, ordered the Nevada Consolidated Copper Corporation to reinstate with back pay four men who had not even applied for work!" *Newsweek,* October 7, 1940. Page 40.

2. *Das Kapital* (Method and Call to Action), Karl Marx, Modern Library Edition, 1867. Page 366.

3. *Industrial Production—United States and Foreign Countries.*

	United States	*Great Britain*	*France*	*Germany*	*Canada*	*Japan*	*Chile*	*World*
1928	100.0	100.0	100.0	100.0	100.0	100.0	100.0	100.0
1929	107.2	104.8	112.4	101.4	108.2	111.5	123.6	107.6
1930	86.5	98.9	114.8	87.1	91.7	106.7	124.7	97.1
1931	73.0	93.1	101.7	68.5	76.5	102.1	96.3	87.4
1932	57.7	89.4	78.7	54.0	62.8	109.0	107.5	74.3
1933	68.5	94.7	90.0	61.5	65.2	126.2	118.4	83.5
1934	71.2	102.1	84.2	80.9	79.5	142.9	129.9	91.7
1935	81.1	106.4	80.7	95.3	87.9	158.1	148.5	103.2
1936	94.2	112.8	84.6	107.8	97.1	168.5	153.2	117.8

(1928 = 100)

Sources: United States. Federal Reserve (*Economic Almanac*).
World—League of Nations, *World Production and Prices,* 1938-39.
Remainder—*League of Nations' Yearbook,* 1937-38, 1939-40.

According to the *World Economic Survey* 1936-1937, published by the League of Nations, the acceleration of the rearmament program in Great Britain began early in 1937. In February of that year, the government announced its decision to spend £1500 million. Expenditures on defense totaled £137 million in 1935-36, £186 million in 1936-37, and £262 million in 1937-38. In this connection, the recent findings of A. L. Bowley, the British economist, are of interest.

In a comparison of national income in America and the United Kingdom, appearing in *Economica,* August, 1942, pages 227-236, Bowley finds that from 1924 to 1938 total income in the United States in current dollars fell 9%; in constant dollars it rose 10%; in constant dollars *per capita* it fell 4%. In contrast, he finds that total income in the United Kingdom between these years increased 12% in current units and 24% in constant units; in constant units *per capita* it rose 17%. "The contrast between the changes in the two countries," he concludes, "is so marked that no adjustments of definitions or of methods of estimates can explain it away."

4. In the speech of the Chancellor of the Exchequer on April 17, 1934, he directed attention to the existence of a surplus of £40 million. Income taxes were reduced from five shillings for each pound of income to four shillings and sixpence (i.e., from 25% to 22.5%).

5. *Economic Almanac,* 1942-43. Pages 151, 152.

Industry	*Employment Annual Average (Thousands)* 1929	1940	*% Increase Decrease*
Agriculture	10,539	10,580	0.4
Manufacturing	11,059	11,288	—2.1
Forestry & Fishing	267	208	—22.1
Transportation	2,465	1,948	—21.0
Mining	1,067	756	—29.1
Construction	3,340	1,907	—42.9

6. *Economic Record,* August, 1942. Page 263.

7. Colm and Lehmann's *Economic Consequences of Recent American Tax Policy*. Page 51. Colm adds: "The higher percentage of tax-exempt securities for 1935 is also in part due to lower stock prices in 1934 and 1935."

8. *Economic Almanac,* 1942-43. Page 285.

9. *Economic Record,* August, 1942. Page 263.

10. *The Managerial Revolution,* James Burnham, New York, 1941. Page 261.

11. *Economic Almanac,* 1942. Page 432.

12. *Ibid.* Page 187.

CHAPTER V

1. Data in this chapter compiled largely from Joseph Dorfman's *Thorstein Veblen and His America,* Wesley C. Mitchell's *What Veblen Taught,* and Veblen's works, especially *The Theory of the Leisure Class, The Engineers and the Price System,* and *Absentee Ownership.*

2. *Thorstein Veblen and His America,* Joseph Dorfman, New York, 1940. Page 32.

3. *Ibid.* Page 165.

4. *The Theory of the Leisure Class,* Thorstein Veblen, Modern Library Edition, 1934. Page 142.

5. *Thorstein Veblen and His America,* Joseph Dorfman, New York, 1940. Page 248.

6. *Ibid.* Page 184.

7. *Ibid.* Page 185.

8. *Ibid.* Page 372.

9. *Ibid.* Page 500.

10. *The Engineers and the Price System,* Thorstein Veblen, New York, 1940. Page 110.

11. *Ibid.* Page 150.

12. "The Men Behind the Scenes in Washington," *Forbes Magazine,* August 15, 1942. Pages 10, 11.

13. *The Engineers and the Price System,* Thorstein Veblen, New York, 1940. Page 150.

14. *Ibid.* Page 168.

CHAPTER VI

1. Italics are the author's.

2. *Ibid.*

3. It may not be a coincidence that the theories the T.N.E.C.

hearings sought to establish and prove are also the principal theories propounded by Karl Marx. Marx's tenets were, firstly, that in capitalism competition ends in monopoly and concentration of economic power; secondly, that the "accumulation of wealth at one pole is at the same time accumulation of misery, agony, toil, slavery, ignorance, brutality, mental degradation at the opposite pole." This is the Marxian theory of increasing misery. Thirdly, Marx predicted these results would cause a chain of crises ending in the collapse of capitalism. Conclusions substantiating each of these Marxian theories could be and in fact were drawn by the monographs from the testimony that was permitted before the committee as well as other ideologically compatible sources.

4. To quote from Moulton: "The continuous expansion of the public debt, the various practices and policies which confuse and obscure the fiscal situation, and the developing philosophy that a permanent expansion of public credit and public debt is not only inescapable but essential to economic and social progress inevitably cause profound concern with respect to future financial and economic stability and also with respect to the future of the system of private enterprise. They seem clearly to indicate a definite, if not perhaps wholly conscious, movement in the direction of socialization. Taken in conjunction with other forms of restrictive legislation and recurrent attacks upon the system of private enterprise they *inevitably* create an atmosphere unfavorable to the assumption of the risks involved in private enterprise, particularly in the field of long-term capital investment." (*Capital Expansion, Employment and Economic Stability*. Page 327.)

Dr. King has said: "The only sane policy after the war will be for the government to levy taxes and pay off its bank debt with the greatest speed possible. Only by so doing can we hope to avoid suffering severely from one of the following things: (1) continuance for an indefinite time, of price controls and government interference with business: (2) extreme increases in the prices of commodities, which increases will rob the thrifty classes of the population of large proportions of their savings, including insurance. If, after the war, instead of paying off its bank debt the government continues to borrow more and more, the results will be disastrous."

5. Cuno Corporation *vs*. Automatic Devices Corporation. 314 U.S. 84, 92, November 10, 1941. Cited in monograph #31, T.N.E.C., "Patents and Free Enterprise."

6. *Economic Almanac,* 1942-43. Page 204.

7. *Economic Record,* August, 1942. Page 263. "Assets of all manufacturing enterprises were $62,118,000,000 in 1930 and $51,580,000,000 in 1940. They were 17% below corresponding 1930 total."

8. Edward Stettinius in a two-hour review traced the history and outlined the financial structure of the United States Steel Corporation.

He stated that in the year previous, the corporation attempted to sell one hundred million of its stock to its shareholders but during delays attending the necessary preparation of registration statements for the Securities and Exchange Commission, the stock market fell and they finally issued, in April, 1938, one hundred million of ten-year debenture. There was considerable maneuvering during the testimony by Mr. Henderson to elicit from Mr. Stettinius an admission that they would never again require capital funds. The following bit of testimony is typical: *

Mr. Henderson: Well, you don't have in mind, then, at what point of acceleration in demand that might be sustained you might have to consider an expansion of your capacity?

Mr. Stettinius: That is, to add to our facilities, to produce more goods?

Mr. Henderson: Yes. Do you foresee that, or have you any point in mind at which that might take place?

Mr. Stettinius: We haven't prepared a statement of that kind. We would be delighted to have our market analysis department apply themselves.

Mr. Henderson: I think you have answered my question. In the discussion of the future of the Corporation, that particular consideration has not entered. Isn't that what you mean?

Mr. Stettinius: That is correct.

Mr. Henderson: So in the foreseeable near future the prospect that you will be in the market, tapping for any large sum for an expansion of your capacity is just not there?

Mr. Stettinius: I mean, if you want to take for example that an automobile normal year is a 5,000,000-car. . . .

Mr. Henderson (interposing): Pardon me, I wouldn't. We will

* *Investigation of Concentration of Economic Power.* Part 9: *Savings and Investment.* Pages 3589, 3597, 3622, 3627, 3657.

get into a discussion of normality, and I don't think 5,000,000 is a normal year.

Mr. Stettinius: There are sufficient sheet facilities in the steel industry today to meet the requirements of the automobile industry, for example, as far as we can see ahead.

Mr. Henderson: Do you get the point?

After this, the chairman, Mr. Lubin and Mr. Henderson all had to go over the witness, leading him through his depreciation accounts, his capacity, his number of employes on hourly and salary payroll, and finally while he was in the midst of talking about the number of employes, Mr. Henderson shot in: * As I see it, just to try to put your testimony on savings and investment in a nub, you are not in any time in the immediate future going to give any great amount of business to underwriting firms; in other words, you are not going to tap individual savings very much, isn't that about correct?

Mr. Stettinius replied: *That is correct.*

Later Mr. Owen D. Young talked at length on the history and development of General Electric Company. He inveighed against the capital gains tax. Then, as usual, Messrs. Lubin and Henderson took the witness. After talking about taxation in the larger brackets, the following conversation took place: *

Mr. Henderson: The English have had a much better experience than we. Have you talked to Josiah Stamp about that?

Mr. Young: Yes, I have.

Mr. Henderson: Other English observers besides Stamp, as they have come into this country, have said that we failed to get at some of the proper uses of taxation to reach that thirty-two billion.

Then Mr. Henderson lunged again, quickly: As I gather from your testimony, you see probably, like Mr. Stettinius, no time in the immediate future in which your company will be needing new financing?

Mr. Young: *I can't.*

Toward the end of Mr. Young's appearance apparently Senator O'Mahoney believed that Mr. Young had been taken off guard, so he asked: * Well, is the electrical industry still a growing industry?

Mr. Young: I think it is still—the last few years don't indicate it very well in gross business, but I think it is an expanding industry still.

Senator O'Mahoney: Well, assuming that is only a temporary—

Mr. Young: I do.

Senator O'Mahoney: Development, then, in the electrical industry there is now the opportunity, in your opinion, for adventure capital and equity capital?

Mr. Young: I think undoubtedly.

After Mr. Sloan had given a lengthy statement covering the history and development of General Motors, Mr. Nehemkis talked about General Motors Acceptance Corporation and the insurance phase of it and then asked: * You have an affiliated or subsidiary company, do you not, which is engaged in the business of financing your output?

Mr. Sloan: Yes; that is the General Motors Acceptance Corporation. We also have an affiliate dealing with the insurance phase of it.

Mr. Nehemkis: Would it be a correct statement, Mr. Sloan, to say that General Motors is in a position today to do most of its internal financing out of earnings, and, in addition, to finance the ultimate consumers of your product as well?

Mr. Sloan: *I think that is a correct statement of fact*—I mean in a practical sense. One could imagine what certainly doesn't seem at all likely, a tremendous expansion when it might get beyond our capacity, but if things continue in a reasonable way, the way we expect, that is true. Mr. Bradley gives me a note that G.M.A.C. borrows from the banks. We do not, but General Motors Acceptance Corporation does. I am sorry I omitted to point that out. We do not in the corporation, but the finance company, General Motors Acceptance Corporation, does, and I should say about twenty-five per cent of the funds we use in financing the consumer through the General Motors Acceptance Corporation is their capital derived from a dollar investment basis; the balance is the borrowing. I am sorry I overlooked that.

The words which the author italicized constitute the only parts of these witnesses' testimony that was used in Monograph #37, which supposedly interpreted this phase of the hearings.

9. *Investigation of Concentration of Economic Power,* Part 9: *Savings and Investment.* Page 3633.

10. "Capital Not Wanted," Stuart Chase, *Harper's Magazine,* February, 1940.

11. "Business in the Wood Shed," Raymond Moley, *Saturday Evening Post,* April 6, 1940. Page 64.

12. *Ibid.*

CHAPTER VII

1. Testimony of Conway P. Coe, Commissioner of Patents, before the T.N.E.C., February 19, 1941.

2. Assistant Attorney General's report for year ended June 30, 1941:

ACTIVITY AND APPROPRIATIONS OF ANTI-TRUST DIVISION OF DEPARTMENT OF JUSTICE
Fiscal Years Ended June 30, 1938, 1939, 1940, 1941, 1942

	1938	*1939*	*1940*	*1941*	*1942*
Personnel	111	187	312	325	583
Appropriation	$413,894	$780,060	$1,309,000	$1,325,000	$2,325,000
	Sherman Act Cases				
Complaints	923	1,375	3,412	2,032	3,674
Major Investigations (new)	59	90	215	180	236
Defendants (new)	265	512	2,485	2,797	2,517

(In reply to an inquiry, the Department of Justice advised that 3661 defendants were awaiting trial on June 30, 1942.)

3. Statement made before House Committee on Patents, March 11, 1941. (Taken from article in *Atlantic Monthly*, July, 1942. "We Depend on Invention," Lawrence Langner.)

CHAPTER VIII

1. An excellent review of the T.N.E.C. Monographs appears in "Fact and Fancy in the T.N.E.C. Monographs" by John Scoville and Noel Sargent, published by the National Association of Manufacturers.

2. A.T. & T.'s proxy statement, March 7, 1942, showed its directors owned 6140 of the total of 18,687,000 shares outstanding.

3. Letter from Winthrop Aldrich, Chairman of Stockholders' Committee, sent to Standard Oil Company of Indiana stockholders, February 8, 1929.

4. National City Bank of New York Monthly Letter, May, 1942.

DIVIDEND PAYMENTS IN 1940, AND DIVIDEND RECEIPTS BY NET INCOME CLASSES

	Amount	*Per Cent of Total*
Total dividend payments (excluding intercorporate):		
Dept. of Commerce (a)	$4,150,000,000	
Dividend receipts reported on federal income tax returns, by net income classes (b)		
Over $1,000,000	72,704,000	1.7
500,000 to 1,000,000	50,443,000	1.2
300,000 to 500,000	67,859,000	1.6
150,000 to 300,000	138,402,000	3.3
100,000 to 150,000	126,763,000	3.0
50,000 to 100,000	311,415,000	7.5
25,000 to 50,000	413,324,000	10.0
10,000 to 25,000	597,867,000	14.4
5,000 to 10,000	427,679,000	10.3
Subtotal over $5,000	$2,206,455,000	53.0
Under $5,000 (c)	1,224,888,000	29.5
Total reported by Treasury	$3,431,343,000	82.5
Bal. not reported by Treasury	718,657,000	17.5
Total	$4,150,000,000	100.0

(a) From Dept. of Commerce *Survey of Current Business*, June 1941, page 17. (b) From Treasury Dept. *Statistics of Income for 1940*, Part 1 (preliminary), page 12. (c) Partly estimated by the Treasury.

"It will be seen that 53 per cent of the total dividend payments was received by individuals having net incomes of over $5,000. The remaining 47 per cent was reported to the Treasury by individuals having net incomes under $5,000 or was received by non-profit institutions (hospitals, schools, churches, etc.) as well as by individuals not filing returns or individuals filing returns but failing to report dividends (evidently small shareholders)."

5. *History of the Business Man*, Miriam Beard, New York, 1938. Page 223.

6. *Ibid.* Page 225.

7. *Ibid.* Page 235.

CHAPTER IX

1. T.N.E.C. Monograph #21, "Competition and Monopoly in American Industry."

2. Roy A. Foulke in Dun & Bradstreet's "Behind the Scenes in Business," 1937.

	Concerns in Business	*New Enterprises*	*Percent*	*Discontinued Enterprises*	*Percent*
1920	1,821,000	459,000	25.2	353,000	19.3
1925	2,113,000	496,000	23.5	451,000	21.3
1930	2,183,000	423,000	19.4	493,000	22.6
1931	2,125,000	355,000	16.7	413,000	19.4
1932	2,077,000	338,000	16.3	386,000	18.6
1933	1,961,000	345,000	17.6	461,000	23.5
1934	1,974,000	379,000	19.2	366,000	18.5
1935	1,983,000	387,000	19.8	378,000	19.1
1936	2,009,000	408,000	20.5	382,000	19.0
	Average, 1930-1936		18.5		20.1

3. *History of the Business Man,* Miriam Beard, New York, 1938. Page 187.

4. *Soviet Money and Finance,* L. E. Hubbard, London, 1936. Page 127.

In his introduction to *The Living Thoughts of Karl Marx,* New York, 1939, Trotsky wrote: "Abolition of private ownership in the means of production is the first prerequisite to a planned economy."

CHAPTER X

1. *History of the Business Man,* Miriam Beard, New York, 1938. Page 13. (Italics are author's.)

2. *Victory Through Air Power,* Major Alexander deSeversky, New York, 1942. Page 222.

3. William Bradford Huie wrote, in *The Fight for Air Power,* "We were working with planes at least seven years behind the commercial planes." And: "It seems unbelievable that seven years after Lindbergh's flight to Paris and only five years before the beginning of this war, the United States Army Air Corps attempted to carry the air mail in ancient steel-tubing-and-fabric biplanes which had a

cruising speed of ninety miles an hour!" . . . "In the summer of 1941, a tactical genius named Claire Chennault addressed recruits for his Flying Tigers. 'Remember, boys,' he said, 'you've *got* to be good out here. When you tackle one Jap Zero in an American P-40, you are already outnumbered three to one!'" (New York, 1942. Pages 4, 44 and 45.)

4. *Victory Through Air Power,* Major Alexander deSeversky, New York, 1942.

5. Recent Annual Reports of Postmaster General.

6. *Public Finance,* Professor Harley L. Lutz, New York, 1936. Page 247.

7. *Science Advisory Board Report,* 1933-34.

8. 1941 OPERATIONS OF TVA AND OF MUNICIPALITIES AND COOPERATIVES RESELLING TVA POWER

Classification	*Kwhr. sold by TVA (Millions)*	*If Sold at Rates of Tenn. Elec. Power Rate (¢)*	*If Sold at Rates of Tenn. Elec. Power Total Bill*	*Actual Revenue TVA*	*Gain, under TVA Rates*
Residential Service (a)	503	2.52	$12,675,000	$10,364,000	$2,311,000
Small Light & Power (a)	267	2.72	7,262,000	5,838,000	1,424,000
Miscellaneous other uses	70	3.96*	2,772,000	1,112,000	1,660,000
Other Electric Utilities	627	0.30*	1,881,000	2,361,000	(480,000)
Large Light & Power (a)	1,213	0.916	11,111,000	9,348,000	1,763,000
Industrial Power (b)	1,810	0.50(b)	9,050,000	7,781,000	1,269,000
Total	4,490		$44,751,000	$36,804,000	$7,947,000

* Actual average, Tennessee Electric Power Co., 1938.

(a) By municipalities and Cooperatives (Private Company rates of 1938 trended to 1942).

(b) Firm and secondary power; sold to 10 large customers under special contracts. Tennessee Electric Power Co. had no business of this kind and the average revenue from sales of all its power does not apply here. Several companies in the USA have rate schedules for interruptible power service to large customers which will give an average price of 0.5 cents per kwhr. or less. (Niagara, Lockport & Ontario Power Co. Rate #2 *FPC Rate Book,* N. Y., page 36), (Ohio Power Co. Rate E P (16A) *FPC Rate Book,* Ohio, page 46), (Portland Electric Power Co. Rate P 8, *FPC Rate Book,* Oregon, page 22), (Pacific Gas & Electric Co., contract with Todd-California Shipbuilding Company for production of magnesium; R.R. Com'n of California docket 24,232). "Interdepartment Sales" of TVA to itself are not included here.

TVA itself received $10,321,000 from sales of electricity to outside customers. Of the above 15.6% of revenues, 2.0% represents the proportion arising from 3.3% Federal excise tax on the sales of residential and retail commercial service, which the TVA does not supply. The remaining 13.6% of revenues, applied to the $10,-321,000 of direct TVA revenues, shows that the TVA would have paid $1,300,000 in Federal taxes on this revenue. Total Federal taxes escaped are thus $5,431,000.

Interest not paid by TVA—"Funds for construction and operation have been obtained from Congressional appropriations, requiring no return of interest, and from operating revenues." (*Annual Report*, 1941, page 57.)

The following money has been spent upon the TVA up to June 30, 1941:

Net Expenditures by War Dept. at Muscle Shoals	$ 40,119,301
Net Expenditures by War Dept. at Sheffield Steam Plant	12,326,392
Total Congressional Appropriations for TVA	336,569,270*
Proceeds from sale of bonds to U. S. Treasury	52,272,500
Proceeds from sale of bonds to RFC	8,300,000
Total	$449,587,463

* Since June 30, 1941, Congressional appropriations to the TVA have doubled, bringing the total as of the present date to more than $776,000,000.

Assuming that the total funds invested in TVA (excluding the municipalities and cooperatives retailing power produced by TVA) amounted to $525,000,000 on June 30, 1941, the annual interest, at 2½%, which was paid by the general taxpayer amounted to $13,125,000. Against this amount stands $336,000 in interest actually paid by the TVA on bond issues, leaving a net difference of $12,789,000 owed to the taxpayers. Edison Electric Institute.

9. *Report of the Subcommittee of the Committee on Appropriations Pursuant to Senate Resolution #223, a Resolution for an Investigation to Determine Whether Certain Governmental Employes May Be Temporarily Transferred to National Defense Agencies to Expedite Prosecution of the War*, U. S. Government Printing Office, July 22, 1942.

10. T.N.E.C. Monograph #19, "Government Purchasing—An Economic Commentary."

11. *The Wealth of Nations,* Adam Smith, Book III, London, 1819. Page 250.

12. *Astoria,* Washington Irving. G. P. Putnam's Handy Volume Edition. Page 21.

13. Tax Foundation's *Discussion of War Finance and Industry,* New York, May 19, 1942. Page 9.

14. *End of Economic Man,* Peter Drucker, New York, 1939. Page 223.

15. *Ibid.* Page 166.

CHAPTER XI

1. Since this chapter was written, the President has sent to Congress two reports of the National Resources Planning Board, which cover some phases of the planners' post-war plans.

Document Number One, nicknamed "the telephone book," weighs five and a half pounds and contains over 400,000 words presented on 640 pages. Document Number Two, not printed at the time of presentation, contains 500,000 words.

More reports are to be expected, for these reports do not cover post-war plans for agriculture, international relations and international trade and finance. In main, however, those which have been released to Congress on two subjects, not only cover most of the plans outlined for them in this chapter but go further.

Document Number One, suggesting social security "from the cradle to the grave," includes: protection from fear of old age, want, dependency, sickness, unemployment and accidents; jobs for everyone, but only through federal employment agencies; and educational grants for youth.

Document Number Two suggests, among other things: retaining control of war plants for which government supplied funds; deciding what concerns will be permitted to continue in operation; granting funds for plant rehabilitation; developing new industries by research work within the government; retaining government partnership in such industries as aluminum, shipbuilding and aircraft; and distributing orders as government deems best. It further suggests consolidating railroads on a national basis; setting up T.V.A.'s in most of the nation's water basins; rebuilding cities, terminals and housing; and continuing, "temporarily," rationing, price control, wage control and allocation of raw materials. Yet, without blushing, it has the temerity to suggest that all this will "encourage healthy business competition."

National Resources Planning Board reports may be obtained from the Government Printing Office, Superintendent of Documents, or through one's own Congressman. Research on these reports to remake America was directed by Dr. Eveline M. Burns, who immigrated to the United States in 1926.

2. Stuart Chase in a speech before the Institute of Public Affairs, Charlottesville, Va. July 10, 1942.

3. National Resources Planning Board pamphlet, "After Defense—What?" August, 1941.

4. "Freedom from Want," Stuart Chase, *Harper's Magazine,* October, 1942. Page 467.

5. "The Economy of Abundance," Stuart Chase, New York, 1934. Pages 310, 313. (Italics are author's.)

6. "Freedom from Want," Stuart Chase, *Harper's Magazine,* October, 1942. Page 462.

7. National Planning Association (Alvin H. Hansen, Chairman Executive Committee) pamphlet #11, *For a Better Post-War Agriculture,* May, 1942. Page 44.

8. National Planning Association (Alvin H. Hansen, Chairman Executive Committee) pamphlet #8, *Guides for Post-War Planning,* November, 1941. Page 16.

9. *Ibid.* Page 17.

10. National Planning Association (Alvin H. Hansen, Chairman Executive Committee) pamphlet # 9, *Britain's Trade in the Post-War World,* December, 1941. Page 33. Also, pamphlet #15, *International Development Loans,* September, 1942.

11. National Planning Association (Alvin H. Hansen, Chairman Executive Committee) pamphlet #6, *United States' Co-operation with British Nations,* August, 1941. Page 23.

12. National Planning Association (Alvin H. Hansen, Chairman Executive Committee) pamphlet #15, *International Development Loans,* September, 1942.

13. National Planning Association (Alvin H. Hansen, Chairman Executive Committee) pamphlet #6, *United States Co-operation with British Nations,* August, 1941. Page 22.

14. *Ibid.* Page 25.

15. *Ibid.*

16. *Ibid.* Page 21.

17. National Planning Association (Alvin H. Hansen, Chairman Executive Committee) pamphlet #15, *International Development Loans,* September, 1942.

18. Vice President Wallace's speech, *Free World Association,* New York, May 8, 1942.

19. Net earnings on capital invested in manufacturing corporations averaged 3.15% from 1925 through 1939. (*Economic Record,* August, 1942. Page 265.)

20. "Freedom from Want," Stuart Chase, *Harper's Magazine,* October, 1942. Page 468.

CHAPTER XII

1. *History of the Business Man,* Miriam Beard, New York, 1938.

2. *Looking Backward,* Edward Bellamy, New York, 1926. Introduction by Heywood Broun. Page iv.

3. "The International Economic Organization of the Future" contained in *Toward International Organization,* Jacob Viner, New York, 1942. Page 121.

CHAPTER XIII

1. National Resources Planning Board pamphlet, "After Defense—What?," August, 1941. Page 13.

2. These are estimates obtained in response to inquiries addressed to Messrs. Muir and Fuller by the author.

3. Bureau of Advertising of American Newspaper Publishers advises that the gross revenue of all newspaper publishers in 1935 was 760 million dollars, of which 500 million was derived from advertising.

4. *Madam Curie,* Eve Curie, New York, 1937. Page 167.

5. *History of Civilization in England,* Henry Thomas Buckle, New York, 1873. Page 162.

CHAPTER XIV

1. *Soviet Money and Finance,* L. E. Hubbard, London, 1936. Page 68.
2. "Economic Consequences of Mr. Churchill" (Essay in *Essays in Persuasion*), J. M. Keynes, London, 1925. Page 27.
3. "The Federal Debt and the Future," Alvin H. Hansen and Guy Greer, *Harper's Magazine,* April, 1942.
4. *Ibid.*
5. *Ibid.*
6. *Ibid.*
7. *Ibid.*
8. *The Road We Are Traveling,* Stuart Chase, New York, 1942. Page 93.
9. *The March of the Barbarians,* Harold Lamb, New York, 1940. Page 283.
10. *Ibid.* Page 307.
11. *Ibid.* Page 117.
12. *Fiat Money and Inflation in France,* Andrew Dixon White, New York, 1933.
13. *Economic, Financial and Political State of Germany since the War,* Dr. Peter Reinhold, New Haven, 1928. Page 22.

CHAPTER XV

1. Described fully in L. E. Hubbard's *Soviet Trade and Distribution,* London, 1938.

CHAPTER XVI

1. *Thorstein Veblen and His America,* Joseph Dorfman, New York, 1940. Page 451. Harold Laski said: "He [Veblen] was an entrancing companion. . . . I remember particularly his admiration for Marx. . . . It was profoundly moving to watch his shy

delight in realizing that his long struggle was at last beginning to bear fruit. . . . His kindness to a much younger teacher remains one of the abiding memories of my years in America." Laski was Veblen's assistant at Columbia University.

2. In this connection, it is interesting to note the language of Article 12 of the U.S.S.R. Constitution of 1936: "Work in the U.S.S.R. is a duty and a matter of honor for every able-bodied citizen, on the principle: He who does not work shall not eat." (*The Truth About Soviet Russia,* Sidney and Beatrice Webb, New York, 1942.)

CHAPTER XVII

1. (From *Editorial Research Reports,* Vol. 1, 1933):

"On December 3, 1907, at the commencement of the depression which followed the financial panic of 1907, in his annual message to Congress, President Roosevelt recommended a national incorporation law. He said: "The Congress has power to charter corporations to engage in interstate and foreign commerce, and a general law can be enacted under the provisions of which existing corporations could take out federal charters and new federal corporations be created . . ." The proposal for a national incorporation law was renewed by President Taft in 1910, and the proposal for a federal licensing law by President Wilson in 1919 and 1920, but no action to these ends was taken by Congress."

. . . .

(From a letter written by Frank Altschul, Chairman of the Committee on Stock List of the New York Stock Exchange, addressed to the Senate Banking and Currency Committee in February, 1934.)

"The competition between states in this [incorporation] field is a matter of common knowledge and the tendency of many states to liberalize the provisions of corporate charters with a view to making their laws attractive for the incorporation of companies has led to the practices which have often given us concern. . . . The remedy for much of this we have long felt lies in a federal incorporation statute."

. . . .

F. W. Lehmann said, before the Bankers' Club of Chicago in 1910: "Having the power to deal with the corporation, the National Government should do so. The state neither can nor will. . . . It is absurd to say that one state may be safely trusted to charter corporations with power to conduct business throughout the entire country and with investors in every state in the union, but that the United States cannot be trusted with like power. In either case, the power may be abused, but how much more probable is such abuse when the power is exerted by a part over the whole, than when it is exercised by the whole, equally over and equally for, the benefit of every part."

. . . .

Herbert Hoover has from time to time proposed that a national incorporation law be enacted and that it be made optional to corporations to register under it. Attached to his proposals was another that he believed vital to promote small business. That was the exemption of corporations of less than $500,000 or $1,000,000 capital from corporation taxes and subject them to income tax in the same way as partnerships.

2. *History of Journalism in America,* G. H. Payne, New York. Page 243.

3. *History of the United States,* James Truslow Adams, Vol. II, New York, 1933. Page 236.

4. *History of Journalism in America,* G. H. Payne, New York. Page 242.

5. The following appeared in the *Chicago Daily Tribune,* January 15, 1943: "Time Magazine recently estimated that the Chicago Sun lost about three million dollars on its first year of operations. The losses all came out of Mr. Field's pocketbook. The Sun is not a corporation, but a personal, checkbook venture of Field's.

"Actually, the paper is financed out of millions that could go into the pay of soldiers, the building of battleships and tanks, the construction of aircraft and tommy guns. That portion of Field's fat, fabulous, unearned income which is poured in to cover up the paper's losses is exempt from the high war surtaxes. His losses on PM are likewise exempt.

"When the Senate recently tried to amend the tax laws to prevent this escape of war revenue, the administration quickly intervened and had the provision eliminated to save its Chicago baby.

"Majority Leader Alben W. Barkley, Democratic senator from Kentucky, according to authoritative sources, frankly told members of the joint conference committee considering the tax bill last October 15 that the amendment in question would hurt Field's out of pocket financing of his failing newspaper ventures, which were supporting the administration's domestic and foreign policies."

6. *Baltimore Evening Sun,* January 27, 1942.

7. In tracing the course of civilization and progress, Buckle comments, on laws which restricted man's initiative and freedom: "The most valuable additions made to legislation have been enactments destructive of preceding legislation; and the best laws which have been passed, have been those by which some former laws were repealed. In the case just mentioned, of the corn-laws, all that was done was to repeal the old laws, and leave trade to its natural freedom. When this great reform was accomplished, the only result was, to place things on the same footing as if legislators had never interfered at all. Precisely the same remark is applicable to another leading improvement in modern legislation, namely, the decrease of religious persecution. This is unquestionably an immense boon; though, unfortunately, it is still imperfect, even in the most civilized countries. But it is evident that the concession merely consists in this: that legislators have retraced their own steps, and undone their own work. If we examine the policy of the most humane and enlightened governments, we shall find this to be the course they have pursued. The whole scope and tendency of modern legislation is to restore things to that natural channel from which the ignorance of preceding legislation has driven them. This is one of the great works of the present age; and if legislators do it well, they will deserve the gratitude of mankind. But though we may thus be grateful to individual lawgivers, we owe no thanks to lawgivers, considered as a class. For since the most valuable improvements in legislation are those which subvert preceding legislation, it is clear that the balance of good cannot be on their side. It is clear, that the progress of civilization cannot be due to those who, on the most important subjects, have done so much harm, that their successors are considered benefactors, simply because they reverse their policy, and thus restore affairs to the state in which they would have remained, if politicians had allowed them to run on in the course which the wants of society required." (*History of Civilization in England,* Henry Thomas Buckle, New York, 1873, Vol. I. Page 200.)

8. That the specter of huge war debts faced other generations and other nations but was dwarfed in the course of time by the progress of enterprise, is interestingly pictured by Macaulay in his essay on

"Southey's Colloquies." Southey, a contemporary of Macaulay and then poet laureate of Great Britain, had ventured, as a solution to the problems of their day, which arose out of the Neopolitan wars, an omnipotent state:

"We cannot absolutely prove that those are in error who tell us that society has reached a turning point, that we have seen our best days. But so said all who came before us, and with just as much apparent reason. 'A million a year will beggar us,' said the patriots of 1640. 'Two millions a year will grind the country to powder,' was the cry in 1660. 'Six millions a year, and a debt of fifty millions!' exclaimed Swift; 'the high allies have been the ruin of us.' 'A hundred and forty millions of debt!' said Junius; 'well may we say that we owe Lord Chatham more than we shall ever pay, if we owe him such a load as this.' 'Two hundred and forty millions of debt!' cried all the statesmen of 1783 in chorus; 'what abilities, or what economy on the part of a minister can save a country so burdened?' We know that if, since 1783, no fresh debt had been incurred, the increased resources of the country would have enabled us to defray that debt at which Pitt, Fox and Burke stood aghast, nay, to defray it over and over again, and that with much lighter taxation than what we have actually borne. On what principle is it that, when we see nothing but improvement behind us, we are to expect nothing but deterioration before us?

"It is not by the intermeddling of Mr. Southey's idol, the omniscient and omnipotent State, but by the prudence and energy of the people, that England has hitherto been carried forward in civilization; and it is to the same prudence and the same energy that we now look with comfort and good hope. Our rulers will best promote the improvement of the nation by strictly confining themselves to their own legitimate duties, by leaving capital to find its most lucrative source, commodities their fair price, industry and intelligence their natural reward, idleness and folly their natural punishment, by maintaining peace, by defending property, by diminishing the price of law, and by observing strict economy in every department of the State. Let the Government do this: the People will assuredly do the rest."

9. In an address delivered at Westminster College, New Wilmington, Pennsylvania, May 21, 1942.

10. *Recent Changes in American Constitutional Theory,* John W. Burgess, New York, 1923. Pages 89-91.